the
babysense
secret

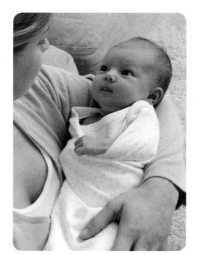

the babysense secret

The painless routine for
happy days and peaceful nights

Bestselling author **Megan Faure**

LONDON, NEW YORK, MUNICH,
MELBOURNE, DELHI

*I dedicate this book to Philip, the love of my life, father of
my children and my partner in everything Baby Sense.*

Project Editor Emma Maule
Project Designers Emma Forge, Tom Forge
Designer Charlotte Seymour
Senior Art Editor Nicola Rodway
Senior Production Editor Jennifer Murray
Senior Production Controller Man Fai Lau
Creative Technical Support Sonia Charbonnier
Photography Vanessa Davies
Art Direction for Photography Emma Forge
Managing Editor Penny Warren
Managing Art Editor Glenda Fisher
Publisher Peggy Vance

First published in Great Britain in 2011
by Dorling Kindersley Limited
80 Strand, London WC2R ORL

Penguin Group (UK)

A CIP catalogue record for this book is
available from the British Library

ISBN: 978-1-4053-4823-2

Printed and bound by Tien Wah Press, Singapore

Discover more at **www.dk.com**

contents

about the author

Megan Faure BSc, OT, OTR is an occupational therapist who has worked in paediatrics in the USA and South Africa for more than a decade. She is an active member of the South African Institute for Sensory Integration (SAISI), which is the body that oversees all therapists specializing in sensory integration in South Africa. It is affiliated with the sensory integration organizations in the USA.

As well as being a lecturer for SAISI on the treatment and theory of sensory integration disorders, Megan regularly lectures to both professionals and parents on various baby and childcare issues, in particular how to help infants with extreme fussiness, poor sleep habits and feeding problems. Megan is the founder and chairperson of the Infant Sensory Integration Training group, which provides courses for therapists to equip them to understand and treat infant behaviour.

Megan is a journalist and author in the field of child psychology, parenting and child development. Passionate about her work and her research into the field of infant development, particularly sensory integration, she felt that an understanding of the way a baby processes the world and the impact the sensory world has on sleep, feeding and development needed to be communicated to parents. With this goal in mind, she has written extensively on this method – she is the author of three previous books and writes for several regional and national publications in the UK and South Africa. She has made numerous television appearances and delivers talks on child rearing at NCT conferences and at the Baby Show in the UK and at many locations across South Africa. Megan runs a practice in Cape Town where she sees babies and toddlers with sleep problems and sensory processing difficulties. She is married with a son and two daughters.

introduction

You are about to embark on the most exciting part of your life. Over the next 12 months, you will meet, fall in love with and form a lifelong commitment to a new human being. In the process you will grow yourself, becoming someone altogether different from the person you have been until now. This little life and your new role as a parent will develop you in ways you will not be able to anticipate.

As with any new relationship and any new role in life, there will be days when you feel a little out of your depth and wonder whether you are doing the right thing. You are likely to focus your concerns on three main areas over the next year at least: how to understand and soothe your little one, when you can next expect a good night's sleep, and whether you are feeding your baby adequately. Your own well being and how you are feeling and coping as a parent will be an ongoing but secondary concern – how life changes!

The Babysense Secret addresses these key aspects of parenting from a unique perspective. I am an occupational therapist fascinated by the developing brain, and I believe that your baby's brain provides the key to these critical areas of babycare. The secret is to look first at how your baby's brain processed the world inside the womb and then at how it is affected by our own busy world. Once you understand both worlds through your baby's eyes and other senses, you will hold the key to her contentment, sleep, feeding and general development – and also to your own growth into a confident parent.

The first three chapters of the book look at your baby's senses and how they affect her emotions, sleep patterns and development. By understanding your baby's sensory world and learning to spot and act on her signals, you will become a sensitive parent who knows how to react to your baby's needs and is ready to be guided by her into a gentle and flexible routine. For most parents, the promise of a routine brings a return of some longed-for predictability.

Chapter 4 reveals your baby's secret language and shows you how to communicate with her in a simple and accessible way. You will find out when she needs to sleep, whether she is hungry, or if she is ready for stimulation and learning experiences. By Chapter 5 you will have absorbed all the easy principles of the Baby Sense approach and have found a little more equilibrium as you and your infant develop a baby-centric routine for feeding, sleeping and play. You can then turn to the practical tips in the age-banded chapters that make up the second half of the book.

Almost every parent I have ever spoken to has longed for a manual explaining exactly how to "read" their baby and understand the hows, whys and whens of sleeping, feeding and stimulation. It's right there in your arms – your baby holds all the answers. She will tell you what she needs and when she needs it.

As you take *The Babysense Secret* on your path into parenthood, may you have many happy days and peaceful nights.

Meg Faure

chapter 1

understanding your baby's sensory world

Kate is so relieved to be in labour. She has been very uncomfortable in the last trimester and is looking forward to meeting her baby. Deep inside her, tiny Jess is experiencing the labour quite differently. Jess has been very comfortable in her perfect womb world. In fact, she found the last trimester particularly soothing as the tight uterine walls contained her movements and provided a deep calming hug. Jess will soon enter a place that is as foreign as it is overwhelming. Over the next twelve months, Jess will discover how to make sense of her new environment. Likewise, her mum Kate has twelve months ahead of her in which she will learn how to read her little one, soothe her, and help her to make sense of our busy world.

learn how to ...

- Understand how your baby's senses develop.
- Discover your own personal sensory experience.
- Understand how and why your baby behaves in response to sensory information.
- Recognize why babies are so different.
- Identify your baby's unique sensory personality.

the secrets of the senses

We live in a sensory-rich world and spend each waking moment taking in information from the world through our senses. The intricate nervous system and brain process this sensory information and we respond emotionally and act on it. As we encounter various situations, we develop the ability to select which sensory information to attend to and how to respond. Your young baby's brain, however, has yet to develop such skills. For the first few months of life she is unable to control what sensory input she takes in, or how she responds to that information.

why the senses are important

There is always a good reason for crying or resisting sleep. Understanding your baby's immature nervous system will help you to appreciate this and perceive the world as she experiences it. Calming a newborn is all about understanding the effect of your baby's environment on her behaviour. The key to keeping her content is recognizing the signals she uses to indicate when, why and how you should nurture, stimulate, and calm her. Then, instead of following rules and strict routines or feeling your way in the dark, you will discover the reasons behind her behaviour. Even better, you will learn the secret of providing appropriate stimulation and thereby make the most of your baby's inborn potential.

sensory experience

The nervous system is made up of the brain, spinal cord, and nerves. The brain's role is to take in information (input), decide what is important and relevant, then interpret the information so that we can perform an appropriate action in response. This input is delivered to the brain through the senses. Our sensory experience is not limited to input from the external world via the five senses of touch, smell, sight, hearing, and taste. There are also three "body senses" that give the brain information about our internal world: movement (vestibular sense), body position (proprioception), and information from our organs (interoception). In order to understand your baby's behaviour, it is useful to see how these senses help us to build a picture of the world.

five external senses

- **Touch** Skin is the body's largest organ and receives information from the world about temperature, pain, touch, and pressure. Touch is the first sense to develop in the womb and plays a critical role in intelligence, mood, and survival. A well-developed sense of touch gives us a picture of ourselves and the world, telling us where we have been touched, how hard or soft, and what we are touching. The sense of touch helps the

sense-able secret

Touch affects bonding and attachment. Touch and cuddle your baby as much as you can to create a positive body image and establish self-esteem.

brain to plan body movements and so affects sporting ability later in life. On a survival level, your newborn will turn to feed in response to a touch on her face. Later the sense of touch can protect her from danger, for example from a bath that is too hot. You use touch to care for and comfort your baby, so building an emotional bond.

● **Smell** Chemical receptors in the mucous membranes of the nose perceive smells. Unlike the other senses, which pass through a relay station in the brain, sensations from the nose go directly to its emotion centre. This explains the strong emotional response we have to scents and odours and the strong memories evoked by familiar smells. We can return to childhood emotions in a flash when we encounter a smell such as the perfume our mother wore as she kissed us goodnight.

● **Sight** The eyes perceive form, light, and colour. At birth the sense of sight is the least developed, but newborns do take an interest in bright lights and contrasting colours. Within a week or so the eyes begin to orient to and track interesting objects, such as mum's face.

● **Sound** This is carried by airwaves and picked up and registered by receptors in the inner ear. Babies quickly learn to identify the direction of a sound, and then attach meaning to different sounds.

● **Taste** Perceived by receptors on the tongue, the sense of taste is closely linked to smell. The chemical receptors on different parts of the tongue are sensitive to salty, sour, bitter, and sweet tastes. Babies prefer sweet tastes, to prime them to seek out the sweet taste of breast milk.

eye to eye At birth, your baby's sight is fuzzy, so she will focus best when you hold her 20–25cm (8–10in) away from your face. At this distance, you are the centre of her attention.

three internal senses

● **Movement (vestibular)** Receptors in the inner ear sense changes of body position, most specifically, movement of the head. When this sense functions well, we know in which direction we are moving, how fast and whether we are speeding up or slowing down. If it does not function well, we may feel nauseous or threatened by normal movement.

● **Body position (proprioception)** Muscles and joints give us information about the position of our body in space and how our limbs are moving. Movement against resistance, exercise, and deep pressure touch are linked to proprioception. Many people make use of this sense to manage stress or when feeling disorganized by taking a long jog or a yoga class or enjoying a deep hug. The information sent from our muscles and joints during these activities can have a soothing effect.

● **Interoception** Our internal organs give information about how comfortable the body is and its survival needs. Messages are sent from the digestive, temperature regulation, and elimination systems. These internal messages result in action and a feeling of well being or general discomfort, which we might experience as indigestion or the urge to urinate. Your newborn finds it difficult to interpret this, making her a little unsettled.

discovering new tastes Your baby enjoys sweet tastes so that she is primed for breast milk, but as she grows you can introduce her to a wide variety of flavours.

social butterfly baby Very alert and delighting in attention, the social butterfly loves being around people and having fun.

slow-to-warm-up baby This baby may take a while to adjust to new situations and so will like to observe the world from the safety of your arms.

the babysense secret

every baby is different

Just as computers are set with different levels of spam filter, so each of us filters sensory input to a varying degree. Some people naturally filter a large amount of sensory input and therefore do not register or react to unimportant stimuli. Since less sensory input is taken in, these personality types are generally much less susceptible to over-stimulation. On the other hand, those who are hyper-responsive to sensory input perceive every little sensation and may be easily over-stimulated.

getting to know your baby

Every baby is different. Spend just an hour at a parent-and-baby group and you will be able to pick out the really laid back, easy-going babies from those who are more high maintenance and maybe a little fractious. As a mother, how you interact with your baby will have a significant impact on her response to the world. If, from the early days, you start to take notice of your baby's temperament, you can alter the way you interact with her to positively affect her approach to life and the way she gets on with others. There are four main sensory personalities:

social butterfly This baby loves interacting with others and her world. She is alert and seems to be constantly on the move, inviting interaction and smiles from everyone. A walk to the shops takes a long time because she makes eye contact with strangers. Life with a social butterfly is never dull but can be exhausting, especially in the toddler years when these babies tend to be busy and a little impulsive. She is not happy when left alone for long because she just loves being in the company of others. These personality types love to be carried and you may find yourself getting frustrated that you never have your hands free.

The social butterfly loves sensory input and stimulation through the senses, which she uses to interact happily with people. If she gets too little stimulation, she can become grumpy because she is not getting enough information from her world. She can also become over-stimulated with little warning because she seeks so much sensory input.

slow-to-warm-up baby Some babies are sensitive to change and take a while to adjust to new situations and people or unfamiliar sensory information. This can make them appear shy. But unlike the sensitive baby (see opposite) who is fractious, the slow-to-warm-up baby is calm as long as she is near her parents. As older babies and toddlers, they may be known as "Velcro babies" because they are happiest when next to mum or on her lap. This baby loves a routine because it makes her life predictable, and is easily upset by changes in her schedule. A slow-to-warm-up baby with no routine is very hard to manage, often needing to be soothed by being carried or fed. As older children, they are quiet and a little anxious. They are shy and tend to withdraw rather than embrace new situations. But once they feel comfortable with a friend or in an environment, they warm up and can be the life of the party.

Your slow-to-warm-up baby's brain is not good at filtering lots of sensory information – she is easily overwhelmed by sensory input and novelty. As her brain gets used to a new sensation she will start to filter better and so will settle and become calmer. Since she is initially sensitive, she tends to avoid situations that are new and potentially overwhelming.

settled baby Easy to care for because she is so placid and calm, the settled baby is the most laid back of the personality types.

settled baby If your baby seems much more laid back than others, she may be a settled baby, the most easy-going of all the sensory personalities. This type of baby sleeps and feeds with ease wherever she is, copes well with stimulation and interaction and is flexible enough to cope with changes in her routine. By the time she is a few weeks old, this baby will be starting to settle into a routine, sleep well, and will be generally content. It is predominantly settled babies who sleep though the night early in life. But their development may be a little slower than that of other babies. There is no rush to roll or crawl because this baby is quite content to lie back and watch the world go by. As a toddler, the settled child is as happy at home reading books as she is going out and about.

This baby has a natural capacity to filter a lot of sensory information. She doesn't register sensory input that is not clear and strong. The brain filters sounds so well that your baby will not easily be woken by noise; and touch is filtered so effectively that she is not bothered by a dirty nappy.

sensitive baby Some babies are just more fussy and sensitive than most. The sensitive baby is very tuned in to the world. She often takes a long time to settle and is more fussy than other babies. Parenting a sensitive baby can be a challenge. Breastfeeding may get off to a rough start because she is sensitive to the feel of your nipple, the touch of your skin, and the smell and tastes involved in breastfeeding. She is best fed in a quiet room with dim lighting soon after a sleep, when she is calmest. Your sensitive baby does not learn to soothe herself as easily as other babies. In addition, it may be a challenge to calm her yourself. She may act as though she does not like being swaddled (she is sensitive to the blanket and pressure) and does not take to dummies (her mouth is sensitive as well). It is important to persist with swaddling and sucking strategies because this will make your life much easier. A sensitive baby is overwhelmed by sensory information because she does not filter it well – every stimulus feels like a potential threat. She needs you to filter the sensory environment for her, especially as a newborn (see pp.23–27).

sensitive baby With greater needs than other babies, you will need to keep the sensitive baby's world calm because she can easily become over-stimulated and upset.

sense-able secret

Disturbing sensory input, such as your toddler's boisterous play, may overload your newborn with too much information. Part of your role as a parent is to shelter your baby from excessive stimulation.

sensory processing

At all times our complex brains are processing endless streams of sensory input. Since there are five times more nerves entering the brain with sensory input than leaving it with messages for action, it stands to reason that the brain has an enormous task in making sense of all this information. Luckily, much like an email inbox, the brain has a "spam filter" (referred to as "habituation") that prevents excess sensory information from being registered. This process of filtering begins when sensory information reaches the nervous system and prevents the brain from becoming overwhelmed by sounds, sensations, and sensory input.

filtering sensory information

In the delivery room, Kate is completely focused on her breathing and the voice of the midwife who is coaching her through each contraction. She has absolutely filtered out the cricket game that her husband is intermittently following on the television.

When sensory information is irrelevant or very familiar, the brain's spam filter kicks in and we do not even register the stimuli. The background sound of the TV in the delivery room will not interest or disturb you during the final stage of labour. Likewise, you probably can't feel your shirt on your back nor smell your fabric softener. These are all examples of the brain filtering out unimportant information, in a process of habituation. This is why people who live near railway lines aren't woken up by the sound of trains at night; because they get used to hearing the same sound at the same time, they filter it out. But the brain does not filter sensory information that is important or relevant.

Returning home after the birth of Jess, Kate feels the overwhelming responsibility of caring for her new baby. As she goes to shower, she wonders anxiously if she will hear Jess cry. She needn't worry because Jess's cry will seem louder to her than any other sound in the home.

If the sensory information is vital or life threatening, we do the opposite from filter: we become sensitized to the input and it grabs our attention. This is the reason that Jess's cry (above) seems louder to Kate than that of any sound in her home.

Filtering is vital. It allows us to focus on important information without becoming over-stimulated by irrelevant "noise". If this process doesn't work as well as it can, a great deal of unimportant information bombards the nervous system, creating over-stimulation or sensory overload. How well a baby filters information depends on his or her personality type and also three other factors: time of day, stress, and age (see opposite). Adults are also subject to these factors, except that personality type is more important than age in filtering stimuli.

filtering sensation

The ability to filter sensory information is linked to our individual sensory capabilities – whether we ourselves are a social butterfly or slow-to-warm-up – but it is not static. For instance, there are times in life when you behave like a sensitive mum, even though you are usually a settled type. Likewise, your settled baby may have periods in the day when she is more sensitive. Three main factors affect your baby's ability to filter sensory information:

1 time of day Ask any seasoned mother and she will have a name for the early evening: "horror hour", "witching hour", and so on. At this time, you and your baby will have lower tolerance for sensory information and stressful situations, while your toddler may become fractious, argumentative, and a lot busier. Your newborn is more likely to experience colic at this time, and you have lower levels of breast milk, and a lower tolerance for your little one's antics.

2 stress Any new situation increases our stress levels. If we can meet the requirements of the situation, for example, bringing your new baby home, we cope, but if for any reason we experience the situation as threatening, we become stressed. In this state adults are more sensitive to stimuli than when they are relaxed. The stress of a new baby may cause you to become hypersensitive to sounds, touch, and smells. This sensory overload can result in tension in the home as you become over-sensitized to your baby's cry or toddler's voice, or to your partner's demands or offers of help.

3 age This is one of the biggest factors affecting your baby's ability to filter sensory input. In the first three months, she does not have the ability to fully filter sensory input and so is particularly susceptible to over-stimulation. This book is banded by age (chapters 7 to 13), and each chapter offers strategies to help you work with your baby's developing ability to filter sensation. This will help you to develop healthy routines.

Once you understand your baby's sensory personality (see pp.14–15) and her current stage in filtering input, you will be better equipped to stimulate her, keep her content, and develop gentle routines that foster healthy sleep and feeding, and you will have an easier life as a mother.

sensory story

time of day In the late afternoon when Jess and Kate are both tired and Kate's milk supply dips, Kate finds that she is much more sensitive. If her sister drops in with her two-year-old at this time of day, Kate feels hypersensitive to the toddler's shrieks and becomes irritated and easily upset.

stress When Jess was only three weeks' old, Kate went on her first outing to her mums' group. Jess was sound asleep and Kate felt great to be out and about. After an hour, Jess woke and began to cry. Kate was suddenly confronted with the stress of changing a screaming baby's nappy in public and breastfeeding her. Jess screamed incessantly and the stress was all too much for Kate. She became hypersensitive to the crying and found her eyes prickling with tears.

age Like many babies, Jess niggles in the late afternoon because her ability to filter sensory input is low at this time of day. Kate tries bathing and massaging Jess to soothe her. Unfortunately, all this additional, well-meant stimulation only makes Jess cry all the more. But at around nine weeks old, Kate notices a shift and suddenly Jess becomes easier in the evenings.

"The process of filtering prevents the brain from becoming overwhelmed by sounds, sensations, and sensory input."

chapter 2

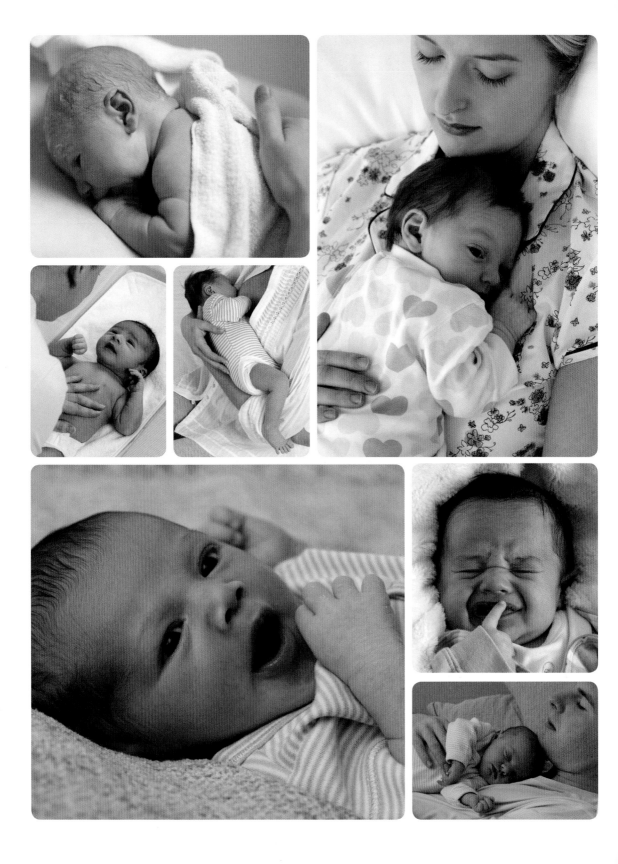

from the womb into the world

James stands at Charlotte's side holding her hand, his face wet with tears as their little boy makes his entrance. James has never felt so overwhelmed with pride and love. Nicholas takes his first breath and cries softly, searching the room for his parents' eyes. His senses are bombarded by this new world of light, sound, and smell. As Nicholas is handed to Charlotte, his mum, he is assaulted by a barrage of new sensory input: the cold air of the delivery room, the smells of Charlotte mixed with pungent, sterile odours, and the bright lights that prevent him from finding her face. Nicholas is overwhelmed by the abrupt change and in order to smooth his transition from womb to world, his parents will need to adjust the environment as much as they can, once home. At the hospital, they could start this process by asking for the lights to be dimmed and reducing unnecessary sound, to make his transition gentle.

learn how to ...
- Understand your baby's sensory world in the womb.
- Smooth his transition from womb to world.
- Provide sensory care straight after birth.
- Create sensory soothing "mum-space" and "baby space".
- Prepare your newborn's nursery.

sensory world of the womb

The womb is the optimal place for the developing foetus. Nutrients are delivered in just the right quantities and your body releases hormones that cross the placenta and regulate growth and development perfectly. Your baby can sleep and wake in a constant temperature, in a bespoke incubator, as it were. The sensory environment of the womb holds the key to many aspects of your baby's development. This experience *in utero* wires his brain for learning later on.

understanding the womb world

Being aware of the sensory input your baby experiences in the womb will help you smooth his transition to the outside world. It will also make him feel more contented during his first days and weeks as his new senses develop. Consider the following factors:

touch Beginning to develop at only three weeks' gestation, when your baby is only the size of a tiny bean (13mm / ½in long), the sense of touch is the first sense to appear. He has small appendages that will develop into fingers (at around seven weeks), but can feel and respond to touch on these, and around his mouth. By 12 weeks' gestation, his entire body is sensitive to touch, except the top of his head, which remains insensitive throughout pregnancy, possibly because of the impending "big squeeze" through the birth canal! In the weeks leading up to birth, the elastic uterus provides constant, deep pressure, like an all-day hug or massage. The uterine world is devoid of light touch. This tight hug keeps your baby secured in a little ball shape with pressure exerted on his back and his hands guided towards the midline (centre of his body). In this position, your baby can suck on his hands, an important soothing strategy. His reflexes are immature but starting to emerge and are contained by the pressure so that he feels secure. In addition to this, the temperature in the womb is always perfect – known as neutral warmth.

Although Nicholas can't see his mum clearly at birth, he immediately feels her calming touch when she cuddles him; he feels the change in temperature from the warm world of the womb to the cold air of the delivery room. If he is given an injection, he'll also feel the painful prick of a needle, but it will be a while before his sense of touch is advanced enough to discriminate exactly where he is being touched or pricked.

ideal space The pressure in the womb keeps your baby's hands pulled in towards his face, which helps him to start sucking his thumb, an important soothing strategy.

sight Your baby's tiny eyelids open at 26 weeks and at six months' gestation we know that babies are sensitive to light in the womb. If someone shone a bright torch light onto your tummy at 32 weeks' gestation your baby could track the light from left to right. Even though your baby is interested in this bright light, the reality is that he is rarely exposed to bright light and there is very little visual stimulation *in utero*. In general, the womb world is visually muted and is often quite dark, especially if you are wearing dark or heavily layered clothes. There are no bright colours or contrasting shapes in the womb on which your little one can hone his developing visual skills.

Nicholas's sense of sight is his least-developed sense at birth, showing him a fuzzy picture of the world. He can only focus on objects that are about 20–25cm (8–10in) from his eyes – the perfect distance to make out his mother's features as Nicholas lies in her arms or feeds at her breast. Initially he sees high-contrasting colour images most clearly.

sound Your baby's sense of sound develops from the second trimester and before 20 weeks' gestation, he can hear and respond to loud noises. On the day he is born, your baby has about five months' listening experience. In the womb, all sounds are subdued: since the sound waves have to travel through water, they slow down before reaching your baby's ears. He therefore receives sounds at a low frequency. The clearest sound he hears is your voice because it is carried not only outside the body but also through your bones in the form of vibrations. Your partner's voice is the second most familiar sound – within hours of birth your baby will recognize your partner by his voice.

Even when the world outside the womb is silent, your baby hears the quiet gushes of amniotic fluid and blood flowing in your veins and of course your heartbeat and digestive system. These background noises contribute to an audio landscape of constant white noise. The consistent sound of your heartbeat is particularly soothing for babies. Experts have found that babies who are played a beat at the pace of the average heartbeat (72 beats per minute) fall asleep more easily and cry half as much after birth. White noise, such as running water and sounds that resemble those heard *in utero*, helps us to sleep better, regardless of age.

After birth Nicholas hears completely different sounds from those he heard *in utero*. No longer does the amniotic fluid dampen and slow sound down. Every noise Nicholas hears sounds louder and harsher. Those that are loud and irregular he finds stimulating, while quiet, rhythmical white noise helps to calm him down.

movement and gravity The sense of movement and gravity created by the balance (vestibular) system in the ears begins to function at five months' gestation. Like the senses of hearing and touch, the sense of movement is relatively advanced at birth. Interestingly, it will only reach full maturity much later – in adolescence – because unlike the other sensory nerves in the brain, nerves conducting movement

first sight Straight after birth, your newborn will focus intently on your face if held the perfect distance away.

getting to know you Sounds heard in the womb, such as your family's voices, will be familiar and soothing to a baby after birth.

from the womb into the world

21

information take a long time to mature. In the womb your baby is supported by amniotic fluid and floats freely in a contained liquid bubble. Since our bodies feel many times lighter in water than in air, your baby has the wonderful sensation of being much lighter than on earth. He is lulled by the constant rocking and swaying motion of this gravity-reduced world. While you move, your baby is gently rocked to sleep, and when the lulling movement stops – such as when you rest or lie down – he may become wakeful and busy, which you may feel as little jabs and kicks. During the third trimester, his vestibular system will have matured sufficiently to sense gravity and to turn into the appropriate head-down position in preparation for birth.

When Nicholas is born, his movement system is suddenly confronted with feeling many times heavier than before, and he must try to move against gravity. The greatest motor goal of every baby's first year is to gain control against gravity, starting with lifting his head.

sense-able secret
Our bodies move with an element of rotation as we walk. This is why many babies are calmed more effectively when carried than when pushed in a pram.

smell and taste Your baby's senses of smell and taste begin to function at 28 weeks' gestation. During pregnancy, when you eat something sweet, the taste crosses the placenta and sweetens the amniotic fluid. Your baby will swallow the amniotic fluid more frequently when this happens, because he enjoys the taste. By the last trimester your baby's taste and smell are highly tuned and he can taste the food you eat and even smell odours from the outside world (these are carried through the amniotic fluid in chemical signals).

Nicholas's sense of smell is so sensitive at birth that he can identify the smell of his mum's breast milk on a cotton swab. If his mum is his principal caregiver – especially if he is breastfed – by the time he is two weeks old, Nicholas will know and recognize her smell better than his dad's.

what can you do?
By the last trimester of pregnancy, Nicholas's sensory system is quite well-developed and getting ready to deal with the outside world. In the womb, he exists in an incredibly stimulus-rich environment. He hears the gurgles, throbs, and gushes of his mum's body and feels the vibrations of her movements, voice, and heart rate. He can taste the flavour and feel the warmth of the amniotic fluid. This cacophony of sensory input are predominantly calming stimuli. As opposed to becoming over-stimulated by the womb world, your baby begins life in an incredibly calming world. From a sensory perspective, it is the ideal place to develop.

To make your baby's transition into the real world smoother, you can try to model his new sensory world on this *in utero* sensory paradise. Your task is to smooth your baby's transition into the outside world, both on the day of his birth and the weeks after.

breastfeeding benefits Sweet tastes, such as breast milk, encourage babies to suck on their hands, a very important self-calming strategy.

the **babysense** secret

on the birth day

There are various strategies you can use to help your baby become accustomed to being outside the womb. If you are having a hospital birth, you may wish to include some of these in your birth plan.

touch For nine months the only form of touch your baby has experienced is skin to skin – his naked skin against your uterine walls. Once your baby is born the best thing you can do is to lie him skin to skin against your tummy and chest. Place your naked baby against your chest, covering both of you with a blanket or towel to keep him warm (put a nappy on him if you are worried about mishaps). If the room is cold or he seems cool, you can put a hat on his head. In this position your baby can latch onto your breast and begin to feed at his convenience. This perfectly natural position is commonly called Kangaroo Care (see p.81). In the early days, aim to "kangaroo" your baby for as many hours as possible. Even babies delivered by Caesarean section can be warmed up on their mum's chest instead of being removed to a clinical incubator. New mothers' bodies are so tuned in to their babies that their body temperature will adjust to keep the baby at the optimal temperature.

sight In the moments after your baby's birth you may notice small "saccades" – tiny shifts of his eye movements – as he scans the room looking for your face. These saccades have been shown to stop only when a baby's eyes meet his mum's or dad's. To help your baby find your face and to create a visually soothing space, ask for the delivery room lights to be dimmed and bring him to your chest, 20–25cm (8–10in) from your eyes. This is the perfect distance for his eyes to focus on your face.

sound The sound that your baby has been most familiar with *in utero* is your voice. For a period of time immediately after birth, your newborn will be calm and alert, listening to and focusing on you. Both you and your partner can talk quietly to your baby to calm him after birth.

smell The smells your baby loves best are the familiar smell of the womb and the sweet smell of breast milk. Do not wash your baby immediately after birth. Wipe him down if he is a little bloody but do not wash off the vernix (see image, right). There is evidence that unwashed babies bring their hands to their mouths sooner after birth than washed babies. Sucking on his hands is one of the first, really important strategies your baby will use to calm himself. Aside from vernix, the soothing smells of mum are comforting at this stage. Therefore, hold your baby or have him close to you as much as possible in the early days.

when things don't go according to plan

Even with a carefully thought through birth plan and realistic ideas on your ideal birth, there is a chance that your baby's birth day will be very different from the picture you envisaged. If your baby is ill or in distress or if you are exhausted after a traumatic birth, you may need to follow the advice of your medical team and may be separated from your baby for a while. Do not let this negative experience be your focus, rather be proactive. Tell the team that as soon as you are able, you would like to "kangaroo" your baby skin-to-skin. Even if a few days have passed, take the time to undress him and place him on your chest. This will be healing for you both.

natural moisturizer Vernix is a natural white, waxy coating that protects your baby *in utero*. Within days of birth this substance will be absorbed into your baby's skin.

from the womb into the world

23

into the world

In the weeks after his birth, your baby will spend many of his waking hours in "mum space" – in your or his dad's arms. Treat the first three months of your baby's life like a fourth trimester *in utero*. By modelling his experiences in the delivery room, in the nursery, and in your arms on the womb world, you will find you are well on the way to a contented baby. You can help to make your baby's experience of the world and of social interactions as soothing as possible by following these sensory principles:

smell Do not wear any perfume or aftershave lotion until your baby is a few months old; even then only introduce scents slowly and watch his reactions. The artificial aromas of personal-care products and air freshener can easily overload him. This is especially true if you're breastfeeding, which brings him into very close proximity to your body scents. It is sensible for dad to remove his work clothes as soon as he comes home. This eliminates all the smells carried on work clothes, such as the scent of public transport, to which your baby could be extremely sensitive in the late afternoon. Both for his health and optimal sensory development, it is advisable not to smoke in the same house as your baby.

sight Wear a little make-up, especially around your eyes. This will draw your baby's attention to your face, which helps to improve his focus and encourage his interactions with you in the early weeks of life.

touch When handling your baby, use a gentle but firm touch, which will help him to feel secure and contained. Wear soft, comfortable clothing that he can snuggle into. New babies are sensitive to being passed around – have family members or friends handle your baby in a quiet environment when he is content. Each time your baby is held by a new person, his sensory system absorbs a great deal of information about that person, especially about their smell, touch, and sound. You may find that you are sensitive to your baby being handled too much. Listen to your gut instinct and don't be shy about telling people that your little one has been passed around enough.

movement Your baby will find the calming movements of rocking and swaying soothing because they are similar to those he experienced in the womb. If he is awake but fussing, sway gently as you hold him.

A sling or baby carrier is an easy way to carry him, freeing your hands. There are two main types of carrier: the fabric sling in which the baby lies almost horizontal, and the upright carrier. Slings are versatile and can be used as supports for hip carrying in the toddler years. They can also be

baby carriers
❶ Slings are better for a young baby because they support the neck and body fully. He can even feed from this position. ❷ Upright baby carriers should only be used once your baby has a degree of head control (at around eight weeks), but are useful well into the ninth month and even later if your baby is small.

the **babysense** secret

used as an upright carrier later, but not with the same ease as purpose-made upright carriers. In a carrier, your baby can face inwards or outwards, depending on how much visual stimulation you want him to have. If it is sleep time, face him in towards your chest. If it is his awake time (see p.51) and he can be stimulated, turn him to face outwards. In some cultures babies are carried on their mothers' backs, which is also wonderful. If you know someone who can teach you how to tie your baby on to your back safely, try this successful, time-honoured method.

your baby's sleep space

Whether your baby sleeps in your bed, in your room in a cot, or in his own nursery, you will need to prepare for his arrival. His space needs to be calm and conducive to sleep. Obviously a baby will wake for feeds, but by keeping the room calm you will increase the chances of him dropping off to sleep – and staying asleep – for longer stretches as he gets older.

sight A dimmer is useful for winding down at bedtime and for night feeds. Keeping the night feed environment as calm, dark, and quiet as possible makes it more likely that your baby will drop back off to sleep after a feed. If the room is fully lit and your baby is spoken to loudly or played with, he may think the night life is worth staying awake for.

Decorate your baby's room in muted colours if he will spend time there during the first few months. Try traditional baby hues and neutral creams. Wait until your baby is six months old before decorating the room with bright fabrics or colourful wallpaper. Line the curtains or blinds with black-out lining (see Resources, pp.214–15) to make the room darker and more womb-like, promoting calm sleep times. This is especially important for daytime sleep periods, which your baby will need – and you will treasure – right up to three years old. It's best not to put any toys in or mobiles over the cot. The cot must be a sleeping space only, not a play area. Place toys or pictures in contrasting colours (black and white) near the changing mat where your baby will be awake and can be stimulated.

swaddling A swaddled newborn is a more settled baby and will sleep for longer stretches. Swaddling (wrapping a baby snugly in a blanket, see overleaf) is very important in the early days because it's the best way to imitate the tight hug of the womb. This provides calming deep pressure, and stops limbs from shooting out due to the startle or moro reflex (involuntary, jerky movements of the arms and legs), which is a common cause of night waking in young babies. For the first nine to twelve weeks, you may want to swaddle your baby for all sleeps and when he's unsettled or colicky. Make sure your baby has some time to kick free of the swaddle when awake. It's a good idea to have at least two swaddling blankets.

night and day Dim the lights and feed your baby in a quiet environment at night, with limited interaction and gentle movements, so that he associates the night with calm and sleep.

sensory story

preparing Prior to the birth of Nicholas, James would tease Charlotte for "nesting". She was busily putting together a special place for when Nicholas arrived. She was still uncertain what was essential for the nursery or even whether he would sleep there or in her room. However, she did know that she would be decorating the nursery in soothing colours, with a dimmer switch to induce calm lighting, and buying soft cotton sheets for Nicholas to sleep on.

swaddling It is very important to swaddle your baby with his hands near his face so he can suck on them to soothe himself. Swaddling your baby with his hands by his sides is not a good option because he will not be able to calm himself, nor to regulate his temperature. Always swaddle with a pure cotton stretchy blanket as polyester can cause overheating. Either fold a rectangular blanket into a triangle or use a specially shaped swaddling blanket.

how to swaddle

❶ Lie your baby with his neck on the long side of the triangle.
❷ Fold up the lower tip of the blanket.
❸ Wrap one corner of the triangle across your baby, leaving his hand near his face so that he can calm himself by sucking his hand if he needs to.
❹ Wrap the other corner of the triangle across his body and tuck the edge in beneath him.

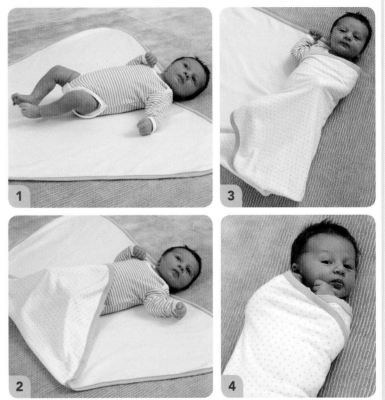

touch Bed linen must be soft. Cotton cot sheets are wonderful, but muslin squares and soft sarongs, tucked in securely, also make excellent bottom sheets. Softness is important, because rough textures are more likely to wake a sensitive baby at night.

smell In the early days, keep your baby's space free from any scent – his olfactory system is very sensitive. As he gets older, lavender in a burner in the room, or as a room spray is calming and will help him to sleep better. Place a small item of clothing or a blanket that smells of you in the cot for comfort and encourage your baby to adopt this as his sleep object.

sound To help your baby fall asleep and to help him develop good sleep habits, try to recreate the intrauterine environment. White noise and womb sounds are calming in the early weeks. You could make a recording of white noise (the vacuum cleaner, washing machine or radio static) to play to your baby, or look for a commercial recording. Also available are CDs of calming music mixed with the steady beating of a heart.

the **babysense** secret

movement A rocking chair is a useful aid at feed times. Your baby will love the soothing rocking motion. Ensure it is comfortable and provides support for your arms and neck – you'll probably spend a lot of time in it in the early weeks. Don't use it to get your baby actually to fall asleep, but rather to calm him into a drowsy state before you put him into his cot to fall asleep on his own. A rocking or suspended cot provides that little extra calming input to settle your baby to sleep.

soothing clothes

Nicholas has been spoilt with the cutest little outfits. James's sister has even bought him some designer denim clothes. James has begun to notice that on the days when Nicholas is dressed up in these trendy outfits, he is a little more irritable than usual. He is wondering if Nicholas is sensitive to the touch experience of stiff fabrics.

- **Touch** Like bedding, vests and clothes may cause your baby to wake and niggle frequently if the fabric is rough or the seams prickly. Denim, corduroy, lace, stiff cotton, scratchy wool, and other stiff or textured fabrics can be irritating. Favour soft fabrics and turn vests inside out if the seams disturb your baby. You can also look for seam-free clothing, or unpick or cut the labels off vests, if these appear to distress your baby.
- **Smell** Cleaning agents leave a smell on your baby's clothes. Even the lightest fragrance that we can barely pick up can upset your new baby's sensitive sense of smell. Furthermore, some fragrances and chemicals irritate a newborn's skin and can even cause allergies. Therefore, the products you use to wash and rinse your baby's clothes may affect how calm and comfortable he is. You might like to wash all new clothes before use to remove the chemical treatments.

developing focus Place a brightly coloured mobile over the changing mat for your baby to look at. This is a place where he is awake and can be stimulated.

your sensory baby

The sensitive baby and the slow-to-warm-up baby are more likely to react negatively to stimulating input in the early days than other babies. Many mothers find that these babies cry easily when confronted with strong smells or excessively bright lights. They sleep best with soft clothes and bed linen. It pays to be especially aware of the sensory input your sensitive baby experiences in the early days.

The social butterfly baby enjoys stimulation and is much less likely to be overwhelmed by sensory input, even when very young. For this reason you can be less concerned about what information he receives from the world and the level of sensory input in his environment.

A settled baby takes the new experiences of the world in his stride. He sleeps easily even in the presence of lots of stimuli and doesn't suffer from colic (see p.112). If you have this type of baby, you may enjoy getting out and about more, because he is less troubled by his sensory environment.

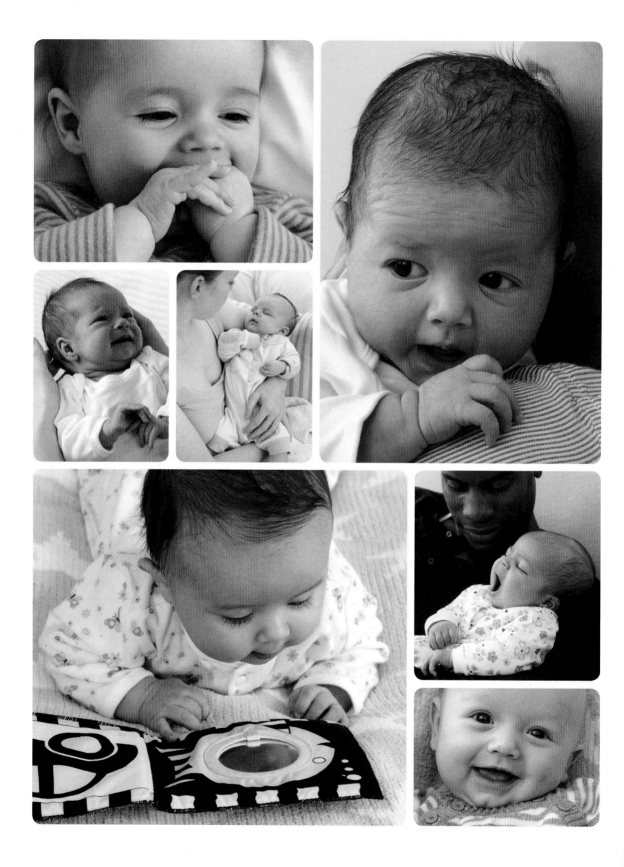

how the sensory world affects your baby

It is one of Matthew's first outings to the shops. After 12 weeks of motherhood, Julia is feeling trapped indoors and just needs to get out. After a morning of window shopping, she sits in the café on the edge of a bustling street with Matthew on her lap facing her. She begins to tickle him and bounce him on her knee. He giggles and shrieks with delight and so his doting mum stimulates him all the more. When her coffee arrives, Julia puts Matthew back in his pram to enjoy her drink. Within seconds he is screaming. Julia wonders if he is bored, and lifts him again for more fun and games, but Matthew just cries all the more. Julia tries feeding and rocking him, but nothing can soothe her baby. Matthew's immature brain has had quite enough.

learn how to ...

- Identify your baby's six states.
- Understand how sensory input affects your baby's state.
- Work out when to soothe and when to stimulate your baby.
- Help your baby to sleep.

sleep cycle

key

1 Drowsy
2 Light sleep / REM sleep
3 Hypnagogic startle
4 Deep sleep / non-REM sleep
5 Light sleep / REM sleep

the process Becoming drowsy and falling asleep, moving into deep sleep and back into a light sleep state is called a sleep cycle. An adult's sleep cycle lasts about 90 minutes, a toddler's sleep cycle is about an hour, and a baby's sleep cycle is 45 minutes long.

During the 45-minute sleep cycle, you can expect that the first 10 to 15 minutes will be a period of light sleep and in the last 10 minutes your baby will also be easily woken. During the middle 20 to 25 minutes, your baby will sleep deeply and this is the time to move your baby if you have to.

your baby's sensory states

Early parenting can seem like you are feeling your way in the dark. If you are frustrated at being unable to predict what mood comes next or how to understand your baby, you are in good company. Most parents battle in the early days to read their baby. Understanding your baby's mood is immensely helpful. It will help you to understand when to stimulate your baby and when to soothe him. These things have a long-term impact on his self-esteem and your attachment to each other.

Babies spend part of each day sleeping and another part awake. In a 24-hour period they pass through six very clear states. Each of these states contains clues that indicate how your baby is feeling and responding.

sleep states

There are two sleep states, light sleep and deep sleep (see also p.33).

light sleep As an adult you have fewer periods of light sleep than your baby, who is in a light sleep state for at least half of his sleep time. While in the light sleep state, your baby will twitch, smile, and flutter his eyes under the lids – this is known as REM (Rapid Eye Movement) sleep. During REM sleep, your baby is dreaming, processing all he has learnt during the day. We believe that this is the period when babies lay down memories and reinforce the brain pathways needed for certain skills. Since he has so much to learn, he experiences more periods of REM sleep as a baby than as an older child or adult. In this state, your baby is easily woken by external and internal sensory experiences.

As your baby falls deeper into sleep, he often experiences a sudden jerk of his muscles, called a hypnagogic startle. Even as adults we experience this jerk, but generally sleep through the minor disturbance. Your baby, however, may be woken by this startle as he falls into a deeper sleep. If your baby wakens within 15 minutes of going down or is a "catnapper", it may be this jerk that is waking him. This is particularly evident in newborns and is best managed by swaddling your baby (see p.26), containing the movement so that he is not woken.

deep sleep After a period of light sleep, your baby sinks into a deeper sleep that we call non-REM sleep. There are no rapid eye movements – your baby is very still and very hard to wake. This vital stage is the sleep state in which growth hormone is released in large quantities, which your body requires for growth and development. In the non-REM state, it is hypothesized that your baby's brain reduces unnecessary connections through a process of pruning. Each sensory and movement experience your baby has during the day results in connections being formed in the brain. You can imagine that in our sensory-rich world, a baby's brain is a rapidly increasing network of connections. Some of these connections are redundant. For instance, if your baby hears Japanese spoken for a few days in a row while you are travelling, he will begin to lay down language connections for learning Japanese. If this experience is not reinforced regularly, once you leave Japan, the connections are redundant and therefore "pruned" while your baby is in deep sleep. This pruning is vital to prevent your baby's brain becoming a muddle of connections and to avoid over-stimulation.

Without a good long period of deep sleep your baby does not get to "recharge his brain" sufficiently for the next awake period of learning. Thus babies who wake frequently or only catnap are generally more susceptible to over-stimulation.

wakeful states

There are four subtle "awake" states that are a little harder to read than the sleep states. As your baby gets older you will more easily recognize his individual signs and signals for each state. See p.33 for photographic examples of each state.

drowsy The drowsy state is seen just before sleep or when your baby wakes. His eyes look heavy and he gets the "thousand-yard stare" – looking into the distance without focusing on much at all.

calm-alert After being awake for a short period, if he has been fed and is comfortable, your baby will cross the threshold into a very responsive and content state. This is the magic calm-alert state. In this wakeful state your baby is focused and really enjoys interaction with you. He has attentive expressions, displays minimal movement, and is focused on specific stimulation, such as gazing at your face. This is the state in which your baby responds best to his world, learning the most from his experiences.

active-alert In this state your baby will kick and move his body excitedly and very vigorously. The active-alert state is not the optimal state for learning because your baby is receiving too much input from his busily moving muscles. This movement stimulation interferes with learning and distracts him. In this state he is at risk of sensory overload.

crying When he is crying, your baby is giving very clear signals that he has had enough. In this state your baby feels disorganized and overwhelmed. You will need to use sensory soothing strategies (see pp.45–47) to help your baby regulate his state and calm down.

sense-able secret
Stimulate your baby and interact with him in the calm-alert state because he will engage with you and learn through the interaction.

sensory story

deep sleep After the outing to the shops, Matthew falls into a deep sleep on the way home. He sleeps so deeply that he does not wake when Julia moves him from his pram to his cot. An hour later he is so still that Julia leans over to make sure he is still breathing. She can't believe her luck at having such an extended period of peace and quiet; usually Matthew is so easily woken from his daytime naps.

Julia has learnt an important lesson about sleep: that her baby has two states of sleep – light sleep and deep sleep.

31

the effect of stimulation on state

Picture your baby's states in descending order, with crying at the top and deep sleep at the bottom.

how sensory input affects your baby

Most babies move between the six states in a relatively ordered and predictable fashion, although social interaction and sensory information affects the states. Stimulatory or arousing input generally moves your baby up a state. Conversely, calming input tends to move your baby's state down a level, by calming his nervous system. We know that in our everyday adult lives, some substances, such as caffeine, act as stimulants, and others, such as tranquillizers, are calming. In the sensory world, the same is true: some sensory information is calming while other input is stimulating. For example, rough handling or jarring sounds make us feel on edge, but few things are more relaxing than the calming smells and the deep touch of an aromatherapy massage with lavender oil.

Knowing which sensory input is calming and which is stimulatory is important in learning how to calm your baby, settling him when he is fussing and helping him to control his state.

responding to your baby

Once you can recognize your baby's state and understand what input is calming and what is stimulating, you will have an easier time settling your baby and helping him to learn from his world.

calm-alert: stimulate It is best to stimulate your baby when he is in the calm-alert state. When he encounters sensory experiences in this state he makes connections between brain cells and learns well. He will be happy to attend to a variety of stimuli and will interact with you.
● Use a variety of different sensory input, for example, start by lying your baby under a play gym. This strengthens connections in his visual cortex, develops hand–eye coordination and strengthens muscles inside and around his eyes. Then, read to your baby, which develops connections in the language centre of the brain.
● Adjust the stimulation as your baby grows older: stimulate one sense at a time if he is less than three months old; combine sensory stimulation as he gets older.

active-alert: calm Once your baby has been stimulated for a little while he will become fractious, a clear signal that he is shifting into the active-alert state. If he is not hungry or uncomfortable, try responding in the following way:
● Try targeting a new sense, for example if your baby has been happy under a play gym (stimulating his visual sense) and becomes fractious,

your baby's six states

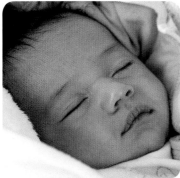

deep sleep Once your baby nods off, he will move into deep sleep. In this state, he will not be easily woken by loud noises. You may find that you can move your baby without waking him.

light sleep A loud noise (stimulatory) can move your baby from deep sleep to light sleep. You can see this if he starts to twitch or grimace in his sleep when he was previously very still.

drowsy Yawning is a good indicator that your baby is drowsy. If he is lying quietly in his cot having just woken and you look into his eyes, he will rouse and shift into a calm-alert state.

calm-alert Your baby will be eager for play and interaction now. But if you put him under a play gym for too long, the stimulus will raise his state and he may move into the active-alert state.

active-alert In this state your baby is a little fractious and trying to cope. If he is exposed to more stimulation, you may find that he raises his state further and ends up crying.

crying If your baby is crying and you rock him gently, you may find that he will settle. He may return to the active-alert state or even calm sufficiently to return to the calm-alert state.

but it is not time for a nap, move him into a space where he can stare at the wall and listen to music (stimulating his auditory sense) or take him for a walk in a sling (stimulating his sense of movement).

● If your baby is fractious, remove the stimulus or carry your baby out of the stimulating environment. Help him to soothe himself, for example by sucking on his hands or by holding onto a comfort object (see p.46).

● When it is time for your baby to sleep, help him become drowsy by using calming and soothing strategies, such as rocking or singing quietly.

how the sensory world affects your baby

1

2

3

help your baby to calm himself
1 If your baby is fractious, help him by bringing his hands to his mouth.
2 This encourages him to begin to put his hands or fingers in his mouth.
3 Once he has his fingers in his mouth, he will begin to suck them. This is an important calming strategy that develops in the womb.

crying: calm When your baby is crying and you have ruled out the basics (hunger, tiredness, wet nappy; see also p.45), over-stimulation is the most common root of crying. Help your baby to shift down a state by using calming sensory input (see chart, opposite).
● You may need to soothe your baby yourself, by rocking him, wearing him in a sling, or giving him a dummy or your finger to suck, especially if he is too upset to soothe himself.

drowsy: calm When using a flexible daily routine (see pp.50–52), you will know approximately when your baby will be tired. Now's the time to use sensory input to calm him.
● Before bedtime, you can help your baby shift into the drowsy state ideal for sleep by giving him his evening feed in a darkened room, and gently swaying him so that his sense of movement is used to calm him.

maintaining the calm-alert state The calm-alert state differs between babies in duration and also in how easily they maintain the state. A full-term newborn initially spends very little time in the calm-alert state: only 15 to 20 minutes in a three-hour cycle. But as each day passes, this time increases, allowing you more time to stimulate your infant and for him to learn. Individual babies have different abilities to filter stimulation. Some can cope with a significant amount of stimulation and still remain in the calm-alert state, while others may rapidly shift up a state and become over-stimulated and fractious. Use this quick guide to help your baby to maintain the calm-alert state or to calm him down as needed:
● **The social butterfly** generally seeks sensory input and maintains a calm-alert state for longer than most babies. He uses stimulation to stay happy and settled. But even the most social of babies may become overwhelmed with sensory input after a time. When your social butterfly begins to niggle, try a change of sensory stimulation and if that doesn't settle him, you may find it is time for a sleep.
● **The slow-to-warm-up baby** has a narrow period of calm-alert and takes time to settle into a new stimulus. These babies need to be calmed and require your attention to stay happily in the calm-alert state.
● **The settled baby** spends more time in the calm-alert state than other babies, and remains settled even when presented with a great deal of stimulation. When he has had enough he is more likely to go into a drowsy state and fall asleep than to start crying. He also gives clear signals of how he is coping.
● **The sensitive baby** has a very limited calm-alert zone. He spends short periods in the calm-alert state and needs to be soothed a lot to prevent him from crying.

calming versus stimulating your baby

Sensory input that is similar to the womb world is calming. Knowing how to calm your baby will help him to get enough sleep to grow and thrive. Use this quick-glance table to help you structure a calm world for your baby. There are some unpleasant things that act as stimulating input for your baby, that you should take care to avoid: noxious smells such as strong perfume, tobacco smoke, and harsh chemicals; foods that taste bitter or salty; very bright, harsh, or flashing lights.

sense	calming	how?	stimulating	how?
touch	• Deep pressure touch • Neutral warmth • Smooth and soft textures • Touch around or in the mouth	• Swaddle • Touch baby's back • Handle firmly • Give deep hugs • Maintain constant temperature • Initially offer smooth-textured food • Use soft bedding and clothing • Guide hands together • Sucking on hands	• Light touch • Unpredictable touch • Touch on the front of the body and face • Extreme temperature • Unpredictable textures in food	• Tickle • Blow on skin • Touch without warning • Lightly touch the face, stomach or head • Big change in environmental temperature, for example, go outdoors, warm bath • Change in food texture or new tastes
movement	• Slow, rhythmical movements • Linear movements	• Rocking • Swaying • Carrying in sling • Rocking chair	• Fast, irregular movements • Angular or spinning	• Swinging through the air (only with a baby over six months)
smell	• Neutral smells • Smell of mother	• Lavender, chamomile • Mother smell • Baby smell	• Strong, pungent smells	• Citrus, cinnamon
sight	• Dim lights • Faces • Calming colours	• Light dimmer • Black-out lining • Pale colours and teal	• Bright light • Contrasting colours • Very bright colours	• Fluorescent light • Red, black and white
sound	• White noise • Familiar sounds • Rhythmical sounds • Low pitch	• Play static • Play white noise • Heartbeat • Lullabies	• Unpredictable noises • High or fluctuating pitch • Loud noises	• Excited voices • Yelling
taste	• Familiar, mild tastes	• Milk	• Strong tastes	• Sour or bitter food

chapter 4

reading your baby's signals

Lucy is Nina's third baby. Nina has been a hands-on mum with her other children and everyone assumed she had mothering sussed. But her experience with Lucy was different right from the start: Nina ended up having an emergency Caesarean, a complete contrast from the idyllic births she had experienced before. In the weeks following the birth, Nina has struggled to take care of a tiny newborn and two toddlers while recovering from the operation and taking painkillers. She's not sure whether the painkillers are blunting her ability to understand Lucy, or whether this baby is just more difficult to "read", but third time round, Nina is feeling lost.

your baby's special language

Your baby's signals in the first weeks of life form the first precious communication between you and her. If you listen and take note, she will get the message that she's important and that you respect her and value her efforts to connect with you. If you can start this relationship by trying to understand your baby and meet her needs, you will reap the rewards and bond more effectively because she feels listened to.

The most effective way to communicate with your baby is to learn her "baby talk". Although each baby is unique, infants have a universal language and you can use it to interpret her needs. Being able to read your baby's signals and determine what state she is in and know whether she is becoming over-stimulated or is calming down is critical. Once you understand this, you can take action to help your baby.

your baby's four types of signal

Unlike adults who can remove themselves from a stimulus, your baby is unable to control her world for herself and must communicate her reaction to you. Luckily, your baby has a language all her own that lets you know exactly how she is dealing with the sensory information.

Your baby will respond to stimuli coming from the world around her in one of four ways. She may be happy and want interaction, she may start to be overwhelmed and appeal for help, she may start fussing, or she may eventually cry. These are the subtle signs she uses to communicate these reactions:

approach signals: "play with me" When your baby is well rested and comfortable, she is in the calm-alert state (see pp.31–33) and interprets stimuli as non-stressful and is ready to respond and use the

learn how to...

- Recognize approach signals, warning signals, and fussing signals.
- Interpret your baby's crying.
- Respond to her signals.

approach signals

- Smiling, or mouthing with an "OOH" expression. Young babies (under six weeks) also "smile", not with their lips necessarily, but with bright eyes, relaxed eyebrows, and smooth breathing.
- Soft, relaxed, but alert facial expression, with open eyes. Your baby makes eye contact and stares into your eyes.
- Cooing.
- Relaxed limbs.
- Generally still body (few large movements of the arms and legs) with smooth body movements.
- Turning towards sounds.

approach signals Your baby will display approach signals when she is in the calm-alert state.
❶ Smiling/mouthing is a classic signal inviting you to play with your baby.
❷ Soft, relaxed expression: this indicates that your baby is calm and in the ideal state for learning.

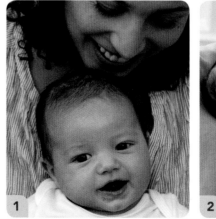

information she gathers to develop her brain. She displays approach signals such as smiling or cooing (see box, opposite) – these indicate to you that she is content and calm. She is ready to interact with the world.

warning signals: "help me" When your baby starts feeling a little stressed by all the input from her environment, she starts to behave in ways that will help her decrease the effect of that stress and bring her nervous system back into balance. She does this in an attempt to help herself stay calm. These signals are generally characterized by self-soothing strategies (see box, right, and images, below) as your baby attempts to organize her brain and nervous system in the face of stimulation. She still has the ability to organize herself or self-regulate – calm herself down – but it takes a lot of effort. This is the time to avoid further stimulation. Remove her from the stimulating environment, and allow her to go to sleep if she needs to.

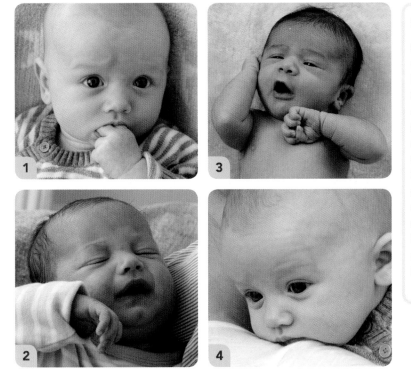

warning signals These are some of the common warning signals that your baby might display. **①** Finger or hand sucking: putting his fingers or hands in his mouth helps your baby to soothe himself. **②** Straightening his legs or bracing his body indicates that he is trying to push the stimuli away. **③** Making fists and putting one hand by the ear is a classic warning signal. **④** Your baby may move into a drowsy state in preparation for sleep so that he can shut out stimuli.

warning signals

● One or both hands on her face, or clasped together.

● Sucking her fingers or hands. She does this to soothe herself. Don't misinterpret it as hunger, unless it is feed time and she is also rooting for a nipple or teat (see p.41).

● Making fists.

● Straightening her legs or bracing her body against the sides of the cot, or into your neck.

● Shifting to a drowsy state.

● Assuming the foetal position.

sensory story

misreading signals Lucy lay under her play gym. She had been there for 10 minutes while her mum made breakfast for her other children. At first Lucy was interested in the bright colours and moving shapes, but now she was starting to kick and squirm a little. She'd had enough and wanted to move away, but at 10 weeks old was unable to roll away from the mobile. Her mum misinterpreted Lucy's response to the stimulation and thought she looked excited to be under the play gym.

fussing signals

- Irritability.
- Gaze-aversion or gaze-locking (glassy eyes or "gape face" – staring into distance with open mouth), looking away.
- Lack of alertness. Staring into space and looking drowsy.
- Finger-splaying or saluting. Your baby may use this sign when asleep or falling asleep. If you disturb her, her hands will go up in front of her face with her fingers spread, saying "Leave me alone".
- Squirming.
- Arching her back and neck, appearing to push away from you.
- Frantic, disorganized, jerky movements, often accompanied by sweaty feet, especially when over-stimulated by a mobile or other visual stimulus.
- Thrusting her tongue out.
- Frowning, grimacing, grunting.
- Yawning, sneezing, hiccups. Your baby may yawn from tiredness if it is sleep time, sneeze to clear her nose, or indeed have hiccups after a feed, BUT before immediately assuming these other causes are correct, look at the circumstances and timing.
- Colour changes such as paleness, mottling, flushing, and a blueish discolouration around the mouth (frequently attributed to wind or gas). This can indicate a nervous system response to fatigue or sensory overload.
- Changes in vital signs such as heart rate and/or respiration, for example panting or irregular breathing.
- Gagging, posseting.

fussing signals: "back off" If your baby is a bit stressed and not removed from the stimulus, put to bed, or helped to calm herself, she will become over-stimulated. At this point she becomes so stressed by the stimulation that she is unable to counteract the effect by calming herself. This period is characterized by fussing (see box, left), such as irritability or squirming, but your baby may not yet actually be crying. When your baby starts to fuss, give her the time out she is asking for by removing her from the stimulus, or removing the stimulus from her environment. Very importantly, teach her how to calm herself by putting her hands to her mouth, and soothe her by using the tips on pp.45–47.

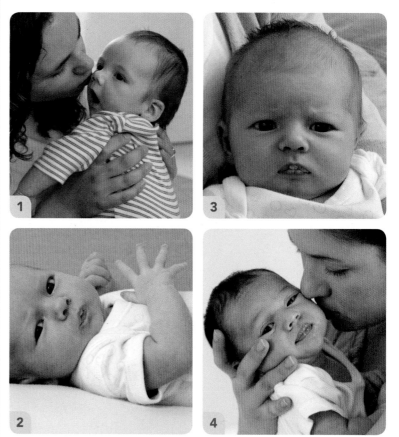

fussing signals These are some fussing signals that you might see when your baby is over-stimulated and asking for help. **1** Gaze aversion: turning his face so he doesn't have to make eye contact and gaping with an open mouth is a fussing signal. **2** Finger splaying/saluting: if you disturb your baby when he is asleep or sleepy, his hands will move up in front of his face, meaning "Leave me alone". **3** Your baby may display signs of irritability with facial expressions such as frowning or grimacing. **4** Pushing away: your baby may arch his back and attempt to push you away, signalling to you to remove the stimuli so that he can calm down.

misreading the signals

It's easy to misinterpret your baby's warning and fussing signs and we all do it, so don't feel guilty. Even the most experienced mum can look back and be amazed at how easily she misinterpreted her baby's attempts to communicate. Part of the reason that we misread signals is because many of us have little hands-on experience of babies before we have our own. As a result, we tend to learn how to parent from books, which frequently steer us towards "medical" rather than behavioural responses.

It is easy to interpret signals as digestive disturbances, wind, hunger, or boredom, or even miss them altogether. If your baby's signals are consistently misread and you feed your baby every time she niggles, for instance, or you take her hands away from her mouth and instead stimulate her to make her laugh, your baby's attempts to soothe herself will be disturbed. You may find yourself in the trap of feeding your baby every time she fusses. Then she may depend on your breast – and indirectly on food – to calm herself. Alternatively, if you interpret fussing signals as boredom and your strategy is to stimulate your baby to make her happy, she may be exposed to many periods of stress. Here are some signals that are commonly misinterpreted:

sense-able secret

If you miss your baby's signals of tiredness or over-stimulation, she will probably end up crying. Do not worry too much, but calm her gently with soft words and soothing movement.

signal	common interpretation	consider this interpretation
Hands rubbing the ears	Ear infection	I am tired
Sucking hands	Hunger or teething	I am tired or helping myself stay calm
Looking away	Lack of interest or boredom	I am taking a break or "time out"
Frantic jerky movements	Excitement	I have had enough and cannot escape the stimuli
Grunting	Trying to pass a stool, or wind	I am over-stimulated*
Sneezing	Getting a cold or needs to clear her nose	
Blue around the mouth	Wind or gas	
Posseting	Reflux	

*The common interpretation may sometimes be correct, but all these signals may also indicate an automatic response in the brain that signals stress.

crying If your baby continues to be stimulated or is not helped to fall to sleep when she is over-stimulated and fussing, it will not be long before she starts crying inconsolably. Few things undermine your confidence and make you feel totally incompetent as a parent more than being faced with a crying baby who you are seemingly unable to comfort. Of course, there are many other reasons why your baby will cry, for example hunger, a wet nappy, environmental discomfort such as bright lights or being too hot or cold, so how are you to know when she is over-stimulated and not hungry, tired or sick? The answer lies in the secret of knowing how to read your baby's signals. Over the next few pages you will learn how to distinguish hunger cries from the whining of tiredness and the irritability of wind.

interpreting crying

It would be great if there were a manual that said when your baby cries long and hard it means X and when she has lots of short gasps it means Y. The reality is that there is no consistent pattern to crying and so no way to interpret it according to its sound. Cries are best understood by eliminating causes and looking at the context. The first step in managing crying is to watch for the signals that lead up to it. For a reminder about your baby's warning and fussing signals, see pages 38 to 41. If you miss these early signals or your baby begins to cry, the following can help you to establish the cause:

the gassy or windy cry

Small babies typically pull up their legs, grimace, and appear to be in pain when crying, therefore it is easy to mistake every cry for a sore tummy or digestive disturbances. Actually, gas, wind, and tummy cramps are not often the cause of most irritability and crying. However, during or shortly after feed time, gas may build up in your baby's tummy, making her feel uncomfortable. If your baby stops feeding and fusses at the nipple, let her come up for air and see if she burps or breaks wind. Some babies like to feed in courses and your baby might just need a breather before resuming the feed.

After a feed, hold your baby upright and pat or rub her back for a while to encourage her to bring up wind. Sometimes a burp will pose no problem and come up quickly; at other times, your baby will not burp at all. Some babies posset and bring up milk curds with the burp, others don't. Wind is unlikely to be the cause of fussing or colic unless your baby is already over-stimulated, in which case the added stimulus of gas may cause her to cry.

crying If your baby shows signs of over-stimulation and she is not helped to calm herself, she may start to cry.
❶ When your baby cries, she may use other body language to signal her feelings, such as rubbing her head and grasping your finger.
❷ Your baby may brace and straighten her body and splay her hands when crying, displaying frantic and disorganized movements.

the hungry cry

Nearly every time your baby cries, you probably will be asked by some well-meaning aunt or shop keeper whether she is hungry. It can be infuriating if you fed her only an hour ago. Of course, you will want to rule out whether hunger is at the root of her distress. In the second part of the book (chapters 7 to 13), the relationship between feeding and hunger is described in detail according to your baby's age, but as a general rule, the following applies:

newborn In the early days your newborn will require frequent feeds, but this does not mean that every cry indicates hunger. Admittedly, her hunger cries may not be clearly differentiated from those of soreness or over-stimulation; it takes time to recognize these cries. Within a few weeks your baby will begin to stretch the time between feeds and you will become familiar with her unique cry of hunger. Until then, if you need clues:
1 Think back to when your baby last fed. Crying less than two hours since then probably doesn't indicate hunger, as long as she is gaining weight.
2 Consider her age. Growth spurts occur at four to six weeks and again at four months and she will need to be fed more frequently at these times.

older baby As your baby progresses to the five- to six-month mark, her nutritional needs may no longer be satisfied with milk alone. If she begins to fuss between feeds and is only satisfied if fed more frequently than before, do talk to your health visitor about the best time to start introducing solids.

the uncomfortable cry

Sometimes your baby just seems uncomfortable and there is no obvious reason for her fussing. This cry is generally accompanied by squirming. These can be possible causes:
● A very wet or dirty nappy or nappy rash can cause tactile discomfort sufficient to make her cry.
● An environment that is too hot or cold. The best room temperature for a baby is 16–20°C (61–71°F), with the ideal being 18°C (64°F). Anything warmer or cooler may cause your baby discomfort.
● Irritation threshold. Each baby has a different threshold for discomfort. This has to do with your baby's sensory filter. Similar to a low pain threshold, a low threshold for sensory changes or irritants will cause your baby to be very reactive and intolerant. If she has a high threshold for sensory information she probably won't complain much and you would hardly know when her nappy is dirty or when she is sore or not. So, for the sensitive baby a dirty nappy may cause misery whereas for a more settled baby, no level of discomfort will concern her.

1

2

burping your baby
1 Shoulder burp: this position is the most popular. Place a muslin over your shoulder. Hold your baby against it with her tummy against your chest. Rub firmly or pat her back.
2 Sitting burp: if the shoulder burp position fails, try the sitting position, on your lap. Place one hand under your baby's chin, against her chest. Pat her back and rub until the burp emerges.

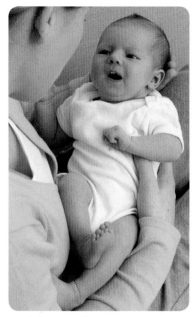

read the signals Remember to pause when your baby seems upset and take the time to interpret her cues.

reflux If your baby cries around feeds and does not like being laid down after being fed, is sleeping for short periods, and is very unsettled, you need to rule out reflux as the root of the crying. Most babies with reflux posset – spit up milk curds – however, not all babies with reflux do this. Benign or silent reflux may also cause discomfort in babies who do not spit up milk curds (see also p.141). If you suspect reflux is causing discomfort, do visit your doctor for a confirmed diagnosis and advice on treatment.

the sick cry

If your baby has been generally happy and suddenly becomes very irritable and cries a lot in addition to a fever or loss of appetite, do check it out with your doctor straightaway. Illness or infection may be the reason behind your baby's crying, or she may have a congenital problem (one that she was born with), such as a metabolic disorder. One relatively common medical cause of discomfort is reflux (see box, left).

the tired cry

If you have ruled out hunger, discomfort, wind, and illness, and your baby is still crying, the chances are she is overtired. Daytime sleeps are crucial in keeping your baby calm while she is awake and easier to get to sleep. In chapter five you will discover how to set up a daytime sleep routine that will help you predict whether your baby's cry is a tired cry.

the over-stimulated cry

When your baby starts to cry inconsolably and there is no obvious reason – in other words she is not hungry, needing a nappy change or ill – you should consider the possibility that she is over-stimulated.

① Look at your baby's environment. Is it too stimulating or full of novel stimuli? If so, it is possible that she has taken in too much information. Her brain is unable to filter or deal with the input and this situation has resulted in crying.

② Think back to the signals she was giving just prior to the crying spell. If she was fussing and giving "back off" signals and yet she continued to be stimulated, she may have reached such a state of distress that she was unable to calm herself, leading to inconsolable crying.

③ Look at the time of day. Towards the end of the day, your baby's cry may well be the result of over-stimulation.

If your baby is constantly over-stimulated and/or deprived of quiet time, she will remain in a state of stress, which may have a negative impact on her overall development. Every baby's cry is individual but you will learn to interpret your baby's over-stimulated cry. She will frequently pull up her legs, become blue around the mouth, and bring her hands towards her face and mouth as she cries, in an attempt to soothe herself.

the sensitive baby If your little one is consistently irritable and gives very little warning before crying inconsolably, you may feel at a loss as to what to do. Sensitive babies are more challenging and will fuss significantly more than all other babies. They will be easily affected by environmental discomforts and may become over-stimulated by the smallest stimuli. If you have a sensitive baby, be extra vigilant with her awake times (see p.51) and watch for signs of over-stimulation.

understanding the causes of crying

1 When did my baby last feed? Is this a hungry cry? → **yes** → Feed my baby

↓ **no**

2 Is my baby too hot, or does she have a dirty nappy? → **yes** → Change my baby

↓ **no**

3 Is my baby feverish, or has she lost her appetite? Is my baby ill? → **yes** → Visit the doctor

↓ **no**

4 Is it late in the day, or is my baby over-stimulated? → **yes** → Try soothing strategies (see below)

↓ **no**

5 Is my baby tired? → **yes** → Settle my baby to sleep

sensory soothing strategies

As your baby's brain processes sensory input, it affects her state. If the sensory information is stimulating, your baby's state may rise – from calm-alert to active-alert, for instance. Calming input will lower the state and calm your baby down or settle her to sleep.

Once you have ruled out the underlying reasons for your baby's crying, you need to move on to soothing strategies (see below). Try the strategies in order and continue with each one for five minutes before changing to another.

five-minute soothing

The five-minute principle is important in calming your baby: try one of the strategies below for up to five minutes. If it doesn't work, try another for a further five minutes. This slows down your responses so that you can sync your timing with your baby. It takes your baby's brain about five minutes to register and fully respond to a calming strategy. If, for instance, you swaddle her and she wriggles and squirms, keep her wrapped for five minutes – this gives her nervous system time to process this strategy and settle.

sensory environment Watch your baby's world for too much stimulation and think about all the sensory input she has to cope with, from sights and smells to sounds. Consider the environment surrounding your baby, and be prepared to alter it or remove her from it, to avoid sensory overload.

sense-able secret
It's better to focus on understanding your baby's cry, rather than trying to stop it. That way, your response is more likely to lessen the fussing, and you will not need to resort to emergency measures, such as driving around in the car, that make your baby dependent on you for calming.

how to respond to your baby's signals

approach signals
- Interact with your baby.
- Talk to her before you touch her.
- Lie your baby in your lap before feeding or playing with her.

warning signals
- Hold her quietly and firmly.
- Tuck her arms in, or swaddle her in a blanket.
- Shade her eyes from glare.
- Let your baby grab your finger.

fussing signals
- Adjust her environment, for example, take her to a quiet place.
- Cut out glare from bright lights.
- Avoid eye contact.
- Play some calming music.
- Hold her firmly and quietly – don't fiddle with her too much.
- Swaddle her: wrap her up with her arms close to her chest.
- Wear your baby in a sling.
- Allow her to suck your finger.

● **Fussing newborns** Take notice of the smells and sights your newborn is trying to process. If her environment is loud and bright, take her to somewhere with dim lights, drawn curtains, and less noise. Your baby is sensitive to loud and unpredictable noises. If she has become over-stimulated because there are too many people around her, remove her to a calmer environment, or at least make sure she is not passed around. Put her in a sling, against your body, to shield her from the barrage of sensory input. Newborns can rarely cope with more than 10 minutes of visual stimulation. Don't wear perfume or aftershave in the early days.

● **Over-stimulated baby** Your baby will cope much better with stimulation as the first year progresses. Watch for her warning signals (see p.39) that say she's had enough. If your baby starts to fuss, remove her to a calm room and rock or sway her gently. Do not surround your baby with hundreds of toys – limit the stimulation so that she can attend well to one activity without being over-stimulated.

self-calming At birth most babies' self-calming strategies are poorly developed. One of your tasks in the first three months is to help your baby to develop strategies that allow her to calm herself.

● Watch out for these solutions and encourage her to do them when she becomes fractious: sucking her hands or fists; touching her face; gazing at you or any object that appears to calm her; reaching for and using a sleep or "comfort" object such as a blanket; looking at her hands; bringing her hands together or in towards the midline of her body.

Your baby will only develop self-calming strategies if you don't over-respond each time she fusses. Try not to pop in the dummy or pick her up to soothe her or feed her as soon as she starts fussing. While you should not let your baby cry for long and it is important to respond consistently, try not to intervene if she is starting to put together the puzzle of how to soothe herself:

● If she is starting to calm herself by sucking on her hands or bringing her hands to the midline of her body, don't interrupt her.

● If your baby is not soothing herself at all (which is very common under nine weeks of age), teach her some self-calming strategies. A good way to do this is to swaddle her tightly with her hands near her face (see p.26 for how to swaddle). In this position she will attempt to soothe herself by sucking on her hands.

swaddling Swaddling your newborn has a wonderfully calming effect similar to a hug or soothing deep massage. Even if you think your newborn does not like to be swaddled, persist: babies who are swaddled are significantly calmer and have longer periods of undisturbed sleep

than babies who are not, because it reminds them of being in the womb. Most babies like to be swaddled until they are nine to twelve weeks old.
● As your baby gets older she may not like to be swaddled as tightly and may push her arms out, but for sleep times do continue to swaddle under the arms.

soothing touch Touch is a tool that mothers use intuitively with their babies, from the soft caress of a kiss on a silky head to a deep hug or swaddling in a cotton blanket. If your baby tends to be fussy, try a daily massage. There are many different approaches to baby massage (see p.105). Explore a few to find the method that works best for you both.
● Massage in the morning at first: some babies cannot cope with a massage late in the day as they are more likely to be fractious at that time. The effect of the deep pressure from the massage will last and your baby will be calmer all day.
● For older babies, massage can be used as part of the soothing bedtime routine. If you find your baby tries to wriggle away, give her a toy to play with or mobile to look at to occupy her during the massage.
● If your baby is crying, use gentle but firm patting to calm her. Premature and very young babies are soothed by still touch. Try placing your hands on her and keeping them still for a few minutes.

sling Soothing movements that mimic the womb are calming for babies. Placing your baby in a sling or carrier when she fusses or when you need both hands free is a great way to keep her calm. Research shows that babies who are carried in this way are significantly less fussy.
● For a newborn, use a sling that provides good support. She will benefit from the calming influence of deep pressure and rocking motion.
● For sensitive babies, a good walk in a carrier or sling is calming.

sounds Soothing sounds are an excellent way to calm a cranky baby. Talk or sing softly to her: she loves the sound of your voice.
● Newborns experience womb sounds as very soothing. You can buy them on CD or de-tune your radio to create white noise, which babies also find soothing. Even the white-noise sound of a vacuum cleaner or washing machine can be sufficient to calm a fussy newborn.
● The rhythm of your heartbeat (approximately 72 beats per minute) was comforting and familiar to your baby for the last six months *in utero*, so hold her close to your heart. Interestingly, the majority of all parents hold their babies on the left shoulder regardless of hand preference, indicating that intuitively we know that babies are soothed by our heartbeat.
● Classical music (baroque music or Mozart are most effective) played softly or gentle lullabies can also soothe a fussy baby.

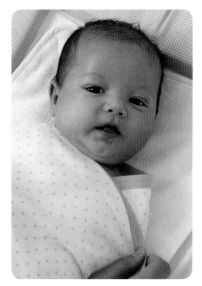

calm and contained If your baby is displaying fussing signals, swaddling is a good way to soothe her.

step-by-step method to soothe your baby

❶ Watch for the signs of hunger, tiredness, or over-stimulation.
❷ If she is crying, use the process of elimination (see box, p.45) to work out what the cause might be.
❸ Look at the first strategy: her sensory environment and time of day. If her environment is stimulating, it may be causing her distress or she may have reached sensory overload.
❹ Allow your baby time (five minutes) to soothe herself.
❺ Move onto the next strategy (see opposite) and pursue it for five minutes so it can take effect.
❻ If your baby is still crying after five minutes, move onto the next soothing strategy.

chapter 5

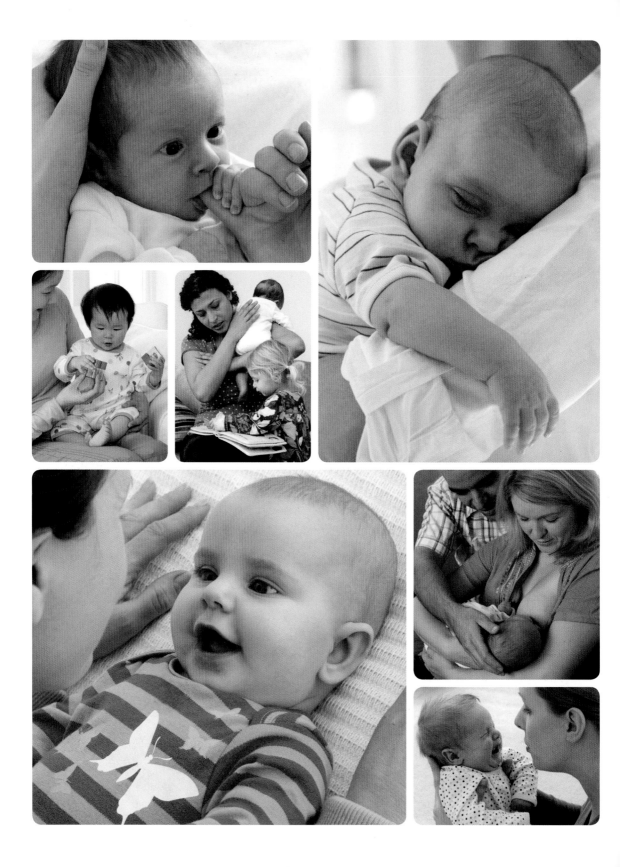

mum sense: your baby's impact on you

Sarah is used to deadlines; she has always worked well under pressure and enjoys the exhilaration of a corporate challenge. So how is it that little Isabella, only a tiny baby, has thrown her equilibrium so out of balance? Sarah feels overwhelmed, anxious, and at a loss for answers. Looking after a new baby is new territory for her and she finds it frighteningly unfamiliar. The advice all seems so contradictory and Sarah doesn't feel that she fits the mould. The burning questions she has are: "How do I fit Isabella into my life and still meet her needs, and how do I ensure that she becomes a well-balanced, happy human being, without losing myself completely in the process?"

learn how to ...

● Balance your needs with those of your baby.
● Create a flexible routine that suits your baby.
● Overcome difficulties in establishing a routine.
● Manage the load of motherhood.
● Understand how you and your baby fit together.
● Recognize and help counter postnatal depression.

sense-able secret

Rigid routines do not take individual families' differences into account, whereas a baby-centric routine allows you and your baby some flexibility. To establish this type of routine, watch your baby and ask yourself the following questions:

● How long has she been awake?
● How does she respond to stimulation?
● What signals is she giving?

routines that work for you and your baby

The transition to motherhood challenges most women. The familiar world of work schedules and timing life to suit your commitments does not suit newborns, who have little sense of routine. Since parenting frequently happens in a relative vacuum – without extended family to help out – new mums often experience isolation and loneliness. Even when their support systems are good, many mothers find the advice they are given by family and friends contradictory. Patterns are hard to establish in the early days, but the key is reading your baby's signals.

the value of routine

There is no question that when babies do start to settle into a semblance of routine, life becomes more manageable. When there is predictability in the day it becomes easier to read your baby's signals and to consider her needs. Some babies fit seamlessly into a routine, but not all, and if your baby is one of the latter, trying to instil a schedule can create more anxiety for you both. So is there a way to read your baby that will make for an easy transition into predictable days?

a baby-centric routine

In the first two weeks, most babies sleep a great deal of the time and your baby may appear to be settling into a pattern of sleeping between feeds and waking only when hungry. This is a protective mechanism: shutting out the world by sleeping for a good portion of every day prevents newborns from becoming over-stimulated by their environment. In these early days, follow your baby's lead and feed on demand. Wake your baby if three-and-a-half hours have passed since the last daytime feed, to encourage her to feed more during the day than at night.

At around two weeks old your baby will become more wakeful and the stimulation of the world around her may prevent her from being able to switch off and go to sleep. This makes it very difficult to establish daytime sleep routines, but in these early days your baby needs to sleep regularly. It is an absolute truth that "sleep begets sleep" – the more your baby sleeps, the more she will sleep and the more settled she will be when she's awake.

Provided her physical and emotional needs are being met – with nutrition, warmth, touch, love, and appropriate stimulation – your baby will benefit from being guided into a flexible routine. If this flexible routine takes place within a structured environment and is built around her natural sleep/wake cycles, she will be calm and content. There are three aspects to guiding your baby into a daily sleep routine:

1 know your baby's internal clock

Your baby's in-built clock primes her to fall asleep with ease and helps to establish a sleep/wake routine. During each day, we experience ultradian rhythms – cycles of our nervous system – every few hours. This internal clock tells us when we are hungry but also when we have a dip in wakefulness. As an adult you will find that your wakefulness dips after lunch and you can easily have a catnap in the early afternoon.

Likewise, babies have dips in alertness but their rhythms are much shorter than ours and so they need to sleep more frequently. The amount of time your baby can spend happily awake – her "awake time" – lengthens as she grows older (see table, below). Making the most of these awake times is the secret to establishing a baby-centric routine that is flexible and meets your baby's need for frequent feeds and sleep. Her sleep/wake routines will change as she gets older and will be influenced by her capacity for stimulation (see step two).

2 recognize your baby's response to sensory stimuli

Some babies cope very well with stimulation: they manage to filter excess information so that they don't become easily over-stimulated. Likewise some babies fall easily into the rhythm of a routine, while others take longer to develop a pattern to their day.

● The settled baby is generally more flexible and can stretch her awake times happily. She falls easily into a routine but a disruption to her day is no problem either.

● The social butterfly may resist routine because, put simply, sleep is boring! She finds it more difficult to get to sleep, but with all that socializing, she needs regular naps desperately.

● The slow-to-warm-up and the sensitive baby become overwhelmed by

mum sense: the value of a flexible routine

● Prevents your baby from becoming over-stimulated.
● Helps you to correctly interpret your baby's moods and cries.
● Helps you to establish whether she is hungry or overtired.
● Gives your baby a sense that you understand and will meet her needs.
● Makes it easier to plan when to do household chores or relax.

approximate awake times

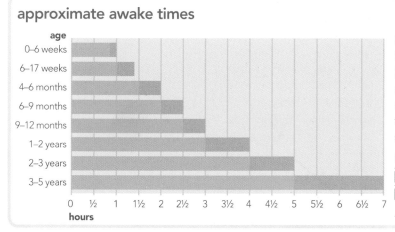

Use this handy table to find out how long your baby's awake time should last, which is determined by how old she is. The table also shows the overlap period between the end of the preceding age band and the start of the next one.

key

▮ Awake time
▮ Overlap period between awake times for next age band

stimulation and need to be guided into a routine carefully to avoid over-stimulation. Slow-to-warm-up babies in particular love a routine and cope well when rested and enjoying a set day.

All babies do well with a flexible sleep/feeding routine, but since each baby is unique, it is not reasonable to expect all babies to adhere to the same routine. Trying to slot a sensitive baby into a routine that expects newborns to be awake for two to three hours simply cannot work and only causes stress for you, the mum. For this reason, most sensible babycare specialists and health visitors do not recommend rigid routines.

3 read your baby's signals As well as considering your baby's awake times and unique personality, you need to be on the lookout for her signs of tiredness when developing her daytime sleep routine. Look out for the common ones (see left) and make a note of your baby's own unique signals too. Ten minutes before your baby's age-appropriate awake time is up (see table, p.51), start to watch for sleepy signals, such as rubbing ears, taking her hand to her mouth, losing interest in toys, and looking away. This is the signal for you to take your baby to her room and start a sleepy-time routine:

● Make sure your baby is comfortable, warm and dry (change her nappy if necessary).
● Draw the curtains or lower the black-out blinds, dim the light, and close the door if the space outside the room is stimulating.
● Play lulling music or white noise to help her to shift into a drowsy state.
● If your baby is less than three months old, swaddle her for sleep. If she is older than three months old and still enjoys being swaddled to sleep, do so. Alternatively, put her in a sleeping bag if the room is cool.
● Encourage her to soothe herself using her sleep object – a comfort blanket or a soft toy (see p.26).
● Hold her close to you so that she is lying in a horizontal position, as this will help to prepare her for sleep.
● Rock her and lull her for a few minutes until she is drowsy (with relaxed fists and body and drowsy eyes) then put her in her cot.

common signs of tiredness

1 Hand by ear: your baby may rub his ear or hold one or both hands by his ear.
2 The same as adults, babies yawn when they are tired.
3 Your baby may bring his hand to his mouth and attempt to suck on his fingers when tired, because he doesn't enjoy this state and is trying to soothe himself.

If you follow these three steps, you will establish a sleep routine that suits your baby's age and personality, and that meets your own need for predictability and patterns. In the age-related chapters (chapters 7 to 13), you will find a flexible routine designed for your baby's age.

Do not become stressed if your baby's sleep times differ slightly from one day to the next, or if your baby has an off-day or falls out of sync. Focus on what you are doing right and know that, in time, if you follow these principles, your baby will be gently guided into a flexible routine – this is the Babysense way.

routines don't come easily?

There will be times when your baby won't fall asleep when you expected and you may feel despondent and a failure for not getting the routine right. Remember that all babies are different and like any other person, they have good days and difficult days. Apart from age, there are two common reasons why your baby's routine may not come easily: over-tiredness and a disrupted sleep/wake cycle.

newborns and routine

As much as you may look forward to some predictability in the early days, newborns do best with flexibility. You will need to feed on demand and trying to establish a routine too soon will create stress for you.

day/night sleep reversed

In the early days, your baby may have her day- and night-time sleep pattern all muddled up. If your newborn sleeps all day and is awake a lot at night, you will clearly struggle to establish a routine. To turn things around, wake your baby if she has been asleep for three-and-a-half hours or longer during the day and make sure you feed her on demand or at least every four hours during daylight hours. At night, feed her whenever she wakes, but do not wake her to feed. When she wakes at night, give her one breast or half a bottle then change her nappy so that she wakes up to feed on the second breast or half bottle. Re-swaddle her and do not stimulate or rouse her once she has finished the feed.

baby fighting sleep

Frequently if your baby is fighting sleep, it is because she is overtired. This happens when she is awake for longer than her awake time allows. A newborn has a very short period of awake time (see box, p.92). When you miss your baby's natural dip in alertness or her awake time (see table, p.51), her brain responds by releasing neurotransmitters and hormones to keep her awake and give her energy. You will find she interacts less happily during this second stretch of awake time, and as it draws to a close you will find it more difficult to get her to sleep because she is overtired. Hormones such as adrenaline (released to keep her alert) and cortisol (a stress hormone) prevent her from falling asleep easily. The consequence of missing the natural dip in your baby's alertness is a battle to settle her, and you may end up in one of two situations:

problematic sleep associations If your baby is overtired she may fight sleep so effectively that you resort to intensive strategies to settle her. They may include rocking or feeding her to sleep, pushing her

how to settle an overtired baby

● Allow for a longer period of settling before she goes to sleep. Drowsy babies may fall asleep in minutes after going to their cot. But a baby who is over-stimulated or showing no signs of tiredness may need a longer period of rocking or gentle music or lullabies to make her drowsy enough to put down awake to fall asleep. It is important to put your baby in her cot drowsy but awake so she learns to fall asleep on her own.
● If your newborn will not fall asleep and you are forced to use a crutch, such as rocking her in the pram or wearing her in a sling until she is asleep, do not worry. Little babies frequently need more sensory soothing to fall asleep and do not form long-term habits before four months of age.
● Avoid rocking, pushing, or feeding to sleep if your baby is older than four months of age as this may result in poor sleep habits.

signals of tiredness

These are the common sleepy signals to watch out for:
● Hands near face, such as fiddling with ears or hair.
● Sucking fists, thumbs, or a comfort object, such as a blanket.
● Shifting into a drowsy state – eyes become heavier.
● Losing eye contact.
● Hiccups.
● Older babies may fiddle with their bodies – picking noses or scratching bottoms.

disruptions to routine

● Temporary growth spurts, when your baby may feed more often. Learn how to deal with these in the age-band chapters (chapters 7–13).

● Travel in a car or train may lull your baby to sleep when she wouldn't typically sleep. Try to travel when she would normally sleep.

● An unusual outing may stimulate your baby making her too alert to sleep. Time outings for her awake time when possible.

● Changing time zones makes following a routine difficult. To manage the transition, watch her awake times; read her fussing and tired signals; and think about how your baby responds to stimuli and how she is soothed (see pp.45–47).

sense-able secret

If your baby doesn't sleep when she needs to, she will get a second wind. This means she is harder to get to sleep at bedtime and may suddenly crash out wherever she is.

in her pram or even driving her around in the car. The difficulty here is that your baby then learns to associate sleep with such invasive techniques, which creates problems because she will demand the same ritual at the end of every day and again every time she wakes at night.

miss another sleep If all your emergency measures fail and you can't get your baby to sleep, you may find she gets a second wind (or a third or fourth) and becomes busier and more irritable and fussy – and even more difficult to get to sleep. In all likelihood, she will collapse in a heap at the end of the day and fall into an exhausted sleep. However, because her sensory system is in such a state of overload, she will struggle to link her sleep cycles (see p.30) and stay asleep for the night. These frequent night wakings will make her more tired and grumpy the next day (because she hasn't slept properly), and so the cycle continues. See the box on page 53 for tips on how to prevent this from happening.

what to do? Even if your baby is not showing signs of tiredness, settle her in her room by the time her awake time ends (see table, p.51). You will find that by enacting soothing sleepy-time rituals in her bedroom, she will eventually settle.

being realistic

When nurturing little ones you should expect the unpredictable and it is unreasonable to anticipate every day to be identical. If you approach your baby's routine with an attitude of flexibility, and base your timings on principles instead of rules, you are much less likely to end up feeling as though you're at fault because your routine is not working.

managing the load It is not unusual in the early days to find yourself still in your pyjamas at 3pm or wonder when on earth you will get the washing done. Everyone seems to advise you to sleep when the baby sleeps – but that's the only time you get to yourself and even then you are getting nothing done! You are in good company. Even your friend who looks like she is on top of it all has her moments when she feels frazzled and disorganized.

There is really only one way to manage the load and that is to shift your expectations of both your day and of yourself. Until you do this you will feel like you are not meeting standards. The only standards for parenting are your own – so be gentle with yourself.

accepting help In years gone by we all lived in communities where care for babies was shared, and the load was easier to manage. Possibly one of the greatest challenges for modern mothers is being able to accept offers of help and time away for yourself. But it is vital for your mental and physical health that you accept any help that is offered. Grannies generally feel a great satisfaction at helping out the newest mum in their family, but anyone can help take the load off your shoulders by helping with simple tasks, such as folding washing or making you a cup of tea.

Your baby's father is probably your greatest support if you will only let him provide it. Build your partner's confidence by encouraging him to provide the babycare – this will help him bond with his child too. If the baby fusses while he is holding or feeding her, try very hard not to sigh patronizingly and snatch her away. Imagine how helpless and excluded he may feel. If the nappy is put on back to front, tell him he has done a great job and leave it as it is. The next time you change the nappy, casually show him how you do it – but don't criticize.

know yourself as a mother

By now you may have identified your baby's sensory personality: is she a social butterfly, slow-to-warm-up, settled or sensitive (see pp.14–15)? Now it's time to look at your own personality. You will probably find you fit one of these four profiles most of the time, too. There will be times when you are stressed or when interacting in a certain setting that your sensory profile will change, but look for who you are most of the time:

the best fit As well as discovering your baby's personality, try to learn about yourself as a mother, to see how you fit together.

● **Social butterfly** You love people and new situations, and you are always on the go. You are probably embracing the new experience of being a mum. Your biggest frustration of early mothering is how holed up at home and isolated you feel. You can help to alleviate this by getting out, for example to parent-and-baby groups, as much as you can.

● **Slow-to-warm-up** Less gregarious than the social butterfly, you like things done your way. You prefer predictability and the disorder of this little life may be throwing you out of your comfort zone. As soon as your baby develops a routine you will thrive and enjoy your "mummy life" more.

● **Serene** You are an easy-going and quiet person by nature – with your baby you are flexible and laid back. You don't always notice her signals and may sometimes miss her needs, such as a dirty nappy. Routines are low on your list of priorities and you prefer to go with the flow.

● **Sensitive** You are quite anxious and susceptible to emotional reactions. You are sensitive to your environment and become irritable in big crowds or when there is too much going on. You are very sensitized to your baby's needs and like things done just right, but a new noisy, smelly baby in your personal space a lot of the time can seem quite disruptive. It's easiest to cope with your mothering role if you take things slowly and don't try to fit too much into a day or make too many social demands on yourself.

making it work When you understand your and your baby's personality, you can build a fun, flexible routine that works for both of you.

your personality match

When you put your own sensory profile (see p.55) together with that of your baby (see pp.14–15), you get a fit between you, like two pieces of a puzzle. You may find you fit well with your baby and the match is an easy one, or you may find that your little one's personality challenges aspects of yours at times. All the mother's personality types will match well with having the same type of baby, except for a sensitive mum and baby, who may find this blend more difficult. If you understand your baby's nature and how it can affect your own moods and feelings, it will be easier to develop a flexible routine. It can also help you to enjoy your new role as a mother by making the most of your different personalities.

When you recognize yourself and your baby in the sensory profiles, you can use this knowledge to enhance your baby's development and to help you play and learn together better. Use this chart to understand how you can make the fit work:

social butterfly mum

baby	fit	making it work
Social butterfly	You two have such fun together. Every day is an adventure and you thrive on the fun and games of your new relationship.	Be sure to watch your and your baby's limits; while life is exciting, you both do need down time, too.
Slow-to-warm-up	Since you love the excitement of life and don't like being holed up at home, your baby's sensitivity and need for routine and predictability may be hard for you.	Try to adjust your pace to your baby. You will need to be sensitive to her need for routine and predictability. Find a friend with whom you can have a regular tea date and your baby will settle into the routine of seeing her new friend.
Settled	Your baby will tolerate your changing moods; she fits in well with your need for excitement and really benefits from the stimulation you bring into your lives.	You can use your animated expressions and general emotional tone to make your baby more alert. This will encourage her development since she may have a tendency to be very laid back.
Sensitive	Your sensitive baby has a tough time with all your excitement. She prefers quiet spaces and muted interactions and your general pace and emotional tone may be too much for her, making her less settled and more fractious.	Take time to slow down and be sensitive to your baby's need for soothing sensory input. Try to use a calming voice, touch, and movements. Don't distract her by speaking while you feed and establish a quiet and predictable bedtime routine.

slow-to-warm-up mum

baby	fit	making it work
Social butterfly	At first you may find your gregarious baby's needs unsettling, but as soon as you get some predictability in your lives, this match works well.	Give your baby lots of stimulation, interspersed with good periods of down time. Try to make a predictable time to socialize since your baby thrives on these interactions.
Slow-to-warm-up	This is a great match because you both move at the same pace. You understand that your baby needs time to adjust and you thrive on routine as much as each other.	Do try to get out and not to isolate yourself from other people. It's important not to be over-protective and to encourage your baby to socialize as part of your routine.
Settled	This is an excellent fit: your baby's calm nature matches your need for predictability.	Make a mental note to stimulate your baby and socialize with her. She is so relaxed and undemanding that it is easy to not take note of her need for stimulation.
Sensitive	You may find yourself thrown by your baby's unpredictable fussing and her lack of clear signals. Your preference for routine and order will be good for her.	Take time to settle your baby into a routine and focus on reading her signals (see pp.38–44) and using soothing strategies (see pp.45–47). Try to accept as much help as you can.

serene mum

baby	fit	making it work
Social butterfly	You are happy to go with the flow but your baby may be frustrated at times with the lack of stimulation and interest in her days.	Make a note to provide enough excitement and stimulation. Try an outing everyday to the park or a parent-and-baby group.
Slow-to-warm-up	You are a great match for your baby because your calm settled nature is predictable for her.	Watch your baby's cues and be sure to notice her subtle baby signals (see pp.38–44).
Settled	You and your baby are like picture-perfect babycare advert – calm and serene. People might call you a "natural mum".	Because you are both so laid back, your baby might end up not having enough stimulation. Watch out for when she is in the calm-alert state (see p.31) and play with her then.
Sensitive	You are a wonderful match for your sensitive baby. You bring calm to what seems to her to be a chaotic world.	Be sure you read her signals (see pp.38–44) and act when she is over-stimulated, then you will find you can short circuit colicky crying.

sensitive mum

baby	fit	making it work
Social butterfly	Your social butterfly seeks stimulation and is noisy and demanding. Her approach to life may be overwhelming for you and you may feel irritable at times.	Try to take good time out from your baby each day. You need adequate sleep, so if your nights are disrupted, sleep during the day. Sleep is a great way for you to recharge your system so you can cope with all the interactions new mothering brings.
Slow-to-warm-up	You are a good fit for your slow-to-warm-up baby because you read her signals and understand her need to approach the world with caution.	Watch out for your baby's signs and signals (see pp.38–44) and when she is ready for interaction, try to provide stimulation and a space for her to socialize.
Settled	A great match for you – your settled baby does not tax you.	Enjoy the ease with which you connect with your little one, but make sure you factor in periods of stimulation to your day, because your baby is very laid back.
Sensitive	You may find that your baby's fussing and the disorganisation of having a newborn in your space makes you feel scrambled and over-sensitive.	Talk to your partner and let him know when you are reaching your limits and are battling to cope. You will need support from your partner, friends and family in the early months.

happy days However you and your baby fit together, there are strategies you can use, such as playing with her and making eye contact, to ensure this precious time is enjoyable and fulfilling.

dealing with postnatal depression

Most women have moments when they struggle with the transition to motherhood and experience anxiety, tears and sheer panic. During those first few weeks or months at home, you may become aware of confusing thoughts or feelings such as sadness, anger, guilt or fears of harming your baby. This usually passes, but around one in 10 mothers of children under the age of two are eventually diagnosed with postnatal depression (PND).

Current thinking on PND finds that the prevailing emotions are anxiety and irritability, mixed with the low feelings. For this reason, a better name for the condition might be perinatal distress. The word "distress" exposes the fact that rather than being depressed, you may just be feeling anxious and at a loss as to how to carry on caring for your baby. These emotions can arise any time around the birth of your baby – from pregnancy to two years after childbirth.

Since PND is potentially serious for you and your baby, it is worth talking to your doctor, health visitor, or a qualified counsellor if you have some of the following symptoms:

- Feeling out of control, frustrated and very irritable.
- Scared or panicky, anxious and worried, or miserable most of the time.
- Unable to laugh or to feel joy.
- Unable to cope.
- Scared to go out but afraid to be alone.
- Unusually tearful.
- Feeling as if you are going crazy.
- Difficulty in sleeping.
- Lack of sex drive.
- Thoughts about harming yourself or your baby.

If you have experienced such distressing thoughts or feelings for more than 10 days, or you feel things are getting worse, not better, seek help immediately from your doctor, midwife, or health visitor, or a qualified counsellor. Perinatal distress robs you of the ability to feel connected, confident and secure. It can be a lonely and isolating experience. The first thing to remember is that it is not your fault. You are not to blame. It is crucial that you tell someone you trust about these disturbing thoughts and feelings, and get the support and understanding you need and deserve. Your inability to cope with daily life is not the problem but may be a symptom of a real, treatable, medical condition. See Resources (pp.214–15) for organizations who can help you with PND.

get enough rest Allow your partner, or friends and family, to take care of your baby while you recover from the strain of giving birth. Getting enough sleep will help your body and hormones recover more quickly.

chapter 6

boosting your baby's development

Dee is savouring every moment of James's life and while some days are a challenge, her overriding feeling as a new mother is one of enjoyment. As a teacher, she wants James to develop as well as he can and succeed in all aspects of his life. She is trying to ensure that his movement, motor, and social skills are the very best they can be. Dee is intent on filling every spare moment with interesting activities and has even gone as far as creating a stimulation activity schedule for her three-month-old son, but wonders if this will be enough to ensure that he is the brightest kid on the block. Unfortunately, this slightly misguided approach may lead to over-stimulation for James. What's needed is a sensible balance between activities, soothing time and sleep.

learn how to ...

● Make the most of your baby's inborn potential.
● Understand the importance of stimulation.
● Know when and how to stimulate your baby.
● Find a sensible middle ground between stimulating and calming.
● Use the TEAT guidelines: timing, environment, activities, toys.

your baby's birth

Birth is a critical moment for your baby and a precarious birth may affect his development for life. Natural delivery is the best method of delivery for most babies. The healthy stress hormones at this time will ensure your baby will manage with mild oxygen fluctuations and be active in the birth process. If your baby becomes distressed and the levels of oxygen he receives from the placenta drops, you may be faced with an assisted delivery or emergency Caesarean to protect your baby's developing brain at this significant time.

your baby's potential

We all feel under immense pressure to give our babies the best start in life. But do we really understand the critical elements that contribute to success and life achievement? There is a vast amount of research on this subject and what is clear is that there is no single factor that makes a difference to a baby's developing intelligence and skills. These are formed by a combination of many things, including his parentage, your pregnancy, and of course, stimulation in the first three years of life. Clearly there is more to giving your baby the best start than just stimulating him at every opportunity.

factors affecting development

There is endless debate on whether we are a product of our upbringing (nurture) or if our genes dictate who we are going to be (nature). The reality is that your baby is a combination of the genes you have passed on, the way you nurture him, and the sensory experiences he is exposed to. In recent years, five factors have been researched in great detail and have been shown to have a direct impact on your baby's physical, intellectual and emotional development:

● **Genes** The genes your baby carries from both of his parents and your families create his aptitude to develop. If your family is very musical, your baby has an increased chance of playing a musical instrument or singing on stage. If you are brilliant on the sports field, he could well carry these athletic genes. Your baby's genes also contribute to his personality and his ability to cope with stress. Since his genetic potential is not an element you can control in any way, we will not explore it further, except to say that the way your baby responds to stimulation will be affected to a large degree by his genes.

● **Pregnancy** You are the greenhouse for this little seed. During your pregnancy you provide the environment and nutrients essential for the prenatal stages of development. By taking care with your diet (see box, opposite) and environment, you can keep your baby safe.

● **Birth** Your baby's birth is the pivotal moment when he emerges into the world and is a critical time for his health and development. Your midwife or doctor will invest energy in ensuring that your baby's delivery is safe for you and for your developing baby's brain.

● **Sensory input** What your baby sees, hears and touches is the key to brain growth and development, and the way you regulate this is probably the most direct way you can have an impact on his development.

● **Love** The emotional context in which your baby develops is the part that makes the magic happen, and is possibly plays the most vital role in growing a healthy person and optimizing your baby's potential.

the influence of pregnancy

During the 40 weeks of pregnancy, you provide the building blocks (nutrients and environment) for the growth of every single cell in your baby's body. Your food choices during these weeks have a direct influence on your baby's development (see right). His brain begins to develop towards the third week of pregnancy and it's during this first trimester that the microscopic newly formed brain cells begin to migrate to their correct position. For example, cells that are important for vision migrate to the specific area of the brain that governs sight. This formation and migration of brain cells is important in determining your baby's potential. Stress and the womb environment also affect your baby's development:

your stress levels Recent research has shown that stress in pregnancy has an effect on the way in which your baby's brain is wired. When you are stressed, increased levels of the stress hormone cortisol are released, which cross the placenta to your baby. As a result, your baby is influenced by your stress, which can have a negative effect on the way his developing brain is programmed and his later ability to cope with difficult situations, such as dealing with problems at work. During pregnancy, it's best to avoid situations that cause you to feel stressed. For instance, ambitious house renovations or big contracts at work. If your relationship with your spouse or family is cause for stress, look for ways to alleviate the pressure by communicating better, seeking counselling, or avoiding family gatherings that increase your feelings of anxiety and anger. If your baby is already here and you had a stressful pregnancy, don't feel anxious or guilty; you can counteract many of the repercussions of being exposed to excess stress *in utero* by being consistent and positive as he grows up.

your womb All the sensory stimulation your baby requires for development *in utero* can be found in the womb. Moving against the deep skin-to-skin pressure of the womb walls, your baby's muscles start the process of creating body sense in his brain. In the last trimester your baby moves to a head-down position, which helps the vestibular (movement) system (see p.13), and contributes to muscle tone. Adequate muscle tone is vital for your baby to be active and to assist you in the birth process and later will contribute to his motor skills. On a visual level, your baby's eyes are protected at a time when they are too fragile to cope with stimulation. Keeping your baby just where he is for 40 weeks and allowing him to gain maximum benefit from the sensory world of the womb gives him the best chance in life. If your baby is born prematurely, you can create a womb-like world in the neonatal unit to help his sensory development (see chapter 7, pp.74–89).

the role of food

During pregnancy, the food you eat forms the building blocks of your baby's cell development. Vital nutrients enter your bloodstream and cross the placenta, so it is important that your diet is healthy in pregnancy. Likewise, when you breastfeed, the nutrients you are taking in help to create breast milk that will nourish your baby.

a healthy diet Eat a balanced diet that includes lots of fruit and vegetables; starches that contain fibre such as wholemeal bread and brown rice; sources of protein such as chicken, lean beef, fish, and eggs. Include foods that have essential fatty acids such as nuts and seeds and eat oily fish twice a week. Drink lots of fresh water and limit the intake of drinks containing caffeine and artificial sweeteners.

avoiding harm Some things you consume may have very negative effects on your baby's brain, such as alcohol, cigarettes, drugs, and many over-the-counter or herbal medications. When ingested, these substances can pass through the placenta to your baby and disrupt the way the brain cells are migrating. For this reason, it is best to avoid alcohol and other potentially damaging substances during pregnancy and also when you are breastfeeding.

areas of development

We tend to measure a baby's developmental progress on a few age-old milestones: walking, crawling, talking, eating solids and so on. But a baby's development is so much more interesting and subtle than this. Curiously, it's the little things we don't notice as parents or which can't easily be measured that can most influence a baby's success later in life, such as his emotional skills and ability to calm himself, alongside the more obvious milestones of movement and speech. So what affects your baby's development? Obviously your baby's genes, your pregnancy, and the early days of life – but you have a significant role too. The way in which you stimulate your baby really does help him to achieve his potential. The second section of this book (chapters 7 to 13) sets out developmental norms in the five areas, age by age, then offers hundreds of ways to adapt your home and lifestyle to enhance your baby's development in each one.

gross motor development The "gross" or large movements of the body are the most obvious area of your baby's development – and the easiest to measure. Your baby's first task here is to gain some control over gravity. At birth your baby is a helpless, curled-up bundle at the mercy of gravity and his immature reflexes. Within a few weeks, he needs to uncurl and integrate his reflexes so that he can first hold up his head and later roll over. Head control is the first step towards learning to walk. As he begins to control his body more, he will be able to sit and later crawl. These are the critical motor milestones of the first year. Walking is the key milestone that many parents focus on, and yet it varies with age and is actually easier for babies than crawling. Good gross motor coordination sets up babies for success in sports later in life, though this is also influenced by genes, such as long legs and good coordination, plus a passion for a specific sport. You can help your baby to develop his potential by playing ball games and by water play.

fine motor development This area of development is more subtle than that of gross movement. Your baby learns to refine his hand and arm movements in order to reach out, grasp, and manipulate objects. Hand–eye coordination is key to this area of development. Within weeks of birth your baby will notice his hands and start to reach and control the way his arms move. By six months he will begin to control his fingers and by his first birthday coordinate reaching, grasping, and manipulating tiny objects, such as the peas on his plate as he feeds himself. Children with a genetic flair for hand–eye coordination may excel at sports such as hockey and cricket. Throw in a creative gene and you may have an artist or a piano player. Though success begins with a child's genes and interests, the way in which you stimulate his fine motor control and hand–eye coordination, for example putting toys just out of his reach to encourage grasping or giving him finger foods to pick up, helps to maximize his potential.

language development It is our ability to communicate using verbal as well as non-verbal language that makes us human, and this is strongly linked to intelligence. Milestones in this area of development include the ability to read non-verbal signals, understand language, make pre-language sounds and of course, at around a year of age, speak words.

Research has shown that the amount of time a mother spends talking to her baby every day and the number of different words she uses have a direct correlation with his IQ. Your baby's genes are the building blocks for intelligence, your pregnancy provides the platform, but it is your interactions, how much you talk and what you say to your baby that will see his potential turn into intelligence.

social and emotional development This is possibly the most important area of development for human beings, allowing your baby to form meaningful relationships with you and to bond with significant caregivers. In the early days and months, your baby needs to bond with a limited number of caring adults, usually you and his other parent and maybe a granny or childminder too. His interactions with these special caregivers set the tone and his expectations for all future relationships. Good bonding requires the following:

● **Tolerance of the sensory world** If your baby enjoys the sensory experiences of social interaction, such as touch, he is more likely to embrace the tactile side of relationships, such as breastfeeding and cuddles.
● **Feeling read and understood** This comes about when you read your baby's signals appropriately and respond to his needs consistently.
● **Happiness and joy** When you laugh with your baby, when you are content with each other, and when you share happy, "feel-good" moments, your baby learns and develops well in all areas.
● **Time and slow space** Bonding and emotional development develop given lots of time and space. The notion of quality time does not apply to babies. Instead they need quantity time with consistent caregivers.

the role of regulation This is not an area of development that many parents are familiar with. Indeed, you may have no idea that you can help your baby develop in this way or the relevance it has in later life. Regulation is all about developing strategies to keep the body's systems in balance. At birth, for example, your baby needs to maintain a steady heartbeat and breathing rate. As he grows, he must learn how to keep his physical or emotional state steady, too, in order to remain asleep or calm.

language development

There are two distinct areas for language in the brain. Wernicke's area is responsible for the understanding of language (verbal and non-verbal) and Broca's area controls speech. Since Wernicke's area develops first, your baby will understand language before he can speak. The connections in Wernicke's area develop rapidly between eight and 20 months, which explains why your baby begins to understand language at eight months and as a toddler understands so much. Broca's area begins to function between 12 months to two years so spoken language can only emerge in the second year of life. The fact that your baby can understand everything about eight months before he can communicate it is a great source of frustration for him.

bonding time Spending lots of quiet time nestled with you nurtures your new baby's emotional potential.

ability to regulate

Your baby may be born with a genetic predisposition to being well-regulated (the social butterfly and settled baby) or may be less able to regulate different areas such as body systems and emotions (the sensitive baby and slow-to-warm-up baby), resulting in crying and difficulties establishing good sleep/wake cycles.

Your pregnancy will also affect your baby's capacity for self-regulation. For instance, babies exposed to drugs in the womb show more signs of not being able to regulate themselves, including fussing in the early days and attention difficulties at school age.

how self-regulation develops As your baby grows, he will gradually learn how to use internal as well as external ways of keeping his body systems in balance. You won't even notice the internal methods because they are governed by your baby's hormones and autonomic system (basic brain system). For instance at birth, the first thing your baby needs to do to adapt to the world outside the womb is to let his hormones and autonomic system regulate his temperature, breathing, and heartbeat, along with other body functions, such as his digestive system. Premature babies take a while to work this out. After a few weeks, your baby begins to be able to regulate his mood and ability to stay calm, too, but it takes most babies around four months to start doing this using both internal strategies – filtering sensory information, such as his brain shutting out the feeling of the clothes he is wearing – and external strategies, such as self-soothing. In the second half of the first year your baby will begin to regulate his sleep and appetite. Later, being able to regulate his attention span will make it easier for him to learn at school.

In the first three months you can help your baby to regulate his mood by not over-stimulating him and by soothing him. You can help him to regulate his sleep by adapting his sensory world until he is able to fall and stay asleep independently. You will find many other effective ways to help your baby regulate himself in the age-band sections (chapters 7 to 13).

soothing your baby At birth your baby is unable to regulate much for himself beyond the most basic tasks of keeping his temperature constant and his heart rate even. You will need to soothe your baby to help him regulate his mood.

what is "normal"?

There is something about being a parent, especially when it's your first baby, that brings out a competitive streak. You may find yourself watching your baby's milestones closely, looking for any sign of brilliance. Before entering the parenting race, you need to understand that comparing babies and measuring your baby's success by his achievement of milestones is at best a pointless exercise, and at worst can cause anxiety, or even animosity between friends. Being individuals, babies should not be judged on the achievement of milestones, which are generally not reliable predictors of either giftedness or handicap. There are a number of good reasons why you should avoid comparing your baby's development with that of other babies:

1 **time span** The time spans in which milestones are reached are quite broad. Not one milestone, from talking to walking, has an exact age for achievement – they are all measured within a range of ages. For example, a normal baby may say his first words anywhere between nine and 16 months of age.

2 **individuality** Development varies enormously between individuals. Some babies advance in one area at a rapid rate and in another area much slower and, just like adults, babies have different aptitudes. You may be a brilliant horse rider and your friend a gifted musician. Likewise, one baby may walk at an early age while another one who walks later may have smiled at two weeks and have an amazing vocabulary by the time he turns one.

3 **one step forward** Development also varies within the individual, regardless of aptitude. One week your baby may be starting to hold his head up while the next he seems a lot more floppy again. Sometime later, seemingly overnight, your apparently gifted 10-month-old may lose all five words he had been happily gabbling. There is a very good reason for this, called "competition of skill". Simply put, this means that different skills compete for the brain's energy as they develop, thus the focus of the brain's energy shifts. For instance, for a few weeks your baby may be focusing on language development then switch to development on a motor level while language appears to take a back seat.

Of course development is not as cut-and-dried as that and most often skill acquisition overlaps so that different levels of skills are established at the same time. Development takes place in spurts because the brain needs to consolidate acquired skills and often when it appears that there is nothing new going on in there, your baby's brain is working very hard in laying down important foundations in preparation for the next stage.

developmental delay

Frequently when a baby has a problem it is his mother who is the first to notice the warning signs. If you are concerned about your baby's development, look for a cluster of signs.

signs of developmental delay:
- Noticeable floppiness of limbs and body from birth or a stiffness that has developed.
- Difficulty sucking or other serious feeding problems.
- Not turning towards sounds by three months old.
- No eye contact from early on.
- No smiling by 10 weeks combined with a lack of interest in people.
- Not babbling to self or others by eight months.
- Never rolled and not crawling by ten months.
- Not moving one side of the body like the other, or asymmetric movement.
- Not reaching for and grasping objects by six months.
- Extreme fussing that lasts beyond six months.

If you notice one or more of these signs, take your baby to your health visitor or GP for a check-up. If you are still concerned even when told that your child is fine, it may be a good idea to make an appointment with a physiotherapist, occupational therapist or paediatrician who specializes in neuro-development; they will be able to interpret your baby's development and can detect problems at a very early age.

giftedness

You may be surprised to learn that giftedness brings its own challenges and truly gifted children do require special handling. It is very unlikely that advanced milestones in the first year will denote giftedness. Most babies who advance rapidly in the first year are completely in line with their peers by eighteen months of age. Possible signs of giftedness are:

● Significantly advanced milestones in every area.
● Very early and advanced language development.

the importance of stimulation

Everybody is born with a genetic code that makes us who we are. This code, sometimes referred to as our nature, is the potential, present at birth, to achieve great things in a certain area. Your baby's code may denote musical brilliance, but if he is never exposed to a musical instrument, that potential will not be nurtured. So it is nurture – the environment within which your baby develops – that determines the extent to which he fulfils his potential.

On the day your baby is born, he has every brain cell he requires for development and for success in his life. However, very few of these brain cells are connected to each other, meaning that he is not making too much sense of his world. As sensory input reaches the brain – say a sound or a touch – it fires a brain cell (neuron) and a message passes from one brain cell to the next. When the baby experiences the same input again, the same pathway fires and so the path becomes reinforced. This is learning.

Much research has been done in the past 50 years on the effects of environment on intelligence. Studies of orphaned infants institutionalized at a young age reveal that the sterile, unstimulating environment of an orphanage causes delays in most areas of development. In fact, babies institutionalized past two years old can have severe long-term problems. Very sadly, even with intensive intervention after the infants were taken from the orphanages, many never reached their potential. The first three years are a crucial period when the brain is most responsive to learning. Studies with animals and babies show that intensive stimulation at this time produces an increase in the connections between the brain cells and enhanced development in the stimulated area of the brain.

emotional context

When considering the key elements for development, we know that your baby's genes are the seeds that carry the code for his potential; that a healthy pregnancy and birth give your baby the best start; and that stimulation is important.

And until recently that was where the equation ended. But in the past decade we have discovered the "glue" – that magic ingredient that makes all this happen and ensures best success: love and a positive

emotional environment. When you stimulate your baby with love and a positive emotional tone, the connections between brain cells develop much quicker and are reinforced more effectively.

This is the reason that babies do not learn in sterile and controlled environments. For example, watching television conveys minimal emotional tone or social interaction, and research tells us that babies learn very little from watching TV on their own, even if the content is educational. A child

can see a pig and hear the word "pig" many times on TV without learning to say the word. But one visit to a smelly pig sty and watching Mum's response to the sensory experiences of this outing may well result in a toddler learning the word "pig" immediately.

Your emotional response to your baby, speaking in your mother tongue (which conveys emotional context) and the sheer enjoyment of his growing bond with you is the fertilizer for your baby's development.

balanced stimulation

Although it is clear that a stimulating environment is essential for development, beware of taking the idea of infant stimulation too seriously. There are many good reasons why stimulation is not a case of "the more, the better". While stimulation is absolutely vital to brain development for your baby's potential, it is essential that it is appropriately timed and well-balanced with opportunities for soothing and sleep.

● **Irritability** Babies who are stimulated a great deal of the time, missing sleeps and without their parents noticing their signals, become irritable and fractious. A fractious baby cannot make sense of what he is learning.
● **Sleep problems** Too much stimulation may lead to an over-stimulated state and your baby will find it difficult to switch off and settle to sleep during the day. Babies who miss daytime naps and are over-stimulated during the day frequently exhibit sleep difficulties and even night terrors (see p.202).
● **Short attention span** Concentration and attention span develop over time. Babies who are bombarded with toys and activities may shift their attention rapidly from one item to the next, without taking time to explore all the qualities of each, which in turn affects their ability to solve problems (an important life skill). You may find that a limited number of everyday household objects – wooden spoons, an apple – will keep your baby entertained for longer, and effectively develop his attention span more, than a pile of random toys scattered over the play area.
● **High activity levels** When life is exciting all the time, your baby may become very active. The stress of being stimulated consistently may cause him to get busier and busier. Watch any toddler at a birthday party and you will see how high levels of stimulation makes toddlers more active and less constructive in their play.
● **Lack of benefit** Contrary to logic, high levels of inappropriately timed stimulation may have no positive effect on development. Connections between brain cells occur best when your baby is in the calm-alert state (see p.31) and also in a loving environment. For instance, reading a book to your baby when he is in the calm-alert state and ready for interaction, will be enormously beneficial for his development. In contrast, stimulation when he is tired and you are impatient will have not any positive effects on his learning.
● **Hampered play skills** If you constantly stimulate your baby he may have limited opportunity to learn to play independently and explore his environment at his own pace.
● **Stress on the family** You may find that the pressures on you to provide your baby with baby classes and state-of-the-art toys is a costly exercise, both financially and in terms of time.

stimulating activities

In the last 30 years there has been intense focus on the critical developmental period of the first three years of life and on how you can stimulate your baby's development. "Stimulation activities" have become the buzzwords of childcare. You can buy a multitude of books, read any number of articles in magazines, buy wonderful toys, and enrol your baby in classes – all with the aim of optimizing development through stimulation. But it seems that this principle may be taken too far. Studies show that, for example, baby intelligence DVDs actually impair language acquisition. This is thought to be because babies spend a limited amount of time awake and alert – if this time is spent in front of a screen, rather than interacting with people, they do not get the same emotional and social experiences that help language to develop.

the sensible middle ground

The secret to stimulating your baby in the best way is finding the middle ground between not enough stimulation and too much. The basic principles of sensible stimulation are as follows:

1 harness your baby's natural desire Your baby is motivated to interact with his world and to master it. This means you can have confidence in the natural process of development and not feel that all the responsibility lies with you. Jean Ayres, a pioneer in the field of sensory integration, believed that children have a natural desire to develop and given a fertile environment will develop well. So you don't need to guide your baby's play at every opportunity; simply provide interesting toys or objects and then observe with interest what your baby does. This will ensure that he feels he has your attention, but is free to explore in the way he would like.

2 provide a fertile environment By providing a fertile sensory environment and age-appropriate toys and books, you can create the opportunities your baby needs to maximize his potential on his own, without the risk of pushing him too hard, or pressurizing your time or relationships as nurturer. Consult the age-related chapters for appropriate ideas (see chapters 7 to 13).

3 read your baby's signals Your baby will learn best from his world and take maximum benefits from the activities and toys you present if he is in the calm-alert state (see p.31). Watch for your baby's approach signals (smiling, cooing, gazing at you with interest) and stimulate him then. By keeping his awake times (see chart, p.51) in mind, you will know when he's ready to stop playing and get ready to sleep.

stimulating your baby
❶ Babies love looking at their reflection in mirrors. You can buy excellent books that include baby-safe mirrors.
❷ Reading aloud in an animated way to your baby and encouraging her to join in by pointing out pictures will boost her development.

4 follow your baby's lead Your best contribution when stimulating your baby is not to be your baby's teacher, it is to assist his progress. Simply set up his play area, or the place you are helping him to explore (such as a safe place in your kitchen or the park) and then sit with your baby for a few minutes while he tries out the activity. Follow your baby's lead and interact with the toys he is interested in.

5 use the TEAT principles Short for Timing, Environment, Activities, Toys, this helpful acronym will help you to remember when and how to stimulate your baby best. At the end of each age-band chapter (chapters 7 to 13), there is a TEAT section packed with ideas for suitably stimulating activities.

the TEAT principles

TEAT is the means by which you can deliver stimulation to your baby, much like a teat (or nipple) delivers milk. When thinking about stimulating your baby remember the word and ask yourself:

T Is this the appropriate **time** for my baby to be stimulated?

E How can I structure his **environment** to make it either interesting and stimulating or calming?

A What **activity** is appropriate for my baby right now?

T Is there a **toy** or two I can offer to my baby that he will enjoy and which will enhance his development?

activities These are the games you play and the interactions you have with your baby that affect his development. They can be either stimulating or calming. Activities should be carried out at the right time of day and in the appropriate place (see timing and environment sections for how to achieve this).

timing

Time your baby's stimulation activities according to his routine (see p.50), awake times (see p.51), and state (see pp.31–33). It is logical to keep visual stimulation to a minimum during the night when your baby should be sleeping. Similarly the best time to develop his visual sense would be while it's light during your baby's calm-alert state in the afternoon. You might blow bubbles to drift around him, which encourages him to track the shapes with his eyes.

Adapt your normal daily routine to accommodate different stimulating activities. By linking activities with certain times of the day, it's easy to boost development without having to schedule special stimulation time.

● Use nappy changing to introduce visual stimulation (unless at night), because your baby will be lying on his back and looking around him.

● A walk in the park can be great for movement stimulation, whether you push your baby in his pram, carry him on you in a sling, or even give him a gentle push in a swing. Playing "This is the way the lady rides" by gently jogging him up and down on your knee will enhance his motor skills.

● Daytime feeds are an ideal time to stimulate your baby's auditory sense – do this by quietly singing or talking to him while you are feeding him.

● Bath time occurs just before bedtime, so try to hold back on stimulation and use calming input, such as gentle movement, to prepare your baby for the night ahead.

toys

A toy is any object that your baby chooses to play with, from everyday household objects, to books, toys, music, and outdoor equipment. In recent years wonderful toys for stimulation have been designed and even a young baby will benefit from appropriate state-of-the-art toys, such as a play gym or soft puzzle cubes.

Once again though, it's a question of timing. Some toys are great for stimulation, but should be used only when your baby is ready to benefit from interaction. For instance, a busy mobile or activity gym can promote eye–movement control and hand–eye coordination. However, trying to interest a tired baby in a mobile or gym is likely to over-stimulate him, pushing him into an overloaded state. He will neither benefit from the interaction nor remain calm. At bath time, you could try some containers for pouring, but keep things calm. At sleep time a more appropriate tool may be a quiet lullaby CD, and just before this when he's tired, no toys at all may be best.

environment

The brain acts like a sponge, taking in sensory information all the time. Unlike the mature brain, which can filter out excessive or irrelevant sensory information, your baby's mind takes it all in! So it stands to reason that his environment will have a major impact on his development.

It is important to structure your baby's environment with either calming or stimulating activities as appropriate – this is the secret to bringing up a calm, contented child. For example, when you want to calm your baby, try swaying him in a quiet room with dimmed lights, or singing to him softly.

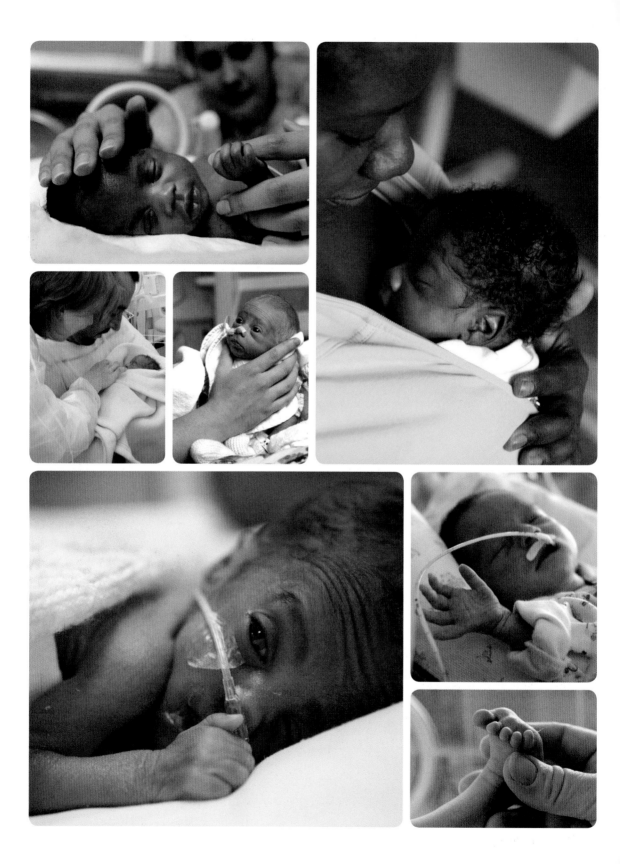

your premature baby

During pregnancy you begin the process of bonding with your little one. You envisage your baby: who she will be and what she will look like. You see yourself as a mum or dad and begin the process of becoming a parent. You build an image of your birth and the way in which you will meet this precious person. Underlying these emotions, possibly on a subconscious level, are the fears that go along with becoming a mum or dad: will the birth be safe; will my baby be healthy; and will I love her the instant I meet her? When your pregnancy ends prematurely (before 37 weeks) you are likely to feel worried and scared, and will need the support of your partner, family, and doctors. Over the next few weeks, you will begin a process of healing that at times may be very frightening. Getting to know your premature baby's signals and how to meet her sensory needs will all help to pave the way for this healing to begin.

life with your premature baby

About seven percent of babies are born prematurely, even in these days of advanced medical care. Some parents may feel anger or sadness, while others may experience denial and become detached or emotionally removed from the situation. Whatever your response, you will have a period of adjustment ahead of you. The information in this section will help you in the process of healing.

adjusting your dream

Seeing your premature baby in a neonatal unit – a special care baby unit (SCBU) or neonatal intensive care unit (NICU) – will seem surreal and upsetting, because it is a foreign and daunting space. Your baby may have been whisked away as soon as she was born, which can be heartbreaking. You have to adjust how you imagined your birth and your new baby. You may feel anxiety, and even grief, on two levels: firstly, you grieve the loss of your dream birth and perfectly healthy newborn. You may feel sad or even angry that your dream has been shattered. Secondly, if your baby is very weak or medically fragile, you may fear that she will die or be disabled. It's normal to contemplate worst-case scenarios, because it is the brain's way of coping as it prepares you to cope with the loss of a healthy baby. It is also very common for parents, especially you as the mum, to experience guilt. You may feel that you have not been an adequate incubator for your baby or failed to meet your own expectations of delivering a healthy baby. Of course, added to these feelings may be complete confusion, worry, and lack of control.

By understanding your baby's basic needs – medical, emotional, and developmental – you will start to know how you and the medical team can cater to her. This will help you to develop a relationship with your baby and understand how to give her the best start possible in less than optimal circumstances. You might like to start by reading *Prematurity – Adjusting your Dream* by Welma Lubbe (see Resources, pp.214–15), which explains the medical, nutritional, and emotional world of the premature baby.

the sensory space The neonatal unit is sterile and can be quite overwhelming for you as the parent. On a tactile level, it is sparse and isolating. You are asked to wash your hands and have to wear a gown or a mask. It smells sterile and medical. Visually you are confronted with drips, tubes, monitors, and bright lights, all sights that make no sense in the context of your baby. The sounds – alarms and voices – in this space are disconcerting. Opposite is an explanation of what you might see and hear in the neonatal unit, as you start getting to know your baby.

sense-able secret

Depending on your baby's medical needs and care requirements, she may be looked after in the special care baby unit (if she just needs to be monitored or is under lights) or a neonatal intensive care unit if she is very small or ill.

understanding O₂ Sats

In the neonatal unit, a saturation sensor is wrapped around your baby's foot or hand that measures how much oxygen is being carried in her blood (her oxygen saturation/O₂ Sats). The sensor monitors the colour of the blood, because this varies according to how much oxygen is in it. Oxygen is vital – your baby may be given extra oxygen via a ventilator or nose tube so that her O₂ Sats remain above 88 percent.

the babysense secret

the neonatal unit

neonatal unit sights

These are the common sights that initially may overwhelm you, but to which you will rapidly adjust:

incubator Your baby will be contained in a see-through perspex crib to keep her warm. It may have a roof with portholes on the side through which you can touch your baby or the incubator may be completely open – a flat bed.

monitor Next to your baby's incubator will be a monitor that reads her heart rate, breathing pattern and breathing rate. If these fall below optimal levels, the monitor will sound an alarm.

pads on chest Your baby's heartbeat and breathing will be monitored via pads on her chest or she may be lying on a mat that registers each breath she takes.

ventilator Your baby may be breathing with the use of a ventilator (the large machine next to her incubator). If so, she may have a tube down her throat or directly into her windpipe. Alternatively she may be breathing on her own with pipes in her nose that keep the air pressure to her lungs steady, reducing the hard work of breathing (this is known as CPAP: continuous positive airway pressure). Or she may simply have a tube with two small prongs fitting snugly in her nose to deliver oxygen at the correct pressure and levels.

lines Your baby may have a needle leading to a tube (line) in a vein in her arm, leg, head, or umbilical cord, which is used to give her fluids and medicine. The line may also be placed in an artery in her arm or leg.

neonatal unit terms

The sounds of the monitors and alarms and the technical terms the staff use when referring to your baby may make you feel out of your depth. However, you will become accustomed to these terms within a period of days, and will adjust to cope with the noxious sensory input. Common terms include:

apnoea A period when breathing stops and oxygen saturation drops.

bradycardia Slower than normal heart rate.

chronic lung disease (CLD) Damaged lung tissue which can result when babies are ventilated (to help them breathe) for a long time.

hydrocephalus Raised levels of brain fluid around the brain as a result of infection or because spinal fluid is not being absorbed well.

hypoglycaemia Abnormally low blood sugar.

hypoxia Low levels of oxygen in the blood.

intubate Inserting a narrow tube into a baby's nose or mouth and down through the trachea to help with breathing.

jaundice Yellow colour of the body or whites of the eyes, due to the liver's inability to process bilirubin, a substance produced as the red blood cells break down.

nasogastric (NG) tube A tube inserted into one nostril and down to the stomach for feeding.

respiratory distress syndrome (RDS) This is a common cause of respiratory problems that results when the lungs do not secrete sufficient surfactant, the substance that prevents the alveoli (air sacs) in the lungs from collapsing.

retinopathy of prematurity (ROP) A visual impairment caused by a problem with the developing blood supply to the back of the eye (retina) when too high levels of oxygen are administered for prolonged periods.

neonatal unit team

The team in the neonatal unit consists of a paediatrician, a neonatologist, a neonatal nurse, and a variety of specialists who will be called in when necessary: cardiologist (heart), audiologist (hearing), neurologist (brain), nephrologist (kidneys), ophthalmologist (vision), pathologist (blood, and other, infections), a radiographer, a breastfeeding counsellor, a social worker, a developmental occupational therapist or physiotherapist, and a speech and language therapist. Add to this team three critical people: your baby, you, and your partner. There needs to be mutual respect and trust between you all so that you communicate properly to help with the care of your baby.

helping your baby

You, the parent, are critical to your baby's care because you bring three unique qualities:

❶ consistency You are the most consistent person around your baby. Nurses come and go, making you the one constant in your child's life. With time you will become the one who knows your premature baby best and who she perceives as dependable and predictable on a sensory level.

❷ speaking for your baby As the most consistent presence and the only member of the team who cannot be replaced, your role is vital. You will observe her responses to interventions and to sensory input. You will learn the pattern of what gets done when and how your baby responds to it. You are the perfect advocate for your baby, able to diplomatically communicate her needs. Within a short time, you will know what sensory input she responds well to, and the effect of interventions.

❸ understanding her state Your baby has a unique language that will tell you what she is coping well with and what is distressing her. Remind yourself of the six states of infancy (see p.33) and the way your baby signals those states (see pp.38–44) – they apply to your prem baby as well as to a full-term baby. Get to know her signals (see p.77) and you will soon be able to translate your baby's responsiveness and her ability to tolerate an interaction at any time.

your baby's sensory state

Your premature baby's states of infancy are similar to those of a full-term baby: she can be in deep sleep, light sleep, a drowsy, calm-alert, or active-alert state, or she can be distressed and crying (see also pp.31–34). The states to encourage are content deep or light sleep and the calm-alert state – times in which your baby grows, experiences optimal oxygenation levels, and begins to interact.

deep sleep This is essential for your baby's growth and when she is in this state she will sleep through most noises and sensory stimulation in the neonatal unit. If she is in a very deep sleep, ask the medical team not to disturb her with painful interventions and monitoring if possible, since this is such a vital time for her growth and development.

light sleep Your baby will spend much of her day in this state. She is processing the interventions and interactions of the day and is easily woken. This is the state in which she gives you "back-off signals", such as splaying her fingers and saluting (see p.40).

drowsy In this state, your baby opens and closes her eyes and is responsive to the world. She takes her time in responding and is not learning much from her world, but she is awake.

calm-alert For brief periods each day, your baby will be in the calm-alert state, breathing smoothly and appearing settled. She is able to learn from her world. This period is very brief for a prem baby and you will need to watch carefully for her signals. Babies born before 32 weeks' gestation will spend almost no time in the calm-alert state and therefore should not be stimulated. The period of calm-alert grows longer as she gets older and you will be able to interact with her for longer periods as she develops.

active-alert In this state your prem baby has a hard time regulating herself and is no longer enjoying interaction. Just a small amount of stimulation or interaction is enough to push her into over-stimulation and the active-alert state. When she reaches this state, she tries to settle herself or protect herself from intervention (see opposite).

crying This is very distressing for your prem baby and uses up energy she requires for growth and healing. It also makes her breathing irregular and her oxygen saturation levels may decrease. Crying is a stress signal that tells you that your baby has had enough. You need to help her to calm down and return to the calm-alert state or go to sleep.

being an active parent

As a parent in the neonatal unit you may feel daunted and at the mercy of the staff, but becoming part of the team and taking an active role in the care of your baby can be very healing. See the box opposite (helping your baby) to see how to play your part by being an active parent. A critical part of being an active participant in your baby's healing is to know and respond to her signals.

signs that I'm coping: approach signals

When your baby shows these signs, she is inviting you to interact with her. Use this time to bond, interact, and build your relationship with her. She will display these signals more often as she gets older and more stable:
● Being awake and calm.
● Stable and regular heart rate and breathing.
● Pink colour and good oxygen-saturation levels.
● Limited body movements.
● Looking at you and perhaps focusing on your face.

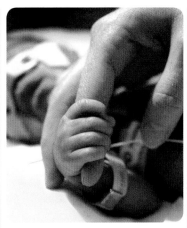

signs that I'm trying to cope: warning signals

Signs that your baby is trying to cope show that she is reaching a level of stress, but is attempting to calm herself. These are healthy signals and show that your baby is growing up:
● Sucking other than for food.
● Putting her hands near her face.
● Placing her hands under her chin.
● Grasping your finger.

signs that I'm stressed: fussing signals

Stress may affect your baby on a variety of levels. At first, she may not be able to continue interacting with you. If further stimulated, she may become irritable and fussy and cry or even go into a stress-induced sleep state. Then, she may react on a movement level by waving her arms and moving frantically or by not moving at all. Finally, she may become so stressed that her medical stability is compromised. Obviously the last of these effects of stress is the more serious and debilitating.

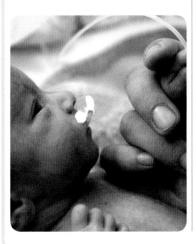

When your baby is crying and stressed, she uses energy that otherwise should be used in growing and keeping her medically stable. By watching for stress signals, you can avoid this negative outcome for your baby. Stress signals include:
● Arching her back and stretching out her arms and legs.
● Heartbeat becoming too slow or too quick and oxygen saturation (see p.74) decreasing.
● Becoming blue around the mouth as her breathing changes.
● Yawning, hiccuping, or sneezing.
● Moving frantically or looking away to escape the stimuli.

If you see these signals, tell the team so that an intervention, such as having a line changed, can be paused to decrease her stress levels.

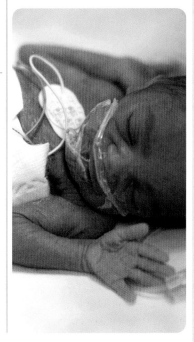

sense-able secret

Your premature baby is very sensitive to touch. Use still pressure touch, such as placing your hand on her, to soothe her.

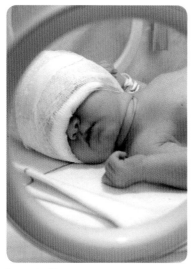

keep it dim Very young premature babies are not able to close their eyes intentionally. Your baby may have gauze wrapped tightly around her eyes to keep them closed.

your prem baby's sensory world

The womb is the ideal sensory environment for your baby, but the premature baby does not have the luxury of the calming womb world. The sensory world of the neonatal unit is far removed from this. Take time to look around the neonatal unit and pick up on all the ways it differs from the womb world, listed here by sensory system. This will help you to understand what must be unsettling for her.

Each individual sensory input in the neonatal unit is potentially overwhelming for your premature baby, and so in combination it has the ability to shift your baby up a state and make her feel stressed. Being aware of this will allow you to monitor your baby and help her if she becomes stressed when she's received too much unpleasant input. The types of input listed here are all very negative, but over in the next section (pp.80–83), we will look at how to adjust your baby's environment to decrease the level of distressing elements.

touch Your prem baby has a fully developed sense of touch and can perceive both soothing and painful interventions. She can feel changes of temperature and is especially sensitive to light touch. Deep, still touch feels calming to her while light touch is disconcerting. She would prefer the soothing deep, constant skin-to-skin touch of the uterine walls, but has instead to deal with the following in the neonatal unit:

● Lack of physical boundaries to make her feel contained.
● Changes in temperature.
● Light touch, such as when changing monitors and nappies.
● Lack of skin-to-skin sensation – even her hands don't come into contact with her own body much.
● Pain, such as when a tube or line are put in.

sight If your baby is born before 26 weeks' gestation, her eyelids may still be fused but will open shortly thereafter. By 32 weeks, she will be able to see and track a light, but she cannot close her eyes intentionally nor can her pupils constrict to limit the amount of light she takes in. Your prem baby finds bright lights and contrasting colours disconcerting. Instead of the muted, dark, and visually soothing world she would have in the womb, she has to deal with the following in the neonatal unit:

● Contrasting colours and patterns.
● Constantly changing levels of light.
● Very bright light – when a nurse comes over to change a line or monitor your baby she will light up the incubator very brightly so that she can see what she is doing.
● Ultraviolet lights if your baby is under lights for jaundice treatment.

sound Your prem baby can hear and respond to sounds. She prefers subdued sounds and is upset by loud and varied sounds. In the womb, the quiet continuous sounds are rarely above 72 decibels and are accompanied by calming vibrations. The sounds of the womb are the consistent, white noise naturally made by your body such as the gushes, gurgles, and beats and rhythms of your cardiovascular and digestive systems. In the neonatal unit the sounds are far from calming sounds:

● Alarms and conversation varying between 60 and 90 decibels and even rising to 120 decibels.

● Tapping the incubator or closing its perspex porthole sounds loud and echo-y to your baby because she is enclosed within the space.

● The sound of instruments and objects being placed next to or even on top of the incubator will be amplified to your baby.

● The crying of other babies can be loud and very disconcerting.

movement and gravity Your prem baby can feel the effect of gravity and movement. In the last trimester your baby would, under normal circumstances, invert herself in the womb and turn head down in preparation for birth. This head-down position provides intense vestibular input (input to her movement system). In addition to the intense input of the head-down position, your baby would experience continuous lulling and rocking movements in the womb as well as the sensation of being able to move almost weightlessly as if floating in a bubble, because water decreases the effect of gravity. When babies in the womb move, they meet the resistance of the womb walls, which is essential for the development of muscle tone. Instead, your prem baby experiences the following:

● Stillness, which feels unnatural and unsettling to her.

● No protection from gravity by being positioned in flexion (curled up in a ball) like in the womb or by the water that contains her little movements *in utero*.

● When lying on her back, your baby's arms and legs fall outwards similar to a frog as she does not have the muscle tone to resist gravity.

smell and taste Your prem baby can smell and taste scents and flavours. In the womb she responds favourably to sweet flavours. Your prem baby is very sensitive to the following smells and tastes:

● Alcohol swabs used to clean the skin before inserting a drip or tube.

● Strong-smelling cleaning agents used to keep the neonatal unit clean.

● Antiseptic soap and alcohol spray that is used to clean your hands before you touch your baby.

● Lack of sweet flavours and no soothing taste of breast milk until she is old enough to be fed orally.

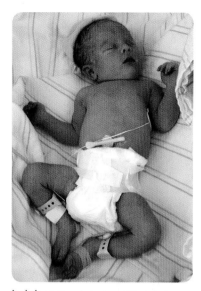

helpless Your baby is not likely to have enough muscle tone to keep herself curled up like a full-term newborn. Therefore her arms and legs will fall outwards when she lies on her back.

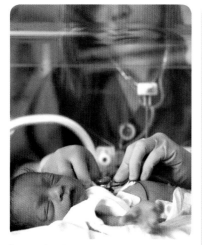

keep checking When prem babies are closely monitored to prevent sensory overload, they have a better developmental outcome for at least 36 months; can come off the ventilator and tube feeds earlier; have a lower incidence of internal bleeding and long-term lung disease; and a shorter hospital stay.

your baby's sensory systems

This table outlines the negative effects that being in a neonatal unit can have on your baby's senses and development in the long term. See pp.82–83 for how to protect your baby's systems.

prolonged sensory input	threat to her senses
Overwhelming input – excess input from all the senses at once	• The combined effect of intense sensory information from all your baby's senses results in an over-stimulated state, which causes her stress and may delay her healing. • Crying, using up her precious energy required for growth and repair. • Increased pressure in the brain, a potential cause of brain injury. • Long term, your baby may have difficulty soothing herself and regulating her state. • Delayed development of sleep/wake cycles.
Painful touch	• Not liking being touched (tactile defensiveness). • Difficulty in feeding.
Strong visual input	• Sleep deprivation. • Lack of day/night sleep differentiation, making it hard to get your baby to sleep at night later on. • Low oxygen saturation (see p.74). • Damage to the retina resulting in visual problems.
Loud sounds	• Low or high heart rate. • Being woken at a time when sleep is important for the body's growth. • Low oxygen saturation (see p.74). • Hearing loss.
No movement and the effects of gravity	• Low muscle tone or shortening of the muscles of the back and the hamstrings. • Flattened head. • Sensitivity to movement: your baby may be distressed when you pick her up or carry her. • Delayed motor milestones (crawling, walking).
Strong smells and tastes	• Difficulty in bonding. • Difficulty with feeding. • Crying when exposed to strong smells.

the **babysense** secret

your baby's sleep

Don't worry if your prem baby sleeps for most of the day; it's good for her. Deep sleep and light sleep (see p.30) are both important for her growth and the development of her brain. Unfortunately your baby's natural sleep cycles and sleep states will be disrupted by the sounds and procedures of the neonatal unit.

helping your baby sleep Sleep is so vital for prem babies that she will probably only have brief awake periods for medical procedures and feeds. Don't worry; your most important role is to watch your baby's signals and help her to sleep as much as possible, especially when she shows signals of over-stimulation (see pp.39–40). Ask the staff if you can do the following:

● Dim the neonatal unit at night so that she learns the difference between day and night.
● Not interrupt her natural sleep rhythms with interventions.
● Allow her to sleep for two to three hours uninterrupted at a time without disturbance.

your sleep Rest and sleep are vital for parents (particularly mum). The temptation to be with your baby at all times is strong, but in the early days you need plenty of sleep to recover physically from the birth, cope with the high levels of stress, and optimize the production of your breast milk. You do not need to be there for every nappy change and feed. Nobody will be judging you.

sleep: what to expect at this stage

● Your premature baby will benefit from sleeping for most of the day.
● Expect your baby to take longer to settle into good sleep habits than a full-term baby. The disruptions of medical procedures, the light and sounds of the neonatal unit, and the need for frequent feeds at night will all prevent her from developing a normal sleep routine.
● Make sure you sleep during the day when your baby sleeps.

kangaroo care

This is very beneficial for your baby and is used extensively in neonatal units worldwide. Place your prem baby on your naked chest wearing only a nappy and possibly a hat. Cover her with a blanket or wear a kangaroo care top. Your chest temperature will rise a degree or two to warm your baby and will maintain a constant temperature for her. "Kangaroo" your prem baby as much as possible as soon as your team gives the go-ahead – usually when she is relatively stable. You can kangaroo your baby when you are both asleep: settle your baby on your chest and find a comfortable position. The benefits of kangaroo care are:

● Better weight gain as your baby uses less energy to maintain a calm state and a constant temperature.
● Encourages earlier breastfeeding.
● Stabilizes heart rate and breathing which helps maintain good O_2 Sats.
● Reduced incidence of hospital-acquired infections.
● Earlier discharge because your baby gains weight more quickly.

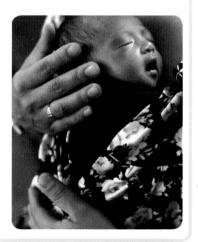

your premature baby

81

sensory developmental care

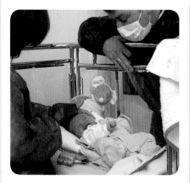

care in the neonatal unit

Since the sensory environment of the neonatal unit is not ideal for your baby's long-term development, "sensory developmental care" has been developed by neonatal nurses and therapists and is used in many neonatal units across the world. Sensory developmental care is a programme that tries to alleviate the stress that your prem baby must endure by being in the neonatal unit, by making it more calming. It is the best care you can provide for your baby and helps to protect her long-term development. When your baby is still medically fragile, her medical needs may take precedence over this care. So do engage with the team, asking them when it is reasonable to start sensory care.

touch

This sense is often the most negatively affected in the neonatal unit. Fortunately, you can use touch in a positive way to counteract the unpleasant experiences of the neonatal unit.

Hold your baby as soon as possible. Do not be put off by all the tubes and drips. Your touch is what she craves. Ask if the medical team can cluster painful medical interventions so that your baby can have as many undisturbed periods of sleep as possible. If any intervention becomes too much for her and she becomes stressed, ask the medical team if they can offer her time out by stopping the intervention while you try giving deep still touch, as follows. Deep still touch helps your baby feel calm, replicating to some extent the containing touch of the womb walls. Warm your hands and place your open palms over your baby's body using gentle but firm pressure. She may take a few seconds to adjust to the touch. Do not move your hands, but do relax your shoulders and keep the pressure deep – your baby finds light touch disconcerting. Within a short time you will feel her relax and her breathing become steady. Use this strategy after painful medical interventions and whenever she needs to become more settled.

Create boundaries for your prem baby to move up against. She finds a boundary around her head particularly soothing since it creates a sense of containment similar to that in the womb – use rolled blankets or special positioning aids to contain her. Let your baby hold your finger or offer a finger roll (a small piece of fabric rolled into a tube) for her to grasp onto if she splays her fingers.

Sucking is important – your baby has more touch receptors in her mouth than anywhere else on her body. She will be soothed by non-nutritive sucking (on a dummy or finger, rather than for food). During stressful or painful procedures, give her a "prem baby dummy" (especially designed for premature babies, see Resources, pp.214–15) to suck on. As well as soothing her, this will help the sucking reflex mature. Swaddle your baby (see p.26) when she is being removed from the incubator and, once she is older than 32 weeks' gestation, swaddle her in the incubator too. She should be swaddled with her legs slightly bent towards her tummy and with her hands together near her face. When she is old enough for a bath, swaddle her for bath time in a large muslin to contain her reflexes and keep her in a flexed position.

sight

Your prem baby's visual system is her least developed sense and needs to be almost entirely protected until she reaches full-term age or is discharged. Ask that the lights of the entire neonatal unit are dimmed and that direct lighting is used over only the incubator when staff are carrying out medical procedures or generally caring for your baby. When the bright lights need to be switched on, cover your prem baby's eyes.

If your baby is in a closed incubator, you can place a towel or blanket on top of the incubator to further dim the space and protect her eyes. Try to use a dark-coloured towel because white reflects light. Ask if the light in the neonatal unit can vary – brighter lighting in the day and dimmer at night to simulate day and night.

sound

This is one of the senses you will have difficulty controlling in the neonatal unit. Make a mental note to listen for any sound that is louder than a gentle voice, then talk to your team about decreasing the levels, for example by turning down the alarms and responding quickly to them. Turn your mobile phone onto vibrate as the jarring sound of a mobile phone call is very unsettling for a baby. Your team will wear soft shoes in the neonatal unit and so should you. Do not place any hard objects on the roof of a closed incubator or tap the lid since the sound is magnified for your prem baby. Close the doors of cabinets and the incubator's portholes very quietly. If your baby's incubator is positioned near an area of high traffic, ask if she can be moved to a quieter space. Also turn off radios or limit usage to soft music; carry instead of dragging chairs; and try to decrease ambient conversation and laughter. You might ask to play a white noise CD gently in the background to mask some of the jarring sounds of the neonatal unit.

movement and gravity

Sensory care for the vestibular and postural system (see pp.12–13) is important for your baby's later motor development. Since the pull of gravity has a big effect on your baby's low muscle tone, you need to place her in a position as close as possible to the contained, curled-up setting of the womb. Positioning systems or nests will help to maintain your baby in a manner that protects her

muscle tone and the length of her muscles and enhances normal motor development. The hospital may provide a special nest, or you can purchase one (see Resources, pp.214–15). If you don't have a specially designed nest, you could roll up a blanket made of 100 percent cotton (for temperature regulation) to create a soft but firm sausage-shaped boundary to position round your baby. Ask the team to show you how.

It's a good idea to place your prem baby on her tummy in the neonatal unit. This helps her to breath, absorb her feeds and aids development; it also makes her feel secure. Since her breathing is monitored, there is no risk of SIDS (sudden infant death syndrome) in this position. When she is on her tummy, place a roll of fabric (you could use a 100 percent cotton blanket) narrower than her shoulders beneath her tummy and chest, that extends from her belly button up to her head. This encourages her shoulders to come forwards and create a flexed shape rather than flattening her chest. Turn her head to the side and tuck her knees up under her tummy.

smell and taste

Your baby's extremely sensitive sense of smell will be affected by the neonatal unit. Ask if the number of invasive procedures involving her mouth, such as changing tubes and suctioning, can be limited and clustered together. Ask that the team don't open swabs, which smell very strong, near your baby's face. Ask if strong-smelling cleaning agents can

be avoided within the incubator. Before feeding your baby or putting in her dummy, try to make sure that your hands do not smell of antiseptic or your baby could react negatively to the feed or dummy.

Kangaroo care or skin-to-skin contact (see p.81) allows your baby to be contained near the soothing smell of mum or dad. If she is having a nasogastric or tube feed (see p.84), try kangarooing her so she comes to associate your smell and touch with the soothing feeling of a full tummy.

Do not wear perfume or aftershave when visiting your baby and wash your clothes with low-fragrance products. Place a comfort object, such as a blanket or teddy that you have slept with and which smells of you in the incubator with your baby – this may soothe her and help her to sleep. Express some breast milk onto a cotton wool ball and place this inside the incubator. You could also put a drop of expressed breast milk on your baby's tongue to simulate the normal taste experience of the womb.

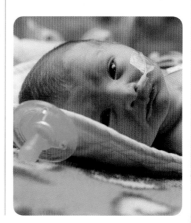

feeding: what to expect at this stage

- Sick or very young premature babies will be fed non-orally, through tubes or even drips in the early days.
- The sucking reflex needs to be established and encouraged by non-nutritive sucking (see right).
- A baby born before 28 weeks can suckle on your empty breast (once you have expressed) so that she develops the coordination of sucking without having to cope with swallowing milk and breathing too.
- From 28 weeks' gestation, a healthy prem baby starts to be able to coordinate sucking, swallowing, and breathing. But many babies only develop the level of coordination needed to feed after 32 weeks.
- Once your baby can coordinate sucking, swallowing, and breathing and can maintain an awake state, she will be ready to start having proper milk feeds, either through breastfeeding or bottle feeding.

feeding your prem baby

Feeding your prem baby may be something you only establish closer to her discharge from the neonatal unit. However, the first steps to feeding your baby effectively starts in the early days.

non-oral feeds If your baby is very small or medically fragile, you may find that a nil by mouth (NPO) instruction is given by the doctors and so she needs to be fed in other ways.

- **By drip** A liquid including water, electrolytes and other nutrients is given to your baby to keep her hydrated. This is may be the only method of feeding for very sick babies or those with severe respiratory problems.
- **Tube feeding** A nasogastric (NG) tube, inserted into your baby's nostril, which passes directly into her stomach, delivers small amounts of expressed breast milk or formula milk. These feeds are started as soon as possible after your baby is born. The amount and frequency of your baby's feeds will be carefully monitored by her team.

non-nutritive sucking Sucking is a reflex that develops by 24 weeks' gestation. Your baby will practise it daily *in utero*, sucking the amniotic fluid that surrounds her and even her thumb or hands. Once your baby is born, this sucking instinct develops into the skill of sucking, swallowing and breathing, which makes feeding possible. In order to be discharged, your prem baby will need to have this skill perfected.

To assist your baby in developing this skill from early on, offer her a prem baby dummy (see Resources, pp.214–15), an empty (expressed) breast or her thumb or your clean finger to suck on. Let her suck in this way for about five minutes before and after a feed, when she is stressed and for at least 10 minutes a day when she is in the drowsy or awake states (see p.31). Suckling on an empty breast after the milk has been expressed is great for a slightly older prem baby: it gives her the experience of sucking and coordinating breathing without the added complexity of trying to cope with swallowing milk at the same time.

cup feeds If your baby is not ready to start breastfeeding, try offering expressed breast milk in a cup (or use the sterilized cap of a bottle). Place the cup near her lips so that she learns to lap the milk, much like a kitten. Do not pour the liquid into her mouth. This method of feeding prior to your baby being ready to breastfeed encourages bonding because you are close to her. It also stimulates her mouth without the complexity associated with feeding from a bottle. You can continue with this method, (rather than bottle feeding) later if breastfeeding is difficult – it is more hygienic than using bottles and teats because cups are easier to clean.

expressing Express your first breast milk as soon as possible after the birth of your baby (preferably within four hours). At first you produce colostrum, a high-protein, antibody-filled pre-milk, which is replaced by breast milk a few days later (see p.98). Your milk will be given to your baby via the NG tube until she is ready to breastfeed. Breast milk is essential for your prem baby's gut and is the best you can do to minimize infection and damage to her intestines. Begin by manually expressing the breast milk by massaging your breast. A breastfeeding counsellor will help you get the technique right. From day two or three (once your milk comes in) you can begin to use a manual or electric breast pump to express milk. If you can tolerate it, dual expressing (both breasts at the same time) using an electric pump is most effective. Keep these tips in mind:

- Initially you will get very little milk by expressing.
- Express for five to ten minutes every three to four hours.
- Continue to express until the flow of breast milk slows right down.
- Do not express for more than 30 minutes at a time.
- Do not wake up especially to express – you need your rest.
- Try to express with a picture of your baby in front of you or where you can see her as this will help with the release of "let-down" hormones – the hormones that stimulate breast milk production.
- After a week or so of expressing, you will find that you can express much more milk at each sitting.

Once you are expressing successfully you will be able to maintain your breast milk supply until your baby is ready to breastfeed. Many mums successfully breastfeed, even when their premature baby has been unable to do so for many weeks. Breast milk can be kept in the fridge for 24 hours or stored in the freezer for up to three months (see pp.158–59).

breastfeeding When your baby is ready to try an oral feed, your team will help you to start breastfeeding or bottle feeding her. The first day, you will probably only give her one feed, gradually introducing more until your baby is off tube feeds and completely onto oral feeds. There is no reason why you can't nurse your baby successfully.

bottle feeding If you find you cannot breastfeed your baby and end up bottle feeding, do not feel guilty. However, it is important to point out a misconception about bottle feeding for premature babies. Contrary to popular belief, bottle feeding is not necessarily easier for your premature baby since the coordination of sucking, swallowing, and breathing is more complicated and the flow of milk harder to regulate, making bottle feeding more tiring for your baby than breastfeeding. In addition you need to mix the feeds carefully and sterilize the bottles extra carefully. The team will help you learn this process.

the sensory experience of feeding

Feeding your baby is a sensory-laden experience. It stimulates every sense: smell, sight, taste, body position, and interoception (internal sensory messages). Your prem baby can only cope with a limited amount of stimulation – input through more than one sense at a time can easily over-stimulate her. Once over-stimulated, she will become stressed and disorganized and her heartbeat, breathing rate, and even oxygen saturation levels may be compromised. In the early days of oral feeds, try not to overload more sensory systems than necessary by following these tips:

- Choose a quiet place to feed and do not talk to your baby or other people while feeding.
- Do not move your baby around or change her position too much.
- Do not wear any perfume and use a fragrance-free detergent.
- If your baby becomes stressed during a feed, stop, help her to settle and try again another day.

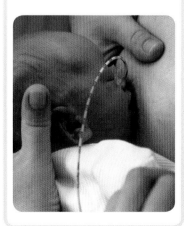

getting to know your baby

Your prem baby may seem nothing like the babies in the mother-and-baby adverts, but developmentally each day she is growing and becoming more like a newborn. A baby who has had a full nine months *in utero* has had all the benefit of a tight womb and being curled up in a very close space for the last two months, which helps to develop lots of primitive reflexes. Your prem baby has not had these benefits so her reflexes may not yet be fully developed.

muscle tone In the last two months in the womb a baby gets to push against resistance which builds muscle tone. Your prem baby has not had the opportunity to work out in a tight space so her muscle tone is very low. This means that when laid flat on her back, her legs and arms fall out to the side. Even her diaphragm, which would normally have built up strength *in utero* by swallowing amniotic fluid, is weak. So her cry is weak and she may not cry aloud at all. She will gradually build up muscle tone as she grows. You can help by putting her in a nest (see p.83) to position her in the right way and to give her a boundary to push against.

primitive reflexes These are our survival reflexes. The baby monkey swinging through the trees on her mum's back needs to be able to hold very tight with her hands (the grasp reflex); find her mum's nipple on the move (the rooting reflex helps her head to turn towards the nipple); suck from her mum's nipple to feed (the sucking reflex) and hold firmer if she feels as if she's dropping (the moro or startle reflex). Even though these reflexes are not all essential to our survival as humans, at birth the full-term baby has all these reflexes, as well as the fencing or ATNR reflex (see p.101).

If your baby is born very premature, she may not have these primitive reflexes initially. As she gets older they will emerge. The important reflexes that will develop between birth and discharge from hospital are the rooting and sucking reflexes which are vital to breast- or bottle feeding. The grasp reflex will help her to feel calm as she holds onto you when faced with situations that cause stress.

target milestones

By the time your baby leaves hospital, she will probably have arrived at the developmental level of a full-term baby: a curled-up bundle with various primitive reflexes, able to regulate her body temperature and breathing, but not much else. Over the course of the first year, work through the book using the target milestones in each section for each particular age. However, as a parent of a premature baby you have to

social interaction

There are three phases of social interaction for a prem baby:

pause phase If your baby was born very premature – prior to 32 weeks – her interactions will be characterized by the word PAUSE: she will pause rather than engage and you should pause before interacting with her. She may not spend any time in the calm-alert state at all. Even the simplest sensory interaction of light touch can cause her to become stressed. She is focusing all her energy on just maintaining stable vital signs (breathing, heart rate and blood pressure) and growing.

touch phase As your baby grows older (between 32 and 35 weeks) she will start to emerge from the pause phase into the TOUCH phase. This stage is characterized by stable vital signs and she will start to gain weight and may even learn a few self-soothing strategies. She is no longer acutely ill and begins to gain weight as she absorbs calories from her feeds. She will occasionally be able to maintain the calm-alert state for longer periods. You will be able to touch her and interact with her.

engage phase From 36 weeks onwards your baby begins to ENGAGE – to interact actively with her environment and invites you to engage with her. She will be less dependent on the machines and will not require constant monitoring. She can actively soothe herself and regulate her body systems.

adjust your expectations of her target milestones by correcting your baby's age to take into consideration her prematurity. This applies to everything, from sleep to feeding and walking to talking, and you'll need to do it until she is about two years old. If your baby was born a month early, for instance, you must expect her to behave like a newborn when she would have been born and to smile when she would have been six weeks old, had she been born on her due date.

To calculate your premature baby's age, use this equation: chronological age – weeks premature = adjusted/developmental age. For example, a six-month-old baby who was born four weeks (one month) prematurely should be as developed as the typical five-month-old: 6 – 1 = 5 months adjusted age.

talk to your doctor If your prem baby was born very early, went through many periods of medical instability, or was at risk of damage to her brain, eyes, or hearing, monitor her very carefully for about two years. If she is consistently not achieving her target milestones in each area of development (see table below) to her adjusted age, of course, bring it to the attention of your paediatrician.

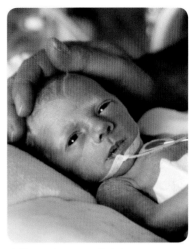

delicate Premature babies are even more sensitive to sensory stimuli and can become over-stimulated more quickly than babies born at full term.

target milestones

Between your premature baby's actual birthday and the day she was expected to be born, you can look for milestones that we would expect to see in a full-term baby.

area of development	target milestones
Gross motor	Bringing her legs up and tucking them near her body as her muscle tone builds up.
Fine motor	Developing a grasp reflex and a sucking reflex.
Hand–eye coordination	Focusing on your face with interest at a distance of 20–25cm (8–10in).
Language	Remaining calm and alert when you talk to her.
Social/emotional	Maintaining eye contact without becoming over-stimulated for short periods.
Regulation	Maintaining the calm-alert state and beginning to soothe herself.

sensible stimulation: TEAT

The purpose of stimulation is to increase the connections between brain cells with the aim of enhancing your baby's learning and development. Connections are best formed when your baby is in the calm-alert state. Since premature babies do not spend much time in the calm-alert state, it stands to reason that you can spend very little time stimulating your baby while she is in the neonatal unit. Instead, spend most of the early days getting to know your baby, reading her signals and sensory state (see p.33), and only start to stimulate her when she is ready, after 32 weeks.

engaging Once she is older than 36 weeks' gestation, your baby will be better able to tolerate social interaction.

timing

On average, no baby under 32 weeks' gestation is ready for stimulation. Between 32 and 35 weeks, if your baby is medically stable, you can begin to interact with her. However, be sure to respect any signs of stress and schedule interactions at appropriate times. Follow the three phases (see p.86) to know when to start stimulating her:
pause phase When she is in the pause phase (under 32 weeks or medically unstable), the most you can do is to sit with your baby, talk quietly and get to know her signals.

As she becomes more stable, you can place your hands on her in a containing way – keep them still.
touch phase Between 32 and 36 weeks, start to bathe your baby and change her nappy so that you gain confidence in handling her. Swaddle (see p.26) and kangaroo (see p.81) her. You can begin with some of the activities but always watch her signals carefully for signs of distress.
engage phase From 36 weeks until she is discharged, stimulate your baby in the short periods when she is in the calm-alert state.

environment

The physical environment of the neonatal unit is very busy in terms of sensory input. Your baby is constantly bombarded by noise, visual input, and novel smells. It may be possible to reduce the level of sound and the amount of light, provide day- and night-time rhythms for light, and reduce the number of times your baby is disturbed (see pp.82–83). You should not attempt to create a stimulating environment

until your baby is home. Just being alive and in our world provides enough environmental stimulation.
visual Try not to overwhelm your baby with lots of visitors, a stimulating nursery, or too many activities once she is home.
movement Use slow rocking and repetitive or rhythmical movements to calm your baby when she is ready to be held. You may like to wear her in a sling to help her to feel secure.

activities

When your baby is medically stable and in a calm-alert state showing signs of being ready to interact, you can begin to carry out some limited stimulation. However, do watch your baby very closely for signs that she is becoming stressed. If she shows signs of stress, becomes less stable (blood pressure rises or falls) or her oxygen saturation levels change, give her a period of time-out and help her to calm herself by sucking or snuggling into a boundary (see p.83). Try again later or the next day.

visual Hold your baby 20–25cm (8–10in) from your face, which is the distance at which a full-term baby can focus. Help her to focus by not stimulating any other sense.

hearing Talk to your baby in "parentese", a soft, slightly high-pitched voice that comes naturally to parents – it's been shown that babies respond to this type of voice with more interest. Read her a poem or a story. Call your baby by her name before you touch her. Play recordings of your voice, heartbeat or white noise to soothe your baby and gently stimulate her hearing.

touch Engage in kangaroo care (see p.81) whenever you are with your baby as soon as possible. Talk to the medical team about when you can start this. Swaddle your baby when you are interacting with her to keep her calm and contained. This is important because the startle reflex causes her arms to fly out, which is very disconcerting for her. Prepare your baby for being touched by speaking to her first. Provide your baby with the opportunity to hold onto your fingers and to suck on them (non-nutritive sucking). Hold your baby's body and head in your hands or support her feet in your hands. Handle your baby firmly but gently. Provide still touch – this is often all she can manage when awake. Begin to massage your baby after 32 weeks if she is stable using firm but gentle strokes (see p.105 for baby massage techniques).

sense-able secret
Stimulate one sense at a time and when your baby looks away or shows any sign of over-stimulation, stop and give her a breather by removing the stimulus.

toys

In the neonatal unit your baby will not have much need for toys. You are her favourite toy!

visual Favour toys in contrasting colours, either black and white or red and white. They will be fun to focus on when your baby is ready. Cut out a picture of your face from a photo and show it to your baby when she is calm.

hearing A soft toy with a white noise or lullaby microchip or recording is a lovely first toy for your baby. Place it in the incubator and play the sounds that will soothe her as well as masking some of the sounds of the neonatal unit.

movement Invest in a fabric sling. By keeping your prem baby close to your body, she will be comforted by your warmth and your heartbeat.

smell Place a teddy or soft toy that smells of you in the corner of the incubator.

chapter 8

your newborn baby

After months of planning the perfect birth and dreaming about just who your baby will be, the big day arrives and you are faced with the reality of becoming a parent. The adjustment in the first two weeks of life is enormous not only for you and your baby, but also for your partner and wider family. You probably feel overwhelmed and anxious at times, wondering how you are ever going to manage to meet the needs of this little life. Coping with the physical after-effects of childbirth, producing adequate breast milk, as well as learning to get by with much less sleep than before, all take their toll on your normal functioning. However, the advice in the following pages will help to smooth this transition, so you can really enjoy spending time with your new baby.

baby-centric routine

- It's best to settle your baby back to sleep once he has been awake for 40 to 60 minutes.
- He will probably be sleeping for a large part of his day, 18 to 20 hours in a 24-hour cycle.
- Allow your baby to feed on demand. Some babies only demand to be fed every three to four hours and are content between meals.
- At night, your baby may go for four to five hours between feeds. Do not wake him at night unless advised to do so for health reasons.

a day in the life of your baby

There is a good chance that no day seems typical to you anymore and that each one brings a whole new set of challenges and questions. The reality is that in the first two weeks you will need to put your life on hold to follow your baby's lead to a large degree. Now is not the time to start guiding your baby into a routine, so stay flexible and follow his lead.

mum sense: a transition

Your birth experience has an enormous effect on how you feel in the days immediately afterwards. If you had the positive birth you planned, you are likely to experience feelings of elation. During childbirth you are flooded with endorphins, "feel-good hormones" that give you a wonderful high for the first few days. These chemicals create a protective shield around you and your baby, giving bonding a good start. Your senses are heightened and you will be in awe of the perfection of your tiny baby; parenthood will seem like an exciting time. If your birth was traumatic and nothing went as you planned or you ended up separated from your baby after birth, however, you may feel inadequate and a sense of loss.

anxiety No one warns you about the very common moments of terror that accompany early parenthood. The thought will enter your head: "They must be crazy to allow me to take this baby home, I have no idea how to look after such a tiny thing." You are in good company. Most mums have these thoughts and our babies survive and thrive in spite

the babysense secret

nurturing Spend time with your new baby, just resting quietly together. This speeds your recovery and will help you bond, making your baby feel secure and content in her first days of life.

of these feelings. This anxiety is normal and it can help to call in your support network – your own mother, your partner, or your best friend: whoever makes you feel better about your mothering skills and supports you. Day by day, you will learn all you need to know to care for your baby. In time you will look back with amusement or astonishment when you recall your fear of even undressing or bathing your new baby.

baby blues From about day three onwards, the hormones that kick in to promote the production of breast milk can trigger a confusing period of lows as well as highs. There will be days when you may feel quite overwhelmed and tearful about the sheer responsibility of caring for this brand-new life. Baby blues can continue for a week or so, but are always short lived and will not have an impact on your relationship with your baby. Try to recognize their effect and talk about your feelings to your partner or a supportive friend. If they continue for more than two weeks, you may be experiencing postnatal depression (see p.59).

germs and bugs You may find yourself concerned about exposing your baby to germs, and wonder if you are being over-protective. Your baby is protected by the antibodies you gave him while he was *in utero*. Colostrum and early breast milk are also full of antibodies that will protect him from illness. However, if he does get ill with a stuffy nose or a fever, your baby will not feed well. This will affect not only his weight gain, but also your milk supply. So it's sensible not to expose him to public places and large groups of people in the early days. If you have to fly on an aircraft or socialize in large public settings while your baby is very young, wear him in a sling that shields him from being handled by lots of people.

sense-able secret

If your baby is ill or in distress or if you had a traumatic birth, you may end up being separated. Do not let this negative experience be your focus – be proactive. Tell the team that you would like to "kangaroo" your baby (see p.81). Even if a few days have passed, take the time to undress him and place him skin to skin on your chest. This process will be healing for you both.

Q&A adjusting to the pace of your new baby

I was a successful account manager prior to becoming a mother. I was so excited to be pregnant and thought I was going to relish motherhood. I do love being a mum, but as each day goes by I am conscious of how much time I am wasting and how little I get done. When can I expect my baby to fit into my lifestyle?

If you have entered motherhood from a busy career or hectic schedule it's common once the dust has settled, a few weeks after your baby's birth, to feel frustrated and as if you get nothing constructive done in a day. It is tempting to try to get back to your former frenetic routines. It's important in the early days to realize that your new baby is a natural slow-you-downer. Breastfeeding, for example, is a labour of love; you need to sit and do almost nothing for 20 to 40 minutes. Try to view this time as a space in which to get lost in a book, watch some TV or just drink in your baby's beautiful features as he feeds. This slow-down time your baby is forcing on you is exactly what you need – time for your body to heal after the birth, time to connect with your child and time to ponder this important new relationship.

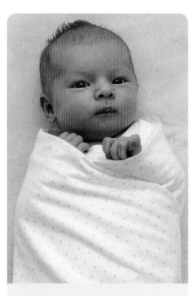

sense-able secret

Swaddling is one of the best methods you can use to keep your baby calm by imitating the snug womb world she has just emerged from. Make sure that you swaddle your baby's hands by her face so she can soothe herself.

baby sense: entering the fourth trimester

Marsupial babies (such as kangaroos) are born too immature to survive in the outside world and are cared for in their mother's pouch after birth. Your tiny human baby does not climb inside a pouch after birth, but is less mature and more vulnerable than most other mammal babies at this point – whales are swimming or foals are walking within hours of birth. Your newborn is dependent on you not only for nutrition and basic care, but also for help in controlling his temperature, his sleep/wake cycles, and even his mood. Your baby's ability to soothe himself, regulate his mood when absorbing information through his senses, and to attend happily to stimulation without becoming overwhelmed develops during the first three months after birth, during the period we call the "fourth trimester".

Although it's the last thing any woman wants to hear after 38 weeks of pregnancy, most babies would really benefit from an extra three months *in utero*. A fourth trimester of pregnancy would allow your baby to be born more mature, able to cope with interactions and stimulation, and to soothe himself. Because of the size of our pelvises and the fact that we walk upright, we are unable to birth babies any bigger than we do. Since a fourth trimester is out of the question, our human babies are born requiring intense nurturing. To provide a fourth trimester of sensory womb-like nurturing, think back to your newborn's experience *in utero* (see pp.20–22) and try to replicate its effects for him.

● **Touch** Swaddle your baby (p.26). Swaddling mimics the womb world since your baby's immature movements press against a boundary, much like the elastic walls of the uterus. Babies find the pressure and neutral warmth of a tightly wrapped cotton swaddling blanket calming.

● **Movement** Carry your baby. Movement is lulling and soothing and most newborns crave being close to mum or dad. You are not spoiling your baby by carrying him; in fact, close contact is good for bonding and will help him to feel secure later on. Use a sling to create a surrogate womb with its deep pressure along with the movement of your body.

● **Sight** Limit visual stimulation in the first two weeks. While it is vital to stimulate your baby's visual skills, this type of input is very potent and can easily over-stimulate him. Time visual activities, such as looking at a mobile or bright toy, carefully. When your baby looks away from you or an activity, respect the time out he requires and remove the stimulus.

● **Sound** Background white noise, such as the dishwasher and TV static (see p.26) settles newborns. In the womb he heard the white noise of your heartbeat and the gushing sound of your blood and digestion. Play womb sounds to your baby (available on CD or as a download).

helping your baby sleep

Have you ever been quite this exhausted? In the first few days, your hormones will carry you through the fatigue and night feeds, but after a week or so, the realization that you are not about to have a full night's sleep any time soon sets in and you may well have feelings of dread each evening as you anticipate the night ahead.

Sleep in the early days is all about adjusting to your baby and meeting his needs. Do not be concerned if your baby wakes and feeds frequently at night. He has to do this to survive. Likewise, do not worry about bad habits developing – in these early days you need to meet your baby's nutritional and sensory need for cuddles rather than worry about the future. When your baby is a bit older (over six weeks) you can start to think about establishing healthy sleep habits, but for now, just go with the flow and follow your baby's lead.

awake time

At this young age, your baby can only really cope with being awake for 40 to 60 minutes before needing to sleep again. This is literally long enough for a feed, a nappy change and a cuddle, and then back to sleep.

Your baby will probably be sleeping for an enormous amount each day. Over the past three months, the tight uterine space and the narrow birth canal have exerted a great deal of deep pressure on your baby's body. This pressure is regulating for the nervous system and may be one of the reasons why newborns sleep so much in the early days. These long periods of sleep are important for survival, ensuring that your baby focuses his energy on growing rather than interacting.

your baby's sleep space

Before your baby's birth you may have decided where you wanted him to sleep – in bed with you, in your room in a cot, or in his own room. Once he is born your preconceived ideas may be thrown aside as you start to make choices that work for you and your infant. Where your baby sleeps is a very personal choice and yet you will find yourselves overwhelmed with advice from health visitors, family, and friends – and this may lead to feelings of guilt. Like every other parenting choice from now, it's up to you to weigh up the pros and cons and make your own decision.

sleep: what to expect at this stage

● In the early days your newborn may have day and night muddled up, feeding more frequently at night and even being more wakeful when the rest of the world is asleep.
● Do not expect your newborn to sleep through the night; accept that he will wake intermittently at night to feed.
● Make sure you sleep during the day when your baby sleeps so you do not become too exhausted.
● During the day, your baby needs to be settled to sleep after 40 to 60 minutes of awake time (see p.51) to avoid becoming over-stimulated and fussy.

"The early days of sleep are all about you adjusting to your baby and meeting his needs. Do not be concerned if your baby wakes frequently to feed at night."

co-sleeping safely

If you choose to co-sleep, follow these guidelines to limit the risk of SIDS for your baby:
● Your baby must sleep on his back.
● Do not use pillows or cover your baby with your duvet.
● Push your bed against the wall and put your baby on the outside of the bed next to you, not between you and your partner.
● You may prefer to use a co-sleeper cot that attaches to the side of your bed (see image).

do not co-sleep if:

● Your baby is exposed to cigarette smoke during the day, or was during pregnancy.
● You or your partner have been drinking alcohol or take drugs or medication that make you drowsy.
● Your baby was born before 37 weeks or weighed less than 2.5kg (5½lb) at birth.
● You are extremely exhausted or have a sleep disorder, for example sleep apnoea.
● You had a Caesarean and are taking painkillers.

co-sleeping Both experts and parents have clear views on the dangers and the benefits of sharing a bed with your baby. There are few things in life as special as cuddling down to sleep with your newborn, breathing in his new baby smell and listening to his snuffles and wispy breaths. For many parents, the idea of co-sleeping is not only romantic, but very practical too. The evidence that supports co-sleeping in the early days suggests it helps your baby feel secure and regulates his breathing and body temperature. For mothers it is also convenient, allowing you to respond with relative ease to night-time feeds. You are likely to continue breastfeeding your baby for longer if you co-sleep.

In the UK, the Department of Health and the FSID (Foundation for the Study of Infant Deaths) and the US-based American Association of Pediatrics have highlighted some risks, such as sudden infant death syndrome (SIDS), and smothering, associated with co-sleeping. They state that the safest place for your baby to sleep is in a cot in your room for the first six months. If you would prefer to co-sleep, but are concerned about safety, you can follow simple guidelines for safe co-sleeping (see box, left).

sleeping separately If you worry about your baby's safety while sleeping in your bed, you might prefer the very safe option recommended by many experts for the early weeks – placing your baby in a co-sleeper cot (a special cot that attaches to the side of your bed, with the mattress at the same height; see Resources, pp.214–15). Otherwise, you can put him in his own cot or Moses basket next to your bed. Wherever he sleeps, he must sleep on his back and be placed "feet to foot" (his feet must touch the foot of the cot) to help prevent SIDS. Safety may have nothing to do with your choice not to co-sleep. If you or your partner is a sensory-sensitive person, the movements and noises of a little body in your bed may prevent you from having a good night's sleep. On the other hand, if your baby is a sensitive baby (see p.15), he may be disrupted by the sensory experience of sleeping next to you and wake more frequently.

Sleep is an essential but rare commodity in the early days and you need to make the choices that allow you to get as much sleep as possible. Choosing to have your baby in his own sleeping environment from day one is a perfectly good choice and most babies settle just as well in their own room as in their parents' bed. You will hear your baby when he needs you since you are sensitized to his sounds and cries after birth. If you are concerned, put a baby monitor in his room so you can respond quickly to him at night. The bottom line when it comes to your baby's sleep space is that all of these options are sensible. In the early days, choose your baby's sleep space according to your own preferences and what gives you the best night's sleep, since you need rest to help you produce adequate breast milk, and to bond with and nurture your baby.

day/night reversal

You should expect your baby to sleep for most of the time during these weeks (approximately 18 to 20 hours out of 24), but if he is waking often at night and sleeping all day, you will need to help him learn the difference between day and night. Day/night reversal is common in newborn babies and usually takes a week or two to resolve. You can help your baby adjust his internal clock to sleeping more at night. Try these strategies:

● During the day, wake your baby after three-and-a-half hours so that he feeds at least four hourly during daylight hours.

● At night, allow your baby to wake himself when he is ready for a feed, provided he is gaining weight and was not premature. It's best not to wake him before midnight to avoid an early morning feed – this prevents him from developing natural sleep/wake cycles at night.

● Help your baby to differentiate day from night by keeping his sleep space dark between 6pm and 6am. Use a muted night light for night feeds and have black-out lining on the curtains (see Resources, pp.214–15).

● During the day, play with your baby, interact and make lots of eye contact and conversation.

● At night, keep interactions subdued. Do not make too much eye contact and do not talk to him so that your baby settles easily back to sleep.

● Do not worry too much about getting him to burp. If he has fed and is drowsy, only burp him for five minutes and then put him down to sleep regardless of whether he burps or not.

● If your baby wakes an hour or so after the last night feed, don't feed him. Re-swaddle him, pat him gently, and let him suck on your finger or a dummy to get him back to sleep.

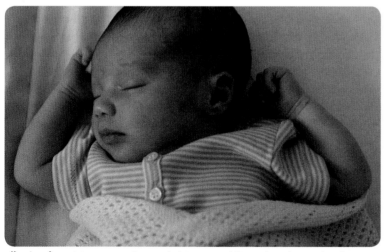

all mixed up It is common for new babies to muddle up their days and nights so that they sleep more during the day and are awake more at night.

Q&A
catnapping

My baby never sleeps for longer than 15 minutes at a stretch. What am I supposed to do?

If you find that your baby is waking as soon as you put him down in his cot or only sleeps for very short stretches (less than 20 minutes), he is what we call a "catnapper". This is a common problem in the early days. Catnapping is caused by a tiny jerk in your baby's body. Initially your baby is in the light-sleep state. Watch how his eyes move under his eyelids as he processes all the sensory information he received during the day. As your baby falls deeper into sleep, he experiences a sudden jerk of his muscles, called a hypnagogic startle. We experience this as adults but generally sleep through the minor disturbance. Your baby is being woken by this startle as he falls into the deeper sleep state.

To limit the effect of this startle and to encourage your baby to sleep for longer, try these tips:

● Swaddle your baby to contain the little jerk so that it does not disrupt his sleep.

● Play white noise in your baby's sleep space; this has been shown to lower babies' states (see p.30) and keep them asleep for longer.

● If your baby consistently wakes after 15 minutes, sit with him, keeping your hand on him after settling him in his cot. When the little jerk disrupts his sleep, maintain the pressure of your hand to help him settle into deep sleep.

feeding: what to expect at this stage

- Breastfeeding takes time to establish and this happens most effectively when babies are fed on demand. It is worth seeking help from a breastfeeding counsellor if you are having difficulties (see Resources, pp.214–15).
- It can take up to six weeks to establish feeding and an adequate milk supply.
- To build a good supply of milk, eat well and rest as much as you can. Establishing your milk supply is more important than doing household chores.
- It's normal for babies to feed almost as frequently at night as during the day in the early days. Feed your baby when he is hungry and don't worry about a routine yet.
- Your baby may demand one or two "cluster feeds" (feeds close together) in the early part of the evening. Encourage one or, at most, two extra feeds in the early evening if this helps him to sleep for a slightly longer stretch later.

feeding your baby

More than any other new skill, feeding can be the toughest challenge in the first few weeks. In years gone by, when we learnt how to mother in a close-knit community, we would have watched a sister or aunt breastfeed and started the learning curve of breastfeeding earlier in life. Sadly for many of us, the first time we see a baby latch on is with our own firstborn in the stressful environment of the delivery room. You may want to buy a book that focuses on breastfeeding to guide you through the early days.

milk supply

Demand feeding is essential in the first days to help establish a good milk supply. Some babies don't feed much in the first 48 hours because reserves from their time in the womb and from the colostrum (the milk that comes before your regular milk supply) are meeting their nutritional needs. Colostrum is a magic milk because it is saturated in nutrients and antibodies critical for your baby's immunity. It is also a mild laxative and helps your baby to pass his first stools of meconium (a dark sticky poo). After the second day your baby will probably begin demanding frequent short feeds, by crying and rooting (turning his face towards you with an open mouth). This is nature's way of telling your body to start producing mature milk and how much of it to produce. Feed whenever he demands to ensure that your body produces adequate milk. You are producing enough if your baby has at least six wet nappies a day, is generally feeding every two to four hours, and is content and sleepy between feeds.

demand versus routine feeds

Do not be tempted to start focusing on routine: demand breastfeeding is very important in the early days for establishing a good milk supply. Breast milk is digested more quickly than formula milk and so breastfed babies usually need feeding more frequently. If you are breastfeeding and your baby is thriving, you can aim to feed two- to three-hourly. Once your milk supply improves and your baby's suck becomes stronger, the periods between feeds may become longer (three- to four-hourly). Bottle-fed babies can be encouraged into a feeding routine earlier than breastfed babies. At this age a formula-fed baby can be fed three-hourly.

the sensory experience of feeding

Feeding is a sensory-laden experience, no matter how old your baby is or how he is fed. Use your knowledge of the soothing womb world (see pp.23–27) to create a sensory space for your baby while feeding:
- At feed time, unwrap your baby, and allow his hands to be free to touch your chest, neck, or face.

breastfeeding tips

Even though breast milk is your baby's natural milk, breastfeeding does not always come naturally. The rewards eventually make up for the hassle.

try these practical tips:

- In the early days breastfeeding is learning a new skill. This is best done in a quiet, calm environment.
- Take an extra minute or two to get organized before starting. Have a glass of water or juice handy. Feeding makes you thirsty, so try to drink at least 250ml (9fl oz) of fluid for each feed. Put the phone on answer-mode, or keep it next to you.
- Choose a comfortable chair with adequate back support and, if possible, a small stool to raise your feet off the ground.
- Try to relax before you begin. Relaxation is important for the "let-down" hormones, which allow your milk to flow. Your baby will pick up on your calmness and feed well too. If you are feeling tense, use a Bach Flower Remedy, such as Rescue.
- Just before feeds, extend your nipple slightly by rolling it between your thumb and index finger. Not only does this create a nice nipple shape for feeding, it also expresses a little colostrum or breast milk, which will encourage your newborn to suck.
- Bring your baby towards you with his entire body facing towards you. His mouth/cheek should make contact with your nipple. As his lower lip touches your nipple, he will open his mouth. At that point bring him in firmly against your breast.
- Correct latching on to the breast is vital to avoid pain for you and to

latching on Your baby's lower lip should cover most of the areola (*left*). **madonna** This is when your baby feeds lying across your tummy (*above*).

encourage milk production. Make sure your baby's lower lip covers almost all of the areola (dark area around the nipple) below your nipple. His top lip should be flipped out to take in some of the areola above the nipple. If not, use your finger to "flip" his top lip out.
- Watch out for incorrect latching on: if your baby only has your nipple in his mouth, the milk ducts in your breasts will be shut off, resulting in decreased milk flow. This will cause your nipples to become cracked and bruised – very painful for you.
- Examine the latching on. If it is correct, your baby will feed well – his lips and jaw will compress the milk reservoirs beneath the areola, ensuring a good flow, while at the same time elongating your nipple to pull more milk out.
- Once your milk comes in (around day three) you may have full, painful breasts. Let your baby suck for a while on each breast. Listen to the gulping as he drinks the watery foremilk that quenches his thirst. As he sucks a

little longer, the creamier hindmilk will be released. Your baby needs both the foremilk and hindmilk.
- Let your baby feed on demand: breastfeeding works on a supply-and-demand basis. The more your baby feeds, the more milk your breasts will produce.
- Try lots of feeding positions until you find the most comfortable one for you. Try the "Madonna" style, with your baby lying across your tummy, or the "rugby-ball" style where you hold his body tucked safely under your arm.
- If your baby does not come off the breast on his own, insert a clean finger into the corner of his mouth to break the suction and gently withdraw your nipple.
- If your milk flows very rapidly, your baby may gulp and choke. This may be exacerbated when you feed sitting in an upright position and can result in excessive intake of air, which may cause wind and gas. Try lying down and allow him to feed while lying next to you.

reclining If your flow of milk is too fast for your baby, resulting in gulping or choking, try lying down for feeds. You may find that she feeds better like this.

● Do not wear perfume for the first six weeks of your baby's life. Your baby is in very close proximity to you at a time when smell is important – while eating. Your own body smell is the most neutral and best for him.

● Keep your voice even, so that it is a soothing sound. Try to relax when feeding since anxiety can make your voice seem strained and high-pitched.

● Watch how your baby reacts to the taste of your milk. Some babies react negatively to certain strong flavours such as garlic or spices.

● Learn to read his signals while he is feeding. For example, if he makes eye contact, reciprocate, but follow suit if he looks away. This will allow him "sensory space" to focus on the task at hand.

● Some babies have difficulty coordinating sucking, swallowing, and breathing in the presence of other stimulation. If your baby is a sensitive baby (see p.15), limit any extra sensory input you give him while he's feeding. If you choose to talk to him, do so quietly and calmly. Limit too much poking and prodding; keep your touch a still, deep hug. Try swaddling him for feeds, as this may help babies who are difficult feeders.

getting to know your baby

Have you noticed how your newborn is all curled up in a little ball, much like he was in the womb? In the early weeks your baby's legs tuck up towards his stomach, in a position we call "physiological flexion". Because this flexion is so stable, it helps your baby to feel organized. When his arms are extended and he is not curled up, he may begin to fuss and his little arms may wave around as if he is attempting to grasp at something. Your baby's first motor (movement) task is to strengthen his back muscles to extend or stretch him out. His neck muscles are very weak and it is important that they strengthen to hold up his head.

primitive reflexes In the early weeks, primitive reflexes govern your baby's movements and he makes very few voluntary movements. The grasp reflex keeps his hands clasped most of the time. The moro, or startle, reflex is elicited in response to his head falling back – he clasps his hands and his arms fly out. It is a redundant reflex, important for survival if he were falling. The rooting reflex is stimulated when you touch your baby's cheek next to his mouth. This causes him to turn his head towards your hand and open his mouth, which is important for feeding. Likewise the sucking reflex is vital for feeding. When his head turns to one side, the fencing or asymmetrical tonic neck reflex (ATNR) reflex results: his arm and leg stretch out on the side his face turns towards (see opposite). This reflex is vital for hand–eye coordination as it allows your baby to see his hand.

target milestones

This stage is a period of uncurling from the womb, physically and socially, and your baby's movements and most of his interactions are affected by his reflexes. These will gradually drop away over the first three months. By two weeks old you can expect him to achieve these milestones:

area of development	target milestones
Gross motor	Holding his head up for a few seconds when held at your shoulder.
Fine motor	Fists closed for a good deal of the time.
Hand–eye coordination	Focusing well to a distance of 20–25cm (8–10in) when his head is supported. Practising focusing at further distances and tracking objects with his eyes.
Language	Beginning to mimic your facial expressions and tongue gestures.
Social/emotional	Making eye contact and holding your gaze. He will also start to turn towards sound.
Regulation	Coordinating sucking and swallowing.

social awareness

Your baby will search for your face immediately after birth because he is primed to be a social being from day one. It is no coincidence that he prefers faces to any other visual information and can identify his home language (the language he heard most *in utero*). Within 24 hours, your baby will recognize your smell. Within days he will know and love your voice above all others, and by the end of the first week, he will recognize your face.

Your newborn spends a lot of time sleeping, but over the next two weeks the drowsiness will give way to a more alert state. Just after birth, before going into a drowsy state, your baby will spend some time in the calm-alert state (see p.31), getting to know his mum and dad. When he is in this state, he will start to make tongue and mouth movements to imitate talking.

curled up Your newborn will remain curled up in a little ball, in a position called flexion, in the first few weeks. This is to help her feel stable and contained.

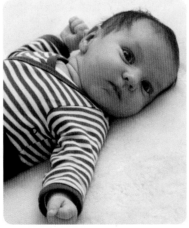

fencing reflex Your baby may stretch out one arm and leg on the same side that his face is turned to. This helps hand–eye coordination to develop.

sensible stimulation: TEAT

The first two weeks are a steep learning curve so don't try to focus on your baby's development, too. Now is the time to slow down and put as little pressure on yourself as possible. From your baby's perspective, just being alive and taking in this new world is enough stimulation.

encourage connections

Your baby's brain is making connections rapidly. These are the primary ways you can support his development:

● Keep his world as calm as possible so that he will enjoy his few settled calm-alert periods.
● Establish happy feeding habits and encourage good periods of sleep so his energy can be used to make brain connections.
● Slow down and look after yourself so you can respond to his needs.

timing

During the first two weeks, your newborn sleeps a lot and therefore filters a significant amount of stimulation. Since his awake times are limited to 40 to 60 minutes (see p.51), you will find there is little time for stimulation. During the brief period before or after a feed, when your baby is comfortable and shows signals of the calm-alert state (see p.31), stimulate him with talk or toys.

In the early days and right up to about three months of age, you will need to adjust the levels of sensory input. The first step is to understand what over-stimulates your baby and how to calm him. Each baby differs in the amount of sensory stimuli he can handle. Finding the right combination of a little stimulation and a lot of calming is the secret at this stage. At around 10 days to two weeks, your baby will become more alert and less inclined to sleep all day. When this occurs, he takes in more and more stimulation and the risk of over-stimulation arises, which may lead to prolonged periods of crying, commonly known as colic (see p.112). By following his cues, you will be able to anticipate his moods and limit crying by removing him from stimuli as soon as he shows signs of irritability or fussiness.

environment

A calming environment is the secret to a settled baby. The best way to nurture your baby so that he thrives is to imitate the environment he enjoyed in the womb.
visual The nursery should be a soothing colour (soft, muted and neutral) and the lights kept low so that when your baby fusses, you can take him to a room that is visually calming. Keep new faces to a minimum, limiting visitors in the first few weeks. If you have to make an outing to visually exciting situations such as a shopping centre, filter out the environment by placing a blanket or a muslin over the pram or wearing your baby in a sling that screens the world.
hearing Soft sounds and white noise are most calming for your baby. Limit visits to very noisy environments as much as possible. He may not fuss while there but might be upset later on.
touch Deep pressure and touch to his back are calming. Since light touch can be disconcerting, check that scratchy fabrics, such as labels in vests, lace, or raised patterns are not touching your baby's skin.

movement Slow rocking, repetitive and rhythmical movements, as opposed to erratic, unpredictable movements, will calm him.
smell Non-distinct smells are better than pungent odours. During the first six weeks do not wear perfume or after-shave. Your own body smell is best for your baby. Wash your baby's clothes in odourless detergent (widely available) and use a tablespoon of vinegar to soften clothes, which is a great softener and leaves no residual smell to over-stimulate your baby.

the **babysense** secret

activities

sleep time

The concept of soothing sensory input is never more applicable than when used in your baby's sleep space.

visual A visually calming room is vital for sleep. Use black-out blinds or curtain lining to help your baby associate sleep time with dark. A light dimmer is useful to keep night feeds subdued and calming.

hearing White noise is particularly calming and can be used to help your baby fall asleep. Examples include running water, a vacuum cleaner or washing machine, and recordings of white noise.

touch Swaddle your baby, especially during periods of sleep. This helps to prevent the startle reflex from making his arms fly out, which is very disconcerting after the contained environment *in utero*. Neutral warmth is soothing for your baby, so keep him at a constant temperature with a muslin or swaddling blanket.

movement Rocking or gently bouncing your baby before sleep will help him settle.

motor development The position your baby sleeps in affects his development. Sleeping on the stomach is not a good idea because your baby can overheat, which increases the risk of SIDS (see p.90). It's safest to put your baby to sleep on his back or side. The side sleeping position is better for muscle development than flat on his back. If he sleeps on his side, make sure you put a wedge or roll (not a pillow) next to him so he can't roll onto his tummy.

smell A small piece of clothing or fabric that smells of you is soothing

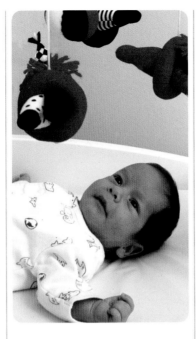

for your little one at sleep time. You could also give him a soft toy, muslin or blanket that you've carried with you to absorb your smell.

on the changing mat

Your baby will always be awake and alert while being changed. This makes it an appropriate time to stimulate your baby, except in the middle of the night. Stimulation is a great distraction for sensitive babies who become fractious when being changed.

visual A mobile over the changing mat will encourage your baby to focus and develop his eye muscles. If your baby is unsettled during changes, this distraction may help. Use mobiles with black-and-white and contrasting colours for very short periods of stimulation.

hearing Talking quietly to your baby in "parentese" – a slightly higher-pitched, sing-song voice that comes naturally to most parents – will help him to focus on your voice.

movement Your baby's neck muscles are weak – support his head as you lie him back on the mat.

bath time

In these early days, you may find bath time stressful as your baby gets used to changes in temperature while undressed. Why not move bath time to the morning when he is less fractious? Or avoid it altogether by just topping and tailing at this stage.

visual Your face is soothing. Bring your head 20–25cm away from your baby so he can focus on your eyes.

hearing Your baby's first few baths are a very new experience for him. Use your voice to calm him and make him feel more secure.

movement Let your baby kick in the bath to stretch out his curled-up legs.

activities continued ...

awake time

Your newborn will only be awake for less than an hour between naps, during which time he is mainly being fed and changed. In the time when he is happily interacting with you, stimulate him and watch the subtle signs he gives you that indicate he has had enough.

visual To encourage your baby's eye muscles to focus, place anything you wish your baby to see at a distance of 20–25cm (8–10in) from his face. When you speak to your baby, let him see your mouth and animate your face. Wearing lipstick will help him to focus on your mouth.

hearing Your voice is one of the most calming sounds to your baby. Talk in "parentese", combining a sing-song voice with long vowel sounds and short sentences.

touch Handle your baby firmly but gently and don't forget to support his head. When he's crying, rub or pat his back. Limit unfamiliar and unpredictable handling by the barrage of visitors who want to meet your new baby. Incorporate baby massage into your day as soon as it seems manageable (see opposite).

movement Carrying your baby in a sling best mimics the containing environment of the womb. As much as dad can't wait to play with your little one, ask him not to make any quick movements, such as lifting him swiftly into the air, just yet. These movements are likely to elicit stress reflexes and are overwhelming.

motor development Place your baby on his tummy a few times a day when he is in the calm-alert state so he can practise lifting his head and strengthening his neck muscles. In the early days, placing your baby on his tummy on top of your stomach when you are lying on your back is a simple way to strengthen his neck muscles in preparation for holding his head up. Speak to him in "parentese" to encourage him to lift his head a little. As his neck strengthens, he will uncurl from the flexed position.

travelling time

Many cultures hole their new mums up for the early weeks to help them recover and bond with their babies. It's a great idea, so see if you can spend time at home and not travel about. If you do go out, shield your baby from stimulation and germs.

visual Cover the front of the pram with a muslin cloth or blanket to keep bright lights and excessive visual stimulation to a minimum.

hearing If your baby fusses in the car, play soothing music and lullabies.

movement A ride in the pram or in a sling helps to calm babies.

feed time

Do not try to stimulate your baby now. He needs to concentrate on survival and you need to get to grips with this new skill.

touch Your baby may be so sleepy in the first few weeks that it's difficult to keep him awake for feeds. In this case you can use sensory stimuli to raise his state: to keep him alert enough to feed, stroke his cheek, wipe his cheek with damp cotton wool, or occasionally tickle his feet.

toys and tools

At this age you are your baby's favourite toy. It is not at all necessary to buy any fancy toys. But if you wish to, here are some toys you can buy or make that suit this age range:

visual Your baby will enjoy black-and-white mobiles, which will help him focus – the visual pathways in his brain respond well to strong patterns. Mobiles, play gyms and any activity that involves movement encourage him to watch, developing his eye muscles. Babies love looking at human faces – cut out a picture of a baby's face from a magazine and put it next to the changing mat or car seat for your baby to look at.

hearing Play soft music, including classical music and lullabies, to your baby. CDs and downloads of womb sounds, white noise, heartbeats and dolphin sounds are all excellent for calming at this stage. You can easily make a white noise track by recording the sound of the washing machine, vacuum cleaner, or radio static.

touch At this stage only use your hands to touch your baby. You don't need any other tactile toys.

movement A baby swing is a fun and novel idea. This type of movement helps to build muscle tone and coordination.

smell Lavender and chamomile are soothing smells. Your baby is not ready to have these essential oils or fragrances on his body or in his bath, but you might like to use them in a burner in the room or in a scented room mister.

the gentle art of baby massage

If there is one activity that should ideally form part of your daily routine with your baby, it is baby massage. Moving from the secure, warm environment of the womb to the cold sterile world outside is a dramatic transition for your baby. Most babies need the close comfort of their parents' touch and in the early days are more settled when in mum or dad's arms. Quiet periods of massage are a wonderful way to connect with your baby, to take a deep breath and relax and to feel as if you are doing something constructive. Massage will increase your confidence in caring for your baby. It's suitable for stable premature babies too, who have been found to gain weight more quickly when massaged. For your baby, the benefits are immense, including:

bonding The sense of touch is one of the most powerful mediums that you can use to bond with your child. Still touch, such as a deep hug, and calming massage will help you to make connections with your baby. It's particularly useful if you are feeling disconnected from your baby if you were separated at birth or if your baby is adopted.

body image Before beginning to massage your baby, you should ask his permission to touch him. It is a great habit to get into when starting massage at any age because it reinforces the recipient's sense of self-worth and respect for his body. Although he can only respond with eye contact and by looking engaged, watch for these subtle signals. If he cries or becomes agitated, it is probably better to stop and try again another day. Massage also creates connections in the brain that are central to the development of body awareness and body image.

calming The deep pressure of massage strokes is calming for the nervous system and therefore is an excellent remedy for "colic" (see p.112).

wellness Massage is good for your baby's health and especially useful for ill and premature babies. The physiological benefits of massage include improved respiration (breathing), better circulation of lymph and blood, and improved gastrointestinal function. Babies who are regularly massaged are less likely to cry, will sleep better, and gain weight quicker.

sleep When your baby is older, massage will help him to regulate his sleep/wake cycle. By associating massage with a bedtime routine, you can prime your baby to fall asleep with greater ease.

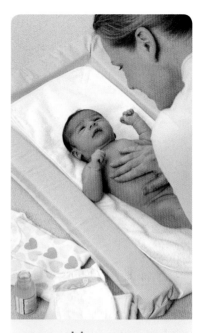

sense-able secret
Massage is an excellent way of bonding with your child. Having everything ready before you start the massage, such as a clean nappy and a change of clothes, will help you feel relaxed during the session.

when to massage?

Your baby is most responsive and will benefit most from massage when in the calm-alert state (see p.31). To identify this state, look for calm movements, open and focused eyes, and regular breathing. Since babies respond well to routine, it is a good idea to try to massage your baby at around at the same time every day. Newborn babies are often most receptive to massage in the morning, after their morning nap. As your baby gets older, you can start to link the massage to the bedtime routine.

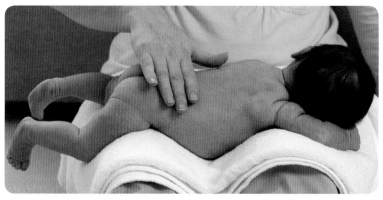

back massage Lie your baby securely over your lap on a soft, warmed towel. Run your hands up and down his back, using gentle but firm pressure.

what you need

Use 3–5 drops of a neutral carrier oil, such as almond, organic sunflower oil, or extra-virgin olive oil. Place a little on your hands and rub them together to warm the oil. Use just enough to keep your hands moving smoothly over your baby's skin.

preparation
● Make sure the room feels relaxing and is free of distractions.
● Position yourself comfortably, leaning against a wall or pile of cushions. Undress your baby and place him between your legs on the floor lying on his back, or on your lap with a towel or nappy under him. You might like to warm the towel in the tumble dryer before you begin.

● Make sure your nails are short, and remove any jewellery that might scratch or catch on your baby's skin.
● Have a change of clothes at hand so that when you are finished, you can dress your baby without having to get up.
● When your baby is older, around four months, it's a good idea to have some toys at hand for him to look at and play with to keep him occupied during the massage.

caution
● Do not massage your baby for a few days after immunizations as his temperature may be slightly raised. This will make him uncomfortable and he may not enjoy the massage.

a massage session

Vary the length of the massage according to your baby's age. You might only massage a newborn for a few minutes, but up to 20 minutes for an older baby. Start at the beginning of these steps with your baby lying on his back and stop when you feel he has had enough.

Start by asking permission. Make contact with your baby by placing your hands on his hips for a moment and ask him if you can massage him. This shows respect and also signals that the massage is about to begin.

your baby's legs

legs Begin at the hips and firmly stroke down one leg from hip to toe, then move one hand at a time back up to the thigh. Hold your baby's leg up if it is easier. Repeat the action towards your baby's ankle.
feet Using your thumb, stroke three times along the sole of the foot from heel to toes. Keep the pressure deep. End by pressing your thumb into the foot for three seconds.
toes Gently squeeze each toe in turn, pulling lightly from the base of the toe to its tip.
Repeat all the steps on the other leg.

your baby's tummy

Always move your hands in a clockwise direction on the tummy – the direction the bowel follows. The following strokes are excellent for babies with colic and digestive problems. If your baby is sensitive to touch on the stomach or chest, skip these steps and move onto the arms.
still touch This beginning stroke tells your baby where you are going

to massage next. Just place your hand on his tummy, maintaining this point of contact for a while.

paddle wheel Place one hand just under your baby's ribs and glide your hand towards the groin area. Before lifting this hand, place your other hand under the rib cage and repeat the same action, gliding downwards. Continue alternating hands, making sure one hand is always in contact with the skin.

I love you Using only your dominant hand, begin the first stroke below the rib cage on your right (your baby's left side) and stroke down towards the hip, making an "I" shape. Then move your hand to your baby's other side, glide your hand across the top of the abdomen, and down to the groin. This forms a sideways "L" shape. Finally, place your hand near your baby's right hip (on your left), stroke up to the ribcage, then across and down the opposite side, making an upside down "U" shape. Say "I – Love – You" as you do each of the three parts of this stroke.

finish the tummy strokes Place your hands on your baby's chest near his shoulders and glide both hands down his body to the toes. Bring one hand at a time up to the shoulders. Repeat. *Finish with still touch again.*

your baby's arms

arms Stroke down one arm, from the top of your baby's shoulders to his hands. Repeat, moving one hand at a time back to the shoulder. Leave one hand in contact with the skin.

hands Press your thumb into the pad of your baby's palm, under his thumb and little finger, maintaining the pressure for three to five seconds. This should encourage him to open his hand.

fingers Very gently grasp the base of one of your baby's fingers and slide your fingers to the tip of the finger, gently rolling and squeezing it. Repeat on each finger in turn. This stroke can be combined with a rhyme about fingers, such as:
"This little piggy went to market ..."
Squeeze the thumb.
"This little piggy stayed at home ..."
Squeeze the index finger.
"This little piggy had roast beef ..."
Squeeze the middle finger.
"This little piggy had none ..."
Squeeze the ring finger.
"And this little piggy cried 'wee wee wee' all the way home."
Squeeze the little finger.
Repeat all the strokes on the other arm and hand.

your baby's head

Cradle your baby's head in your hands, look into his eyes, and wait for him to make eye contact. Place your thumbs at the centre of his forehead and gently stroke out towards his ears. Then stroke your hands down from his neck to his shoulders.

your baby's back

Turn your baby over on the mat or on your lap. Gently stroke down his back from his neck to his buttocks. Use both hands simultaneously on either side of the back on a bigger baby or one hand on a smaller baby, leaving your other hand resting on his buttocks.
Finish with a cuddle.

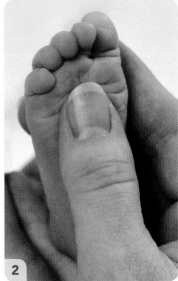

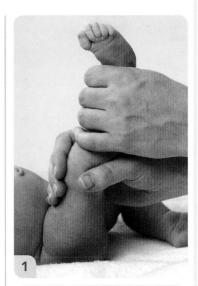

baby massage strokes
❶ Legs: begin at the hips and stroke the leg firmly from hip to toe and back again to the thigh. Repeat the action down to your baby's ankle.
❷ Feet: stroke along the sole of each foot, then end the stroke by gently pressing your thumb into the foot for three seconds.

chapter 9

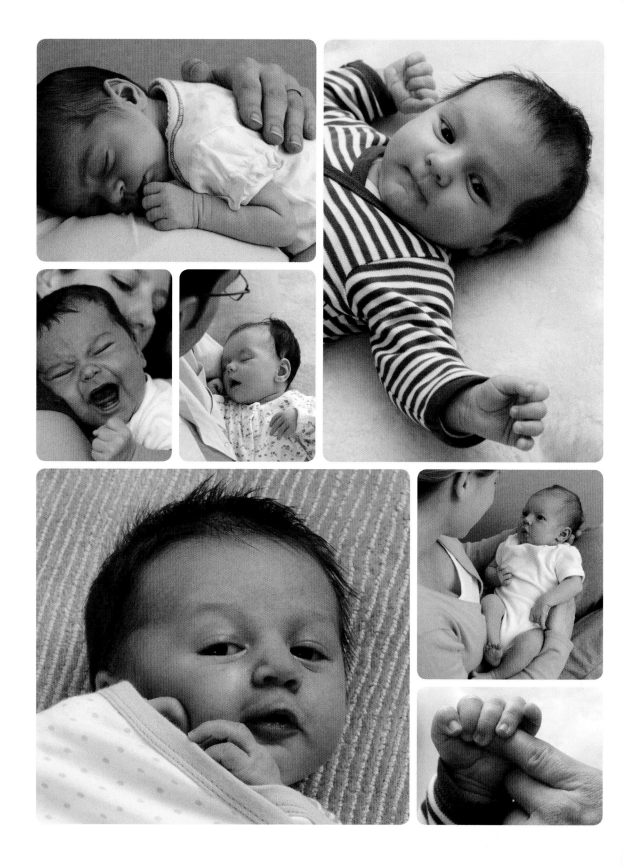

your baby at two to six weeks

It's hard to believe that you will soon be a month into motherhood. Days that fly by (and nights that don't) seem to be a way of life now. If you are having moments of doubt and every day is filled with guesswork, you are in good company. Most parents find themselves asking reams of questions at this point: Is she really still hungry? What could I have eaten that caused this wind? Could she be calming herself or is she trying to tell me that she is sleepy? Where did all these pimples come from? Is it normal for her to skip a night feed? Life seems to revolve around this little being and your anxieties about nurturing her. On the following pages are strategies to help you both through the next month, including how to start to guiding your baby into a gentle routine, which will make your life feel more structured and predictable.

baby-centric routine

● Try to limit your baby's awake time to no more than 60 minutes at a stretch and plan this time for nappy changing, bathing, feeding, and stimulation.

● She will probably be sleeping for most of the day, about 18 to 20 hours in a 24-hour cycle.

● Your baby will be feeding every three to four hours during the day, but continue to feed on demand even if it is more frequent than this.

● Expect a growth spurt, lasting between 24 and 48 hours, to occur when she is about four to six weeks old. During this time, feed her two-hourly if necessary.

a day in the life of your baby

In these early weeks, no day feels typical. You may find that the only similarity between one day and the next is the swing of your emotions. Of course, you will see rays of hope each day as your baby gives you a signal you recognize, or even starts to have her feeds at a regular time. In general though, it is too early to expect a fixed routine.

mum sense: routine debate

You may be advised or tempted to push your baby into a rigid routine before she is ready. As much as you long for some pattern to your days, your baby is too young for you to start a strict sleep or feeding schedule. There are very good reasons for this:

babies are individuals Every baby's ability to filter information differs. Whereas some babies can cope well with interaction and stimulation (the settled baby or social butterfly), others can become overwrought with much less interaction (the slow-to-warm-up and the sensitive baby). The latter are generally more fussy and need to sleep very frequently or will be prone to over-stimulation. Trying to keep a sensitive baby awake for two hours at this age will make her very miserable.

growing understanding As you learn to recognize your baby's signs and signals you will know that when he turns away it's because he's had enough stimulation.

every day is different Some days your baby will wake earlier in the morning than others, sometimes you may find your baby sleeps deeply for more than two hours whereas the same sleep on another day will only last 45 minutes. If you are timing your baby's sleeps rather than watching for her signals of sleepiness, you may feel stressed and be unable to decide when she should next sleep, or worse, you may end up struggling to keep her awake in order to stick to her routine.

feeds vary It is impossible to fit all babies (breast- or bottle fed) into an identical feeding schedule at this stage. Not only are formula and breast milk very different from each other, but every mother's breast milk supply and composition will differ from another's.

These early days can seem never-ending, but the reality is that routine is not far off – a few months down the line you'll be able to follow a reasonably flexible routine. At this stage, a rigid routine is just not advisable, but by following the baby-centric routine (see box, opposite), your days will soon be a little more predictable.

a confusing time

It might not feel like it, but you are slowly learning to read your baby's signals and in time will have a clearer understanding of her needs. Some days a real pattern may appear to be emerging, and the next all predictability goes out the window. Towards the six-week mark, you may start to feel a little trapped by the seemingly endless nappy changes, breastfeeding, and soothing, and may long for one moment of freedom. The weight of the responsibility may overwhelm you, which can lead to moments when you feel down. But seconds later, burying your nose in the new baby folds of her neck, you will be overwhelmed by love and elation. These mixed emotions are completely normal for first-time mothers (and even with subsequent babies!) and should gradually balance out as you become more used to taking care of your baby.

sense-able secret
At this age it is too early to establish a strict routine. Instead, watch your baby's signals and try to gauge what he wants.

Q&A **weight of responsibility**

I consider myself a relaxed mother, but every now and again I find myself checking to see if my baby is still breathing or if the cat is sitting on her head. What can I do to feel more in control?

If you find yourself anxiously watching your sleeping baby and at times are overwhelmed with the awesome responsibility of a new life, you are in good company. This is nature's way of ensuring our babies survive – we become a bundle of nerves and worry over things we never thought we would. The reality is that your baby is very resilient and will thrive. However, if you find that you are paralysed with fear and anxiety about your baby and how you will care for her, you may be suffering from postnatal depression (see p.59).

Q&A
nappy rash

My baby was so miserable yesterday and I could not work out why. I feel terrible because today her bottom is covered in red blisters. Is this nappy rash?

When your baby develops nappy rash, a good case of maternal guilt can set in. Many babies suffer from this, which is caused by ammonia in the urine and faeces burning the soft new skin of your baby's bottom.

to avoid nappy rash:
● Change nappies frequently and clean the genital and anal area thoroughly at each change.
● Avoid perfumed or alcohol-based wipes. The best way to clean the area in the early days is by using cotton wool swabs and cooled boiled water.
● Disposable nappies do not require you to use a barrier cream since the nappy wicks the moisture away from the skin very quickly.
● Make sure that cloth nappies are rinsed well and changed often since they don't wick moisture away from skin as effectively as disposables. Or use a nappy liner with your cloth nappy.

   Occasionally nappy rash is more aggressive and spreads into the folds of your baby's thighs and develops raw lesions. It is possible that this rash is caused by the fungus candida albicans. If this happens, ask your doctor to prescribe some anti-fungal cream.

baby sense: colic

Between 10 and 14 days after your baby's birth, she may begin to have periods of crying where she pulls up her legs and appears to be in pain, especially in the evening. The term "colic" begins to hang like a threat over your head. Colic is much debated by experts, with suggestions for its causes ranging from digestive disturbance to gas to food intolerances to over-anxious mothering! The reality is that colic is nothing to fear. Using the advice that follows, you should be equipped to prevent these periods of unexplained crying, and, if they do arise, to manage them so that the crying lasts no longer than 15 to 20 minutes.

rule out the basics

If your baby is fussing a lot, you need first to rule out physical causes of discomfort before considering colic as the cause. These include:

hunger In the two- to six-week period, your baby still needs to feed regularly, so if she is crying and more than two to three hours have passed since she was last fed, she may well be hungry – feed her.

the wrong formula Breastfed babies are less likely to suffer digestive disturbances because of the protective nature of the antibodies in breast milk on the intestines. If your bottle-fed baby is restless after feeds and has eczema, diarrhoea, or constipation, speak to your health visitor to ensure that she is on the right formula milk.

lactose intolerance It is common for a young baby's immature digestive system to find it difficult to break down the lactose in milk. Most babies grow out of this problem, but it can cause digestive discomfort, explosive stools and general discomfort. This is not a reason to change formula or stop breastfeeding unless your baby is very ill or not thriving. Again, speak to your health visitor for advice.

constipation Difficulty in passing stools is common in young babies and is does not necessarily indicate constipation. However, your baby may be constipated if she is straining when passing stools and her poos are hard small pellets. Your doctor may prescribe a remedy to loosen her stools. This problem rarely occurs with breastfed babies.

reflux Whether your baby possets and brings up milk curds or not, she may have reflux: regurgitation of the stomach contents back up into her gullet, or oesophagus (the pipe that carries food from her mouth to her stomach). Even if she does not bring up milk, she may have reflux that is not easily noticeable, because she regurgitates the milk and swallows it before it reaches her mouth (silent reflux). Regurgitated curds are acidic and may burn the oesophagus, resulting in oesophagitis, an inflammation and irritation of the lining of the oesophagus. Babies with reflux fuss a lot and don't like being laid flat, especially after a feed. In extreme cases they may refuse to feed for a period of time. Reflux is not common, but if your baby is diagnosed with it, you can help her (see p.141).

allergies Although allergies are increasingly more common, it is still unusual for a baby to have an allergy to milk. If your baby has severe eczema or recurrent colds and coughs, you may want to rule out allergies as a cause of unsettledness. Talk to your doctor or health visitor.

disruption of intestinal flora There is some evidence that if you were given antibiotics around the time of the birth of your baby and she was delivered by Caesarean, the healthy bacteria needed for digestion that are naturally present in most babies' guts may have been disrupted. These natural bacteria can be replaced with a probiotic treatment and will result in a more settled baby. Discuss this with your doctor.

illness If your baby becomes very unsettled, stops feeding, or is feverish, rule out illness by taking her to your doctor immediately.

environmental factors To rule out discomfort caused by her environment, check whether the temperature around your baby is too hot or cold, whether her nappy is wet or dirty, or whether bright sunlight, scratchy clothing, or other irritants could be disturbing her.

making sure Watch out for illness: if your baby becomes very unsettled, refuses feeds or develops a fever, she may be sick. Take her to your doctor straightaway.

what is colic?

Having ruled out the possible causes for crying and discomfort (see above), you may be faced with the realization that nothing tangible can explain your baby's unsettledness. If the crying tends to happen between 5pm and 8pm each evening, you may consider the culprit to be "colic". Contrary to popular wisdom, colic does not have its root in tummy troubles and the digestive system. The fact that colic classically happens in the early evening is proof that there is more to these prolonged periods of crying than meets the eye. If it were a digestive problem, it would be as likely to occur at any time of day. The basis of colic is the immaturity of your newborn's brain. Your baby's brain does not filter sensory information very well in the early days, which results in periods of over-stimulation. Interacting and being awake in our world can be overwhelming for your new baby. By the end of a long day of interaction and stimulation, she may become stressed and irritable, resulting in the trademark crying and discomfort.

the low down on colic

The classic "colic curve" which starts at around two weeks, peaks at six weeks and drops off by 14 weeks, is experienced by parents and babies across the world, irrespective of culture.

It is usually attributed to digestive issues because the high-pitched crying is typically accompanied by pulling up of legs, passing wind, grimacing, and apparent abdominal discomfort. But, since this happens only in the evenings, it can't be due to digestive troubles, otherwise it would also occur at any other time of day. The real cause is the immaturity of your baby's brain, leading to easy over-stimulation.

how colic develops

Throughout the day, your baby takes in and processes a great deal of stimulation from the environment and her interactions with people. When newborn, she is unable to filter excess sensory information. These interactions accumulate and lower her ability to tolerate stimulation. This is especially true for sensitive and slow-to-warm-up babies. This reduced ability to tolerate stimulation predominantly affects your baby at the end of the day, especially if she has not slept well during the day (sleep gives her a chance to recharge her sensory system). By the evening, your young baby may reach a state of over-stimulation. In this state, dealing with stomach gas and other internal sensory input (that she could cope with earlier in the day) becomes a challenge. She begins to fuss or cry in response to normal interactions and sensory input, such as the excitement of dad coming home or a bath and massage. This fussing may create anxiety for you and you may inadvertently make the situation worse by patting, rocking, over-feeding, and generally handling your baby too much at a time of day when stimuli are hard for her to

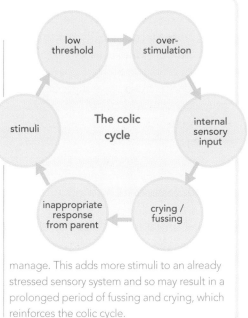

The colic cycle

low threshold → over-stimulation → internal sensory input → crying / fussing → inappropriate response from parent → stimuli →

manage. This adds more stimuli to an already stressed sensory system and so may result in a prolonged period of fussing and crying, which reinforces the colic cycle.

sense-able secret
You can help to prevent colic by:
• Ensuring your baby sleeps regularly during the day.
• Reading your baby's signals of overload.
• Making sure your baby's sensory environment is calming.

preventing colic The key to preventing colic is to encourage regular daytime sleeps. Babies who sleep regularly during the day are significantly less likely to become over-stimulated because their brains have the opportunity to recharge and therefore can cope with more stimulation. Babies who are awake for long periods during the day are generally more likely to fuss and need extensive soothing in the evenings.

Take the time to learn and read your baby's unique signals, especially in the evening when she may signal that she has had enough stimulation. These signals include rubbing her eyes, averting her gaze, or sucking on her hands (see pp.38–39). If you see these signals, adjust her sensory environment by removing or limiting stimulation (for example, by taking her out of a noisy room or putting her in a sling so she feels contained). See p.35 for more ideas on creating a soothing environment.

managing colic Even when you understand colic in the context of over-stimulation and have watched your baby's signals and made sure she has slept well, there may be days when she fusses and cries in the evening, particularly if she is a sensitive baby. When she begins to fuss, start by ruling out physical reasons for it. Could it be hunger, tiredness or discomfort? If your baby is fussing or crying and there is no physical reason for her unsettled mood (see table, p.45), try the 7 S's of calming to soothe her (see opposite).

the **babysense** secret

the seven S's of calming

These are based on your baby's ability to use her sensory systems to calm herself and be soothed. Help your baby to find a self-soothing strategy she can use. Often these involve her mouth and sucking.

slow down When you feel stressed by the demands of your new baby, slow down and give her time to be calmed by one of the six following calming strategies. Your baby's brain takes about five minutes to be settled by any new strategy. Take a deep breath and resist the temptation to swap rapidly between soothing techniques.

sensory awareness Start by calming your baby's sensory environment and remove her from stimulation when she is tired or over-stimulated. Do not make the problem of over-stimulation worse with long periods of burping and general handling, such as passing her from person to person or keeping her in a busy room in the house. Burp her for no more than five minutes – if the wind has not come up by then, it will come out the other end eventually. Pursuing burping may exacerbate fussing, which will result in your baby gulping air and getting more gas bubbles in her stomach.

sucking Your baby has more sensory receptors for calming in her mouth than anywhere else on her body. Sucking is a vital step in soothing. She can suck on her own hands or a dummy or your finger. Help your baby to keep her hands in her mouth by swaddling her with her hands near her face or by holding her hands to her mouth. Give your baby space to develop self-calming strategies herself rather than instantly feeding her simply to calm her. You might like to encourage her to take her hands to her mouth; grab a security toy and suck it; suck a dummy or her hand; or bring her hands towards the midline of her body. If your baby needs a dummy to help her settle, encourage this as they are a great source of sucking comfort.

sleep Make sure your baby is not overtired. An overtired baby will be fractious in the evening – try not to keep her awake for more than an hour at a time, even in the evening. Sleep will calm your baby and help her to reset her sensory state.

swaddle If your baby is unsettled and it is not time for a feed, try swaddling her in a blanket (see p.26) to help her to settle and to drop off to sleep, particularly if she has been awake for an hour or more in the evening. Swaddling is soothing for a fractious baby because it inhibits the reflexes that are disconcerting for her.

swaddling

Swaddle your baby for all her sleeps as well as when she is irritable or fussing. You can swaddle your baby with her knees bent up, instead of straight – the calming effect will be just the same. The important factor is that her hands are swaddled close to her face so she can soothe herself. However, make sure she has some time during the day unswaddled to exercise and bend her hips. Bending at the hips and kicking her legs is important because it is through this motion that the thigh bone "carves" the hip bone into its proper shape.

Q&A
baby resists sleep

My three-week-old fusses a lot and I really battle to get her to sleep. She can be awake for four hours at a stretch and then wakes after 30 minutes. She cries a lot in the evening and at 9pm falls into a fretful sleep. What can I do?

If your baby resists falling asleep and fusses before each sleep, wrap her up in a stretchy 100 percent cotton swaddling blanket, and sit calmly with her in her quiet and darkened sleep space. Hold her close and gently rock her without making eye contact until she is drowsy, then put her into her cot.

Put on a CD of white noise or lulling music to mask any background noise that might be troubling her. If she fusses, place your hand on her body or let her suck on your finger or a dummy. If she has not settled within a few minutes, and begins to cry, pick her up gently and rock her (a sling is useful in this instance) until she is drowsy, then try again to put her into bed. If she continues to cry and is not asleep within 15 minutes, hold her and rock her until she is asleep. Once she is fast asleep, place her gently into her bed.

Although you don't want your baby to develop habits that rely on you calming her until she falls asleep, it is more important at this stage for her to sleep than to worry about how it happens. Babies need to be held a lot, so don't worry about bad habits forming just yet.

sling If your baby is crying in the evening and is not happy lying in her cot, lift her, swaddle her and place her in a sling. Carry her about, protected against your body from the stimulation of the world, rocking and jigging her until she falls asleep. Once asleep, settle your baby in her cot. Do not worry about "spoiling" your baby because babies younger than three months do not develop sleep expectations and long-term sleep habits. Some babies just need a little extra sensory soothing, particularly those who are colicky in the evening. Baby wearing (carrying your baby in a sling) helps your baby to feel calm and secure and, once she is deeply asleep, you can put her back in her cot.

sounds White noise, the sound of your voice and lullabies can soothe a fractious little one. Play a CD of white noise at the same volume as your baby's cry – it works wonders in quieting a colicky baby (see p.26).

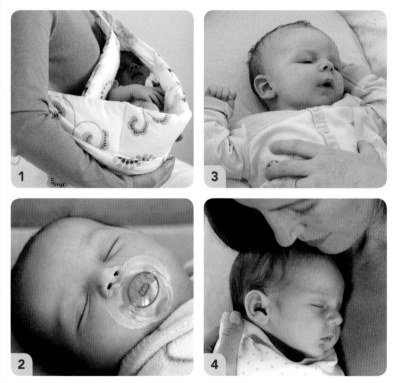

soothing your baby If your baby is crying, try these strategies to calm her and prevent colic. ❶ Baby wearing: carrying your baby in a sling is a lovely way to keep him close and soothe him. He will be calmed by the motion of your body. ❷ Sucking a dummy is comforting. Dummies provide an excellent calming method for babies who struggle to keep their hands in their mouths. ❸ Try placing your hand on your baby in a deep, still touch for a few minutes to help him feel contained. ❹ Wrapping your baby tightly in a swaddle will mimic the calming world of the womb.

the **babysense** secret

helping your baby sleep

Your baby is no longer a newborn and each week brings new sleep challenges, but also draws you slightly closer to having a good night's sleep yourself. Following the Babysense principles will help you with this.

When your baby was newborn, she probably fell asleep with ease and slept for long periods. You may even have had to wake her for feeds during the day. As she reaches the two- to six-week stage, she becomes more alert and may start to resist sleep. Sleep is essential – and the best way to prevent colic and over-stimulation. Although it's still too early to establish a sleep routine, you can begin to guide your baby towards a gentle baby-centric sleep pattern.

awake time

When working towards a sleep routine at this young age, remember that it is how long your baby is awake that determines when she should sleep. There is no recipe for your baby's life, such as sleep/play/feed or feed/play/sleep. Every day is different. Sometimes a feed will fall immediately before a sleep and, on other days, your baby will wake up at around the time a feed is due. At this age, your baby should be awake for no longer than 60 minutes between sleeps. Make a note of the time she wakes from her last sleep. After 50 minutes, watch for signals of tiredness such as yawning or sucking on her hand (see pp.52–53), and take your baby to her sleeping environment to help her settle to sleep.

sleep space

At this tender age, your baby will happily sleep anywhere and may even sleep better with a little noise around. Since babies of this age have not developed long-term memories, they do not have sleep expectations. However, it is wise to put your baby to sleep in a regular sleep space so that soon she will associate it with sleep. Aim to have her sleeping in this sleep space for at least two daytime sleeps and in the evening when she goes to bed. Keep her sleep space soothing and mimic the calming sensory space of the womb to help her fall asleep:

● **Touch** Swaddle your baby for sleep time.
● **Visual** Dim her room and if you are out and about, cover the front of her pram or travel system for sleep times to block out the world.
● **Sound** White noise will help her settle and sleep deeper and longer. Tune out the radio, play a CD of white noise or put on a fan, or perhaps have a small fountain outside her bedroom.
● **Movement** Hold and rock your baby to settle her if she is resisting sleep. Use a sling or baby hammock for rocking.
● **Smell and taste** Your breast milk and mummy smells are calming.

sleep: what to expect at this stage

● It is normal for your baby to wake after 45 minutes, during the light-sleep state. A typical sleep cycle for babies of this age lasts 45 minutes. This means that your baby will go from light sleep to deep sleep and back into a light sleep state every 45 minutes.
● Regardless of how long your baby has slept, monitor how long she is awake for and put her back to sleep after 50 to 60 minutes of awake time (see p.51).
● Your baby will start to sleep for one longer stretch if she is left to wake on her own at night. As long as your baby is gaining weight, you can leave her to wake on her own – you don't need to wake her at night to feed her.
● Accept offers of help during the day so that you can nap when your baby sleeps.
● Your young baby does not necessarily need to feed before she sleeps. Bear in mind that some sleeps might happen before a feed is due. If this is the case, let her sleep and feed her when she wakes up.
● Many babies become more wakeful and harder to get to sleep at this age.

Q&A
separation anxiety?

I think my baby has developed separation anxiety. She is content as long as she is being held, but she won't fall asleep on her own. In desperation I have ended up letting her sleep next to me – so that both of us can get some rest. I am worried that this will create a lasting habit.

Many babies begin to protest about being settled to sleep at around this age. This is not separation anxiety, manipulation or bad habits. Quite simply, your baby needs sensory soothing in order to settle. Your baby is still very little; don't worry about starting any bad habits when she is so young. At this stage, she needs her sleep more than she needs to learn how to put herself to sleep unassisted, so do what it takes to get her to fall asleep.

Ensure that she is not over-stimulated, and make sure that she is not kept awake for longer than 60 minutes at a stretch (including feeding time). If she fusses when you put her down, keep your hand on her: the deep pressure will help her to feel contained. Keep her swaddled for all sleeps. Persevere with this approach, even if she appears to resist swaddling – she will learn to like it. Make sure that you swaddle her with her hands close to her face so that she can suck on them to soothe herself.

daytime sleeps

Sleep is critical to prevent over-stimulation and colicky crying and yet this is the stage when many babies resist falling asleep and/or wake after a very short time. To help your baby sleep, take her to her sleep space 50 minutes after she last woke. Watch for signs of tiredness (see pp.52–53) Even if she doesn't show these signals, help her become drowsy and settle to sleep. If you are out and about, settle her to sleep in her pram or a sling.

getting your baby drowsy Prepare your baby for sleep by changing her, swaddling her, and then settling her into a drowsy state. This will be best achieved by dimming the room, swaddling and rocking her gently, or feeding her if a feed is due. Soothe her in this manner until her eyelids are heavy but not closed.

from drowsy to asleep When your baby is drowsy, place her in her cot to settle to sleep. If she is unsettled, leave your hand on her to help her feel contained. It's best if she falls asleep on her own, but if she still does not settle and is fussing, pat her or lift her and hold her against you until she is settled, aiming to put her down drowsy and calm. Do not be concerned if she occasionally falls asleep in your arms – at this age babies do not have long-term memories or expectations around sleep.

catnapping Some babies still catnap at this age. This happens when your baby wakes within 20 minutes of going to sleep as a result of the hypnagogic startle (see p.30). Your baby is woken by a little jerk of her limbs as she falls from light sleep to deep sleep. Swaddling is the best way to prevent this. If your baby is a catnapper, re-swaddle her, encourage her to suck on her thumb, your finger or a dummy, and gently pat her. If she remains unsettled, pick her up gently and sway, holding her close to you until she is drowsy, then settle her to sleep in her cot. It is more important to get her to sleep than to worry about creating habits at this stage.

night-time sleep solutions

Do not wake your baby to feed her at night, unless you have been instructed to do so for health reasons, for example, if she was premature, is not gaining weight, or is too drowsy to feed well. When she wakes at night, feed her if more than two hours have passed since her last feed. If she wakes an hour or two after the last feed, re-swaddle her and pat or cuddle her back to sleep. If she is just niggling, try not to lift her, which will wake her further and create the expectation of a feed. Keep night feeds (between 6pm and 6am), very quiet and calming – do not take her out of the room she sleeps in, keep the lights dim, and make sure your interactions are muted.

feeding your baby

Feeding your baby becomes easier as you grow in confidence, but in this period, you will still be focused on establishing your breast milk supply or working out the right feeding option for you and your baby.

breastfeeding

Breastfeeding is easier now as you have probably mastered the way to help your baby latch on. However, as with any other stage of mothering, feeding may still trouble you. Your primary concern at this stage might be whether your baby is getting enough milk – with breastfeeding you can never tell how much milk you are producing. By now your baby should have regained her birth weight. Provided she is gaining weight and is generally happy and content to feed every two to three hours, you can be sure that your breast milk supply is adequate. Another way to confirm this is to look at your baby's nappies: she should have at least six wet nappies a day and her urine should not be dark or smelly.

When your baby cries, listen to her cry and use the opportunity to begin to read the subtle signals (see pp.38–39) that reflect her state. In this way you will slowly learn to distinguish hunger cries from those that indicate over-stimulation or tiredness. If she is fussing soon after a feed and you know she does not need to be fed again, calm her by using other methods such as rocking her or using white noise (see pp.115–16).

your breastfeeding diet

By now you will have realized that producing and maintaining an adequate milk supply to successfully meet your baby's nutritional needs requires an enormous amount of energy. Did you know that you expend as much energy to make enough milk to feed your baby for 48 hours, as you do running a half-marathon? This energy will obviously be obtained from what you eat. It is easy to fall into the trap of not eating well, and grabbing snacks or relying on fast food when there's barely time in the day to make yourself a cup of tea. As a result you may not be consuming enough nutrients or drinking enough to allow your body to meet your baby's milk requirements.

In general, keep your diet similar to when you were pregnant, as your baby is familiar with the tastes she encountered in the womb, and try to make sure that it is well-balanced in order to keep up your milk supply. Eat plenty of carbohydrates (wholemeal bread, rice, pasta, potatoes) and protein (fish, meat and dairy products, and eggs), plus lots of fluids (at least two litres/3½ pints a day) and a variety of fruits and vegetables. You may hear a great deal of conflicting advice on what you should avoid eating while breastfeeding. You may have been advised to eliminate all

---

feeding: what to expect at this stage

- Your breast milk supply takes at least six weeks to become fully established. It is important that you eat well and get plenty of rest at this stage and breastfeed regularly (at least every three hours during the day) to ensure an adequate milk supply.
- If you are bottle feeding and your baby wakes more than every four hours at night, consider changing her formula to a more filling one. Check with your doctor before changing formula.
- Your baby may demand one or two cluster feeds (feeds close together) in the early part of the evening. Follow her lead if it is helping her to sleep for a longer stretch at night.
- Your baby will have one longer stretch at night without feeding. As long as she is gaining weight, leave her to wake on her own.
- You can expect a growth spurt at between four and six weeks of age, when your baby will demand a feed more often than before.

avoiding harm Do ask your doctor if any medication you are taking while breastfeeding is safe, as small amounts of it will be transferred to your baby in your breast milk.

sorts of food in an attempt to settle your baby, particularly if she is colicky. Recent research has shown that eliminating food does not have much impact on crying and colic at all. The only foods worth avoiding or limiting are:

● Gas-producing foods, such as onions, cabbage and beans.

● Dairy products if your baby has a lactose sensitivity or severe reflux.

● Caffeine, sugar, cocoa, and stimulants, such as artificial sweeteners, which may cause your baby to become over-stimulated and irritable.

● Alcohol and some medication must be avoided as it is transferred to your baby in breast milk. If you need to take medication while breastfeeding, check with your doctor about its suitability.

● Excessive intake of Vitamin B_{12} – more than the RDA for breastfeeding women: 2.8 micrograms/day – can contribute to decreased milk supply. Liver and shellfish contain high levels of Vitamin B_{12}.

checking your milk supply

If your baby is consistently unsettled between feeds and appears hungry, you might wonder if your milk supply is adequate. Your milk supply may be insufficient to meet your baby's needs if:

● Your baby consistently demands more milk before two hours have passed since the last feed.

● Your baby is fussy between feeds, only settling when she is fed more frequently.

● She is having a growth spurt, which usually occurs at four to six weeks, then again at four, six, and nine months.

● She is bigger or above average weight for her age – her energy needs may be greater than an average-weight baby.

● She has fewer than five to six wet nappies a day.

● She is not gaining adequate weight.

boosting your milk supply

There are a number of ways to increase your breast milk supply:

increase If your milk supply is low and your baby is demanding to be fed frequently, the best way to increase your milk supply is simply to feed her more frequently for a few days. She may be having a growth spurt.

enhance Supplements high in alfalfa protein, with the recommended daily allowance (RDA) of vitamin B, have proved to be beneficial in maintaining a good milk supply. A drink made from blackthorn (sloe) berries can also be beneficial, as well as refreshing and energizing, when mixed with a little water. Alternatively, try drinking two litres of "jungle juice" tonic mixture (see box, opposite) a day.

express Try expressing some breast milk if your baby misses or does not finish a full feed, and always at the end of a feed, too (see pp.158–59 for details on expressing). This fools your body into believing it needs to produce enough milk for twins, or at least for a very hungry baby. Store the expressed breast milk in the fridge for up to 24 hours, or freeze it in plastic feeding bottles with secure tops to seal in freshness, or plastic bags made especially for storing milk (see Resources, pp.214–15 for stockists). Breast milk can be frozen for up to three months, and is useful when you need to have someone bottle feed your baby.

growth spurts

If your baby is unusually niggly during the day for a few days and you have ruled out illness, she may be having a growth spurt. Growth spurts have a specific purpose. They are nature's way of ensuring that your milk supply adjusts to your growing baby's nutritional demands. Your baby will become unsettled and demand to be fed more frequently than before. You should respond by feeding your baby whenever she seems hungry, and ensure that you drink plenty of fluids and increase your protein and carbohydrate intake. Within a day or so, your milk supply will adjust to the new demand by increasing supply and she will be more settled again.

A growth spurt generally lasts 24 to 48 hours. Once your supply has increased, your baby may have some deep sleeps that last a little longer than usual and will revert to three- to four-hourly feeds. Once your baby is over the growth spurt, stretch her feeds as close to three hours apart as you can by encouraging non-nutritive sucking (either hand-to-mouth or a dummy if she is unsettled), and by swaddling her in a cotton blanket, or gently rocking her between feeds.

"jungle juice" recipe

Mix together the following ingredients:
- 50ml (1¾ fl oz) blackthorn berry tonic (from www.weleda.co.uk)
- 1l (1¾ pints) apple or grape juice
- 2l (3½ pints) of water
- 1 sachet fruit-flavoured rehydration solution or 250ml (9 fl oz) rehydration liquid
- 1 dissolvable vitamin tablet, such as Berocca or Redoxon
- A few drops of the Bach Flower Remedy "Bach Rescue Nights"

Keep the mixture in the fridge and drink throughout the day. It should last for two to three days if kept refrigerated.

Q&A breastfeeding not coming easily

I have been breastfeeding for three weeks and really thought I would have got the hang of it by now. No one told me it would be this hard. It is painful to feed my baby and she feeds every two hours. My breasts feel full in the morning but not during the rest of the day. I am tempted to throw in the towel and give her a bottle. Help!

If you are really struggling with breastfeeding, for whatever reason (for example, cracked nipples causing excruciating pain, anxiety about your milk supply, previous breast surgery, or just plain dislike of the whole experience) and you have an unsettled, unhappy baby, it is understandable that you may begin to feel a sense of dread as each feed draws near. It is very easy to begin to doubt your parenting abilities. Many women battle for the first few weeks – if breastfeeding is important to you, you may succeed with some perseverance. Remember that it can take a few months until it feels natural. All it may require is a quick fix, such as a change in latching positions, using the right nipple cream, or increasing your fluid intake. Seek the advice of a breastfeeding consultant in your area.

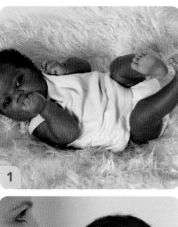

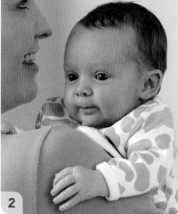

baby's emerging skills

❶ At four weeks, your baby will be less curled up than at birth, as he starts to unflex and stretch his limbs.

❷ As her neck muscles grow stronger, you will notice that your baby starts to hold her head up when at your shoulder.

getting to know your baby

As each week goes by, your baby will appear less floppy, less curled up, and more alert. She is now interested in the world and is learning from every sensory experience.

reflexes and posture At this stage reflexes still govern your baby's movements, although over the next few weeks they will become more integrated and most of the more primitive ones will disappear. You will notice that she still has her fencing (ATNR) reflex – when her head is turned to one side, she extends her arm on the same side. She will start to catch a glimpse of her hand in this position, but because her arms swipe around so much, she will not be able to remain focused on it for long. Her arms and legs move a lot at this stage, especially the arms, swiping wildly through the air. This makes her feel disconcerted and you can help her to feel more composed by cupping your hands behind her shoulder blades and providing some pressure to bring her hands towards the midline of her body. During this period you'll notice that she clasps her hands much less. Occasionally she will open them. She will not start reaching for objects yet, but will stare intently at them, almost reaching out with her eyes.

During this period your baby needs opportunities to work her back and neck muscles, as she becomes less flexed. If you place her on her tummy she will start to lift her head up from the surface and when held in a sitting position she may hold her head upright for a little while. When you pull your baby into a sitting position from lying on her back, she will start to hold her head in line with her body. By six weeks your baby will have uncurled a lot, have straighter hips and knees, and will be able to hold her head up for a few minutes.

visual development Your baby is working hard at developing her eye muscles. The muscles inside her eyes are responsible for her focus and clearness of vision. She will be practising her focus at different distances. She loves mobiles with contrasting colours because they help her to maintain focus and work those muscles. The muscles surrounding her eyes are responsible for coordinating eye movements. This is essential if she wants to watch a moving object. Your baby enjoys patterns of any kind. She will watch people if they are in her line of vision and even turn her head towards them if she hears a sound.

social awareness Your baby recognizes your face and will stare intently at your facial features. If you stick out your tongue, she may copy you. If you smile, she will try desperately to copy it. Eventually the big milestone that makes all the hard work seem worthwhile will happen around the six-week mark: your baby will start smiling. Some babies start smiling with intention (not just for gas bubbles) even earlier than six weeks. Your baby loves language and responds to your voice. When you speak to her she will hold your gaze for longer and may even try to talk by making little throaty noises.

regulation At this stage your baby can just about maintain her body temperature and heart rate. She cannot regulate her sleep/wake cycles or state (calm-alert/active-alert, and so on) yet and that is why she fusses just before she falls asleep. One of your baby's key tasks at this age is to learn to remain calm when exposed to stimulation.

big grin At around six weeks (occasionally before) you will see something that makes everything worthwhile: your baby's first smile.

target milestones

Your baby's big motor goal at this stage is to strengthen her back and neck muscles. This is vital for head control and body strength, which are important for crawling and, later on, walking. If your baby does not spend time on her tummy in the early days, she will not be comfortable on it later, when she should be developing her crawling skills. On a fine motor level, the goal now is to open her hands and become aware of them. Expect your baby to achieve these milestones by six weeks.

area of development	target milestones
Gross motor	Holding her head up for a few minutes and strengthening her back muscles. Beginning to lose reflexes.
Fine motor	Opening her hands when she is relaxed, though they usually remain clasped.
Hand–eye coordination	Working her eye muscles hard to focus on objects that are further away from and closer to her. Beginning to track an object as it moves from the side of her vision to the midline of her body. Starting to bring her hand to her mouth.
Language	Mimicking facial expressions and tongue gestures.
Social/emotional	Smiling at around six weeks old.
Regulation	Starting to be able to shift from an awake state to a sleep state, but will usually need help to do this.

sensible stimulation: TEAT

Now more than any other time, your baby is at risk of sensory overload. Since she cannot yet control or filter sensory stimulation, she is very dependent on you to ensure she does not become over-stimulated. If your baby is colicky, you will have to be extra-vigilant to calm her world down, as opposed to stimulating her.

communication Talking to your baby, even if she can't respond with words, is great for her developing language skills.

timing

You should try to keep most of each day calming for your baby. She will, however, be very receptive to stimulation and interaction when in the calm-alert state, which will usually be after a meal but not just before a sleep, when she is tired. During this awake period, hang mobiles near her changing mat or massage her (see pp.105–107).

Take walks with her in a sling and talk to her but always watch for signs of over-stimulation, such as averting her gaze or frantic, jerky movement.

It's important now that she is in this receptive state when you try to play with her. Watch for her signals, such as focusing intently on you or smiling or cooing (see also p.38), before engaging with her.

environment

Your baby is still becoming familiar with her world and needs to have a soothing space to retreat to when she is over-stimulated.

visual Remember that your baby is very sensitive to stimuli from all her senses, but in particular to visual input. Use black-out or lined curtains or blinds to keep her sleep space dark, especially for bedtime. When you want to stimulate her, choose black-and-white and geometric patterns, faces, and bright colours. Your baby will be able to focus on these best when they are held 20–25cm (8–10in) from her face.

hearing Your voice really is music to your baby's ears! It has been shown that babies who are spoken to a lot in the early years develop speech

significantly faster than babies whose mums don't speak to them as much. It has also been proven to have a positive effect on IQ. Try singing to her, giving a running commentary on what you are doing, or describing things around her.

touch Apply deep pressure to your baby's back to calm her.

movement Focus on calming movements, such as lifting and swaying her gently.

motor development Provide opportunities for your baby to spend time on her tummy to strengthen her neck muscles. Create a safe place in each room where she can lie on her tummy while you are busy in that room. A soft playmat on the floor is perfect for this.

activities

sleep time

It is important that you keep your baby's sleep space calming and use soothing sensory input to settle her into a drowsy state before bedtime, especially if she fights sleep.

visual Keep your baby's world very muted and calming visually, avoiding bright lights or jarring colours around sleep time. A dimmer switch and black-out lining help for night and daytime sleeps respectively.

hearing A rhythm of 72 beats per minute, similar to a mother's heartbeat, has positive effects on sleep. Hold your baby on your left side against your heart and she will settle if fussy prior to bedtime. Set a metronome or play a track with a heartbeat to help your baby fall asleep more quickly. Play recordings of white noise – it has been proven to help babies (and in fact people of all ages) to fall asleep with ease.

touch Continue to swaddle your baby at night and for daytime sleeps.

movement A rocking chair or moving cot is a wonderfully soothing sensory input; use it to rock your baby into a drowsy state.

motor development Your baby should not sleep on her tummy, nor be able to roll onto her tummy at night, as this has been linked to SIDS (sudden infant death syndrome). The best position for your baby to sleep in is on her back, with her feet near the foot of her cot. If you place her on her side, use specially made wedges to keep her from rolling onto her tummy. Alternate the side she sleeps on, to give both sides of her body a chance to develop equally.

on the changing mat

When young, some babies cry and struggle when being dressed and undressed for bath time or nappy changes. If your baby fusses at change time, help her to focus on sensory information. This will distract her from the less pleasant experiences of the task at hand.

visual Hang up a black-and-white mobile – for example, made from toy zebras or black-and-white fabric blocks, or draw black designs on a white paper plate. Place the mobile about 20–25cm (8–10in) from your baby's face. Up to four weeks of age, use a long mobile that hangs down to the mat beside your baby's head, not above the mat, since your baby's neck is not strong enough to keep her head in the middle, looking up. It is easier for her to relax her neck to face one side to work on focusing on the mobile. Change the side that the mobile hangs on daily to that each side of her neck gets some work. Move the mobile towards four weeks, when her neck muscles strengthen sufficiently to hold her head straight. Now you can hang the mobile in the middle, above her head.

bath time

This is the beginning of the bedtime routine, so don't over-excite your baby. Rather, play quietly and keep things very calm after her bath.

touch If your baby is very fussy at bath time, swaddle her in a large muslin cloth or thin cotton blanket before putting her in the bath. This will contain her reflexes and the deep pressure will calm her for bath time. Make sure the room is warm so that your baby is comfortable when naked. Massage your baby's arms and legs as you wash her. Hold one leg with your left hand, then gently squeeze and stroke your hand towards her foot. Repeat with your right hand. Alternate hands in this manner as if "milking" the leg. After doing this a couple of times, move on to the other leg. Do the same with her arms. After the bath, dry your baby with a warm towel, applying deep pressure. Try a towel with a hood – it makes babies feel cosy.

activities continued ...

visual Holding your baby in a baby bath puts you in an excellent position to make eye contact with her. Look at her and talk to her, but watch for the cues indicating that she's had enough.

hearing Play soft music to your baby, especially after her bath or during massage time.

motor development Encourage your baby to kick around in the bath, stretching out her little legs.

movement Some babies cry at bath time because they don't enjoy being tipped backwards to be washed. If yours does this, try an upright bucket-shaped bath (see Resources, p.215); you can submerge your baby without tipping her backwards. Bucket baths also use less water and space than normal baby baths.

awake time

Although your baby is more wakeful, she will probably only maintain the calm-alert state for a maximum of 15 minutes at a stretch. Stimulate her during this time, but watch for her signals that say she needs a break.

visual Make eye contact when your baby is awake or initiates eye contact, but watch her – when she looks away it is a sign that she is composing herself. Use a brightly coloured picture, book or toy to encourage her to focus and maintain visual attention. If you move the toy slowly within her line of vision, she will start to follow it with her eyes.

hearing Talk to your baby as she lies on your lap. As she learns to turn her head to look at you she will strengthen her neck muscles and show off her hearing and visual skills. Sing lullabies and laugh with her.

touch Calming baby massage is a wonderful way to develop your baby's body awareness and to bond with her. Try massaging her after the morning feed, when she is content and in the calm-alert state (see p.31). For baby massage techniques, see pp.105–107.

movement Moving in space is important for the development of your baby's motor milestones. As her brain registers movement, her muscle tone builds up and her balance begins to develop. This helps create body awareness, as she finds out how her body moves through space. To stimulate this sense during playtime, sway and turn around slowly while holding her. Rhythmical linear movement (rocking from side to side or back to front) is calming. If your baby is awake but a little fractious because of visual stimulation, change the sense you are stimulating and rock her. Wear your baby in a sling or carrier every day. Go for a walk with her awake so that she can see out and interact along the way.

motor development When your baby is content, well fed, and after a sleep, especially in the early morning, let her lie on her tummy to help

strengthen the neck. If your baby falls asleep in this position, make sure you turn her – she should not sleep on her tummy. Help your baby if initially she is reluctant to lie on her tummy by placing a rolled-up towel under her chest so that she can lift her head to look at you or a toy. Place your baby on her tummy on your chest. Looking at your face will provide motivation and encourage her to lift her head. Begin the exercise by propping yourself up a bit on pillows so that she doesn't have to battle the pull of gravity so much. Progress to lying flatter so that she has to work harder. Give your baby something interesting to look at when she is playing on her tummy to encourage her to lift her head, such as a brightly coloured toy, picture of a face, your face, or a mirror to see herself. During a massage (see p.105) spend a bit of time working on her hands, opening the fingers and palms. Play finger and hand games with rhymes, so that your baby gains awareness of her hands.

travelling time

During these weeks you will become more confident about taking your baby on outings. Keep her settled when out by watching her signals.

visual Continue to cover the front of the pram or car seat with a blanket to keep bright lights and excessive visual stimulation to a minimum. In a pram that can face forwards or towards you, make use of this option so that you can interact with your baby and she can see your face.

touch Research has shown that babies who are carried in a sling or baby carrier are calmer than those left in a car seat, pram, or cot. This

is due to both the deep pressure and movement. Of course, your baby has to go in her car seat when travelling in the car, but make sure you take her out when you reach your destination.

feed time

While your focus at feed times is nutrition, there are simple things you can do to enhance your baby's development while she feeds.

visual Tie a red, white or pink ribbon and attach it to your bra strap. This not only helps you to remember which side to feed from next if you're breastfeeding, it also gives your baby something to focus on while feeding.

hearing Talk to your baby or read to her so that she becomes familiar with language and changes in the tone of your voice. Speak to her in parentese (the sing-song, higher-pitched tone that mothers commonly use with their babies) since babies respond to this with more interest. If your baby becomes unsettled or stops feeding, this may indicate that she needs quiet in order to coordinate sucking, swallowing, and breathing.

touch Encourage your baby to open her fists against your breast so she can feel your skin as she feeds. This helps her to feel close to you.

toys and tools

At this age, your baby loves playing with you best, but you can invest in some interesting, brightly coloured toys or even make some of your own.

visual A hanging mirror is a wonderful toy; hang it above your baby to reflect light and dark as it swings. A commercially bought baby mirror is the wisest choice, since it's been manufactured to be safe for your baby and will not easily break. If you use your own mirror, make sure it is safe and shatter-proof. Buy or make a black-and-white mobile to hang over the changing mat. Don't put it over the cot – that is a sleep area, not a place to play. Make face cards by using the congratulations cards you received, or cutting out faces from a magazine and sticking them on card. Attach these cards to the head rest in front of your baby's car seat or place them next to her when she's lying down.

hearing Buy or make a rattle for your baby to listen to and turn towards (she won't be able to hold it yet). CDs of calming music or intrauterine sounds are also good.

touch Use your hands to touch your baby – her sense of touch will thrive if you massage her regularly at this stage. See chapter 8 (p.105) for massage techniques.

Make a texture mat by sewing various textured fabrics together. Try felt, fake fur, corduroy, denim, silk and cotton, and sew on a few buttons (very securely). Lie your baby on the mat and allow her to explore the different textures.

chapter 10

your baby at six weeks to four months

At last you've reached the magical six-week mark. This is a significant milestone for so many reasons: you are reasonably recovered from the birth and your breast milk supply is becoming well-established; your baby is smiling and becoming more predictable – you are starting to get the hang of this mothering business. This stage is a turning point for most mums. You will of course have moments when the realization that you are expected to keep this up 24 hours a day for the foreseeable future is a little overwhelming, but your baby suddenly becomes so cute that all the exhaustion and emotional flux of the past two months seems worthwhile.

baby-centric routine

● Try to limit your baby's awake time to 60 to 80 minutes and plan this time for feeding, nappy changing, outings and stimulation.
● Your baby probably will be sleeping for a large part of his day – 18 to 19 hours in a 24-hour cycle.
● Expect to feed your baby every three to four hours during the day.
● A growth spurt at about six weeks of age is common. You will need to feed more frequently over about 24 hours.
● One of the night feeds (usually the 10pm to 11pm feed) may fall away during this time and your baby should now sleep for a six- to seven-hour stretch before waking for a feed between 1am and 2am.

a day in the life of your baby

Although each day is different, by the end of this period you can expect a feeding and sleeping pattern to be emerging. Your baby is ready to lead you into a baby-centric routine. As you will still be feeding your baby an exclusive milk diet, you will need to be flexible. For instance, your feeds may change in length and frequency while your baby has growth spurts and he will have days, perhaps during hot weather, when he needs more milk for rehydration.

mum sense: a learning curve

On every level, the first three months are a period of immense change. Your body has been adjusting rapidly – focused not only on producing milk and adjusting to new levels of hormones, but also recovering after a nine-month assault to your person. During pregnancy, your body changes slowly over 40 weeks, but the recovery is swift – it only takes around six weeks for it to revert to close to how it was pre-pregnancy. As a consequence, you may have been experiencing night sweats, significant bleeding, and contractions of the uterus. Of course, looking at your body, you are probably hoping that this is not all the recovery you will experience. Your tummy is likely to still look like a lumpy pillow and it will take a good part of the first year for it to return to normal, and even then, it may never really be the same.

If your baby has been colicky, you may really be struggling emotionally with where exactly you are going wrong. Remember that every baby is different and that a colicky baby is not an indication of any short-comings as a mother. Caring for an unsettled baby who does not sleep much puts huge strain on you and your partner. Your relationship and the way you support each other may require a vast amount of growth and adjustment as well.

Over the past month or two you have learnt how to fold a soiled nappy so that the contents don't fall out, how to feed your baby, and how to get by on very little sleep! Now comes the next step: guiding your baby towards a flexible routine that suits you both.

establishing a flexible routine

Your baby is ready for a pattern to his day, so now is a good time to start establishing a flexible routine. If you start with a sleep routine, you will find that a daily system, including feeds and play time, will follow automatically. There are three key secrets to setting up a successful baby-centric sleep routine:

1 **watch your baby's awake times** After after an hour of awake time take your baby to his sleep space and settle him to sleep.

2 **observe your baby's signals** When your baby gets tired, he will signal this fatigue – he will probably rub his eyes or ears, or suck his hands (see also pp.52–53 for common signs of tiredness).

3 **recognize your baby's temperament** Your baby is an individual, so try to establish a routine in line with his sensory personality (see pp.14–15).
- A sensitive baby may need to be helped to sleep using a calming strategy, such as patting or rocking, or he may prefer less sensory input. Do not prolong his awake time as he will become over-stimulated easily.
- The social butterfly may not give clear signals of tiredness but needs his sleep as much as any other baby. Make sure that he is not over-stimulated before his sleep times.
- A settled baby can cope with longer periods of stimulation and you may find that he settles to sleep even if you stretch his awake time. Settled babies give clear signals, making it easy to establish a routine.
- The slow-to-warm-up baby loves a routine and will give clear signals when he needs a sleep; he settles best in his own sleep space.

settling into a routine

You might be struggling to get your baby into a daytime routine, but don't worry, there are ways to encourage this. Above all, remember that your baby is still very young. At this age, comforting him and meeting his needs for food and sleep is more important than sticking to a strict routine. Babies need lots of touch and movement, which is why your baby loves to be in your arms.

The first secret is not to focus on a time-based routine – don't try to rigidly put your baby to sleep or feed him at the same time each day. Nor should you strictly follow feed/wake/sleep or wake/feed/sleep regimes. Rather, watch when he feeds and how long he is awake (his awake time, see p.51). At this age, he needs to feed every three to four hours during the day and can only manage to be awake for one-and-a-half hours at most before needing to go back to sleep. So, at one hour and 15 minutes after his last sleep, take him to his cot, rock him gently into a drowsy state and put him down for a sleep. You will find sometimes your baby feeds before a sleep and at other times when he wakes up – this is normal. If your baby just catnaps and wakes after 20 minutes, try swaddling him for his sleeps and shushing him back to sleep. Don't leave him to cry. If he won't go back to sleep, get him up again, but check when his next sleep time is due by monitoring the amount of time he stays awake.

Q&A
self-soothing difficulties

My baby tries to suck on his hands but he seems to "lose" them and become unsettled. How do I encourage self-soothing?

Many babies younger than three months old struggle to keep their hands in their mouths for long enough to soothe themselves due to primitive reflexes that move the hands away from the mouth (the fencing and moro or startle reflexes, see p.100). By the time he is 12–14 weeks, your baby will have more control of his arms, and will be able to keep his hands close to his mouth. This is when he will start to derive some pleasure from sucking on his hands. Until he can keep his hands successfully in his mouth, swaddle him with his hands close to his face so he can easily suck his hands or thumb, or offer him a dummy to keep him calm. It does not matter what your baby sucks on to soothe himself, as long as he has something.

your baby at six weeks to four months

131

sense-able secret
Even though each month you will have a baby-centric routine to guide you, don't feel discouraged or negative if your baby does things differently. Remember that all babies are individuals.

rule out the basics
Address the physical causes of discomfort as the first step to manage crying. See p.112 for more about managing the symptoms.

check for these possibilities:
- Hunger
- Wrong formula
- Lactose intolerance
- Constipation
- Reflux
- Allergies
- Disruption of intestinal flora
- Illness
- Environmental discomfort

baby sense: the colic cycle

If your baby has unexplained bouts of crying every evening he probably has colic (see p.112). If your baby is settled and has not developed colic at this point, he is unlikely to start now. You may be fortunate enough to have a settled baby who will probably remain calm and content. Or perhaps you managed your social butterfly or your slow-to-warm-up baby well (by giving them regular sleeps and sensory "down time") and in this way averted colic. But if your baby is more sensitive or you are having a hard time getting him to sleep well during the day, colic and unsettledness may still be part of your life until around 12 weeks. If your baby remains restless and unsettled, and is generally unhappy when awake, it is worth ruling out the basics once more (see box, left). Once you have done this, you may discover that his crying has its root in his sensory world: he is probably overtired or over-stimulated or both and has reached the end of his tether by the evening.

short circuit the colic cycle

To short circuit colicky crying in the evening, it is important to establish a routine before bedtime: wake, bath, feed, and then sleep.

❶ **Last sleep** After the last afternoon sleep, watch the time your baby spends awake carefully – limit it to 60 to 80 minutes. For example, if your baby wakes at 5pm, be sure to aim for a bedtime of 6pm to 6.30pm.

❷ **Bath** Half an hour before bedtime, give your baby a bath, followed by a massage. But if your baby is frequently colicky in the evening, it may be worth bathing him in the morning because the stimulation of an evening bath can be too much for him.

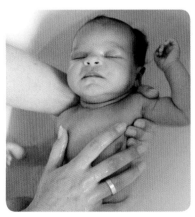

bath Give your baby a bath, followed by a massage, before his night-time sleep as part of his bedtime routine.

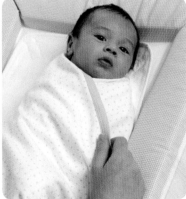

swaddle After his bath, swaddle your baby, as this will help him to feel calm in preparation for sleep.

3 Feed Dress your baby in his sleep space and swaddle him for the last feed of the day. Feed him in a darkened room with few distractions. Play a white noise CD to recreate the soothing sound of the womb. Then place him in his cot to drift off to sleep while still drowsy.

sensory calming strategies If your baby begins to cry, follow these four steps. These will help you to reduce the crying and short circuit colic:

step one

● **Swaddle and burp** Swaddle your baby for the last feed of the day. Once the feed is finished, burp your baby for five minutes only. Pursuing burps in the evening makes colic worse by extending the period of handling. If no burp comes up within five minutes, do not pursue it, and instead put your drowsy baby down to sleep in his cot.

● **Deep pressure** If your baby begins to squirm and fuss in his cot, place your hand firmly on him as he lies in the cot and let him squirm, with you there soothing him. Do this until he falls asleep or for five minutes.

● **Pat and shshsh** If your baby begins to cry, pat him and say "Shshsh", in an attempt to soothe him while he is swaddled in his cot. Many babies will fall asleep within five minutes. If he is crying after five minutes, move to step two.

step two

● **Swaddle and burp** If he is still crying, lift your baby out of his cot and burp him for five minutes. Re-swaddle him if the cloth has become loose.

● **Rock and deep pressure** After he burps or after five minutes, rock him until he is drowsy. Put him down in his cot and place your hand on him, applying deep pressure. Let him squirm with you there soothing him in his cot – do this until he falls asleep or for five minutes.

● **Pat and shshsh** If your baby begins to cry, pat him and say "Shshsh" while he is swaddled in his cot. Do this until he falls asleep or for five minutes. If he is still crying after five minutes, move to step three.

step three

● **Feed** Lift your baby, and offer him a top-up feed (this is called cluster feeding, see p.138, and is appropriate in the evening). Many babies settle well after this second feed.

● **Swaddle and burp** Once fed, swaddle your baby and burp him for five minutes, then rock him until he is drowsy and put him down in his cot.

● **Deep pressure** If he begins to squirm and fuss, place your hand on him, applying deep pressure while he squirms with you there soothing him in his cot – do this until he falls asleep or for five minutes.

short circuiting colic

1 Swaddle and burp: once the evening feed is finished, burp your swaddled baby for five minutes only.

2 Put him in his cot and place your hand on him, applying deep pressure. Let him squirm in his cot while you soothe him.

3 If your baby begins to cry, pat him and say "Shshsh" while he is swaddled in his cot for five minutes.

soothe baby in sling Place him in a sling and rock him until he falls asleep. He will be calmed by the warmth and motion of your body.

the dummy debate

A dilemma that many new parents face is whether to offer their baby a dummy. It is true that sucking really helps to calm young babies. Some learn to suck on their hands from early on. Encourage this, as being able to calm himself is the first very clever, independent skill your baby learns. Your life will be easier if your baby can calm himself, especially at sleep time. However, many babies under three months do not do this efficiently, and need your assistance. Help your baby to find his hands. If this is not enough (a common problem) then try a dummy. The first three months of your baby's life are a period of huge adjustment. Try not to set yourself too many unrealistic goals – such as getting through the crying with no dummy.

● **Pat and shshsh** If your baby begins to cry, pat him and say "Shshsh" in an attempt to soothe him while he is swaddled in his cot for five minutes. If he is still crying after five minutes, move to step four.

step four
● **Carry and soothe** If your baby is crying, lift him, swaddle him and place him in a sling or baby carrier and rock and bop him until he falls asleep, protected from the stimulation of the world against your body. Do not worry about spoiling your baby. Some babies need a little extra sensory soothing, particularly those who are colicky in the evening.
● **Back in the cot** Once your baby is asleep, settle him in his cot. If he begins to stir as you take him from the sling to his cot, place your hand on him, applying deep pressure and let him squirm, but with you there soothing him in his cot – do this until he falls asleep.

other options for coping with colic
By following a sensible daytime sleep routine and using sensory principles for calming your baby and watching for over-stimulation, you should avert colic altogether. If you find your baby is still unsettled, rule out basic needs (see pp.112–13) and use the step-by-step approach when the crying starts (see p.133). You may be advised to try other methods which in certain cases can make a difference:

chiropractic A chiropractor gently manipulates your baby's spine to release tightness in muscles and reduce inflammation in the joints, which is said to reduce mucus production in the digestive system. Reducing this inflammation helps with bloating, cramps, and constipation.

homeopathy Homeopathy is a form of alternative medicine that has few side effects. Speak to a registered homeopath or homeopathic pharmacy if you would like to try this.

traditional remedies Old wives' tales (for example, a warm pad placed over the tummy) and herbal remedies (certain herbal teas) are often recommended. Remember that all these have potentially powerful effects on your baby's system and do check the effects of any remedy (even if it is said to be "natural") with your doctor, health visitor, or a pharmacist before giving it to your baby.

medical approach There are numerous medicines available on prescription from a doctor or over the counter at a pharmacy. Most have a sedative effect and should be used with extreme caution; only give them to your baby with the guidance of your health visitor or doctor.

helping your baby sleep

Some semblance of a daytime-sleep pattern starts to emerge during these weeks as your baby's sleep/wake cycles begin to be more regular. If you give your baby the opportunity to soothe himself, he will do so, and may put himself to sleep and resettle himself in the night, needing less sensory support from you, such as being rocked back to sleep.

awake time

Your baby will probably need three naps a day: usually one long one and two shorter ones, but if all his naps are short, he will need four. At this stage, your baby will manage to be awake for an hour to an hour and a half between naps. After about an hour, watch for his sleepy signals, such as yawning and rubbing his ears (see pp.52–53) and take him to his sleeping space and settle him or feed him if it is time for a feed.

the late afternoon sleep This sleep can be tricky. It's best to aim for a bedtime of between 6pm and 7pm. Treat the last daytime sleep as follows:
● For sleeps before 4.30pm, let your baby sleep for one sleep cycle of 45 minutes (see p.30). If he sleeps for longer, wake him by 5.15pm so that he will settle easily at bedtime.
● If the sleep is due after 4.30pm, let your baby have only a catnap – in other words wake him once 15 to 30 minutes have passed or by 5.15pm, so that he does not have difficulty falling asleep in the evening.
● If the last daytime sleep is due anytime after 5.30pm, just put him down for the night with an early bedtime, if he is exhausted. An appropriate bedtime for babies of this age is any time from 5.30pm to 7pm.

sleep space

Until now you may have been flexible about where your baby sleeps and he would have slept just as well out and about as in a special sleeping space. But everything changes once your baby becomes more alert – now he needs a consistent place for day- and night-time sleeps. Three factors make this important at this stage:

age Until three or four months of age, your baby will not develop sleep expectations, but by the time he is four months old, he will start to expect to be put in the same space and have the same routine for sleep. You may have loved having your newborn close to you as he sleeps and may continue to do so. But, if you are finding that you no longer sleep well with him next to you, or are planning to put him in his own cot or

sleep: what to expect at this stage

● At this age your baby can really only manage to be awake for 60 to 80 minutes. If you act on his sleepy signals (see pp.52–53) and start a sleep routine 60 minutes after his last nap, you will find a pattern of daytime sleeps starts to emerge.
● Depending on the length of his sleeps, your baby will have around three or four naps during the day.
● As soon as you notice a pattern emerging with your baby's nap times, encourage this by being consistent (putting him to sleep in the same place, at the same time) and repeating it each day.
● Aim to have your baby in bed by 7pm at the latest. If you leave him to wake on his own, he may sleep for between six to eight hours without waking for a feed (at around 1am to 3am).
● As impossible as it seems, try to have a lie down when your baby is sleeping during at least one of his daytime naps.

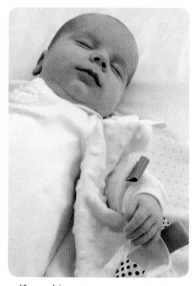

self-soothing Encourage your baby to adopt a comfort object, such as a small blanket or stuffed animal, which will help him to soothe himself.

room for sleep eventually, you should think seriously about moving him before he develops these sleep expectations. It will be much harder to move him into his own sleep space when he is older.

consistency If you have let your baby sleep wherever you happen to be and have not always put him down in the same place for his naps, now is the time to do so, because settling him into a consistent sleep space is vital for establishing a sleep routine. Do not fall into the habit of letting your baby sleep anywhere or at any time. It is understandable that on some days you will be very busy and your baby won't be at home for his daytime sleeps. But on these days, try to ensure that he goes to bed in his sleep space for at least one daytime sleep and, of course, goes to bed in the same space every night.

calming Try to make sure that the environment in which your baby sleeps is soothing, so that he is not over-stimulated. Dim the lights and offer him a sleep object, such as a soft blanket or small teddy, which he can use to soothe himself when he wakes in the night.

time for your baby's own sleep space?

Although guidelines in the UK (from The Foundation for the Study of Infant Deaths (FSID) and the Department of Health) state that the safest place for your baby to sleep is in a cot in your room for the first six months, there is no clear-cut recommendation on when to move your baby into his own cot, out of your bed or bedroom. Think of these three basic principles as a rule of thumb:
● Go by your gut feeling and personal circumstances.
● It is easier to move a baby before three or four months since sleep expectations arise at this age. The older he gets, the more likely it is that habits will form, because he will find the familiarity comforting. This makes the transition to his sleep space harder, but not impossible.
● It is difficult to move a toddler, especially prior to the birth of a sibling, so make the decision well before this time.

still unsure? Look for these indications that it is time to consider moving your baby into his own cot or room:
● You have a space in your home for your baby to sleep in.
● Your baby is disturbing either your or your partner's sleep and you are getting less rather than more sleep.
● Sleep deprivation is causing you to feel exhausted during the day and is affecting your emotional relationship with your baby. Having an emotionally available parent is more beneficial than co-sleeping. It is important that you are rested enough to be able to respond to your baby.

- You have a sensitive baby, who is disturbed by your movements and sounds at night and actually sleeps worse when co-sleeping. Sensitive babies often sleep better in their own rooms.
- You and your partner are no longer in agreement about your baby sleeping with you (whether in your bed or your room). Sharing your bedroom with a baby or toddler is something you need to agree on.
- He is only feeding once at night. After four months of age, nutritional needs during the night decrease significantly, so as long as he is well and healthy, this is a good time to move your baby to his own sleep space.
- You are planning to have another baby. It is unsafe to have your toddler and a newborn sleeping in your bed. It is also unfair to expect your toddler to move to his own room just days before the arrival of a new baby. So move your toddler long before you contemplate having a new baby in the bed with you.

further sleep tips

Regular naps are critical at this age; they not only prevent over-stimulation, making your baby happier and more alert while awake, but also help him to sleep well at night.

For daytime sleeps take your baby to his sleep space 10 minutes before you expect him to be asleep. Swaddle him and hold him (or feed him if a feed is due), while gently swaying from side to side – to help him unwind from the stimulation of the previous couple of hours. This time of unwinding prior to naptime will ensure that he is not overtired or over-stimulated by the time he goes down for his sleep. Once he is calm and drowsy, put him down "happily awake".

Your baby's sleep cycle is 45 minutes long, but by six months old, he will begin to link sleep cycles and sleep for longer than 45 minutes at one or more of his naps (see box, right). Many babies do not link sleep cycles yet and so each nap may only be 45 minutes long. This is quite normal, so don't worry.

At this stage your baby is likely to wake for one night feed. If he wakes more often, try not to respond instantly to every small noise or squeak you hear from him (leave him for a few minutes, as long as he is not crying in distress). If you allow him the opportunity to resettle himself at these times, he will soon learn to calm himself and put himself back to sleep during the night. If your baby cries, respond to him but keep the night feed as quiet as possible. By this age your baby may no longer be soiling every nappy. If he has only passed urine, do not change his nappy at night, which will wake him fully. However, if you are using reusable nappies, you may need to change them at night to prevent nappy rash. You might consider using disposables at night, which effectively wick away moisture from the skin.

linking sleep cycles

To encourage your baby to link sleep cycles to lengthen his day and night sleeps when a feed is not due, try these tips:

- Listen for a few minutes when your baby wakes to see if he resettles himself with self-soothing measures, such as sucking his thumb or hands or bringing his hands together.
- If he does not succeed and remains restless, respond by quietly and calmly re-swaddling him, encouraging him to put his hands to his mouth or giving him a dummy or sleep object and patting him back to sleep.
- Keep trying for about two to three minutes, but if it does not work during the day, accept that the sleep is over and get him up. Watch the period of awake time to work out when his next sleep is due. At night, feed him if more than three hours have passed, then settle him back to sleep.
- If your baby woke after a short sleep and seems irritable with fatigue, you might find that his next period of awake time is slightly shorter than usual. Be guided by his signals and put him back to sleep when he is ready.

feeding: what to expect at this stage

- Feed your baby at least every four hours during the day. It's best not to let him sleep for longer than this without a feed.
- Expect a growth spurt at six weeks and again at four months. Feed your baby more frequently during growth spurts; then your milk supply will increase to meet the demand.
- If you are bottle feeding, your baby will start to feed less often and will drink larger volumes – up to 200ml (7fl oz) per feed – four to five times in 24 hours.
- Provided that your baby is gaining weight, stretch the interval between feeds to as close to three hours as you can by encouraging your baby to suck on his hands or on a dummy (non-nutritive sucking) and by gently rocking him. Swaddle him in a cotton blanket or place him in a baby sling or carrier if he won't settle.
- Your breastfed baby may need cluster feeds (see right) in the early evening. If he is unsettled when you put him down, try a top-up feed of breast milk or a bottle of expressed breast milk.
- Most babies drop one of these night feeds at this stage, requiring only one or two feeds between bedtime and morning.
- Milk provides all the nutrition your baby needs at this stage. Do not consider solids yet, because your baby's digestive system is not ready for them.

the babysense secret

138

feeding your baby

By the time your baby is six weeks old, your milk supply will be well-established. If you have been successful with breastfeeding thus far, you will probably continue to feed for a while. If your choice has been to move your baby across to formula feeds or a combination of breast and bottle, you have no doubt made the right choice after a lot of consideration and should feel comfortable with this decision. Your baby will not be ready for solids for a while yet and so your focus at this stage should still be on getting his milk feeds right.

breastfeeding

By now, you are becoming proficient at breastfeeding and a skill that was foreign to you three months ago is coming more easily. All the signals that you relied on to know you had milk, such as the sensations of let-down and hard, tender breasts, may decrease now and combined with the extra fussiness your baby may display while having a growth spurt, may lead you to believe you have insufficient milk for your baby. The reason these signs of fullness disappear is that your breast tissue is becoming very efficient at producing milk on demand. If you do not feel full before a feed, do not wonder if you are still producing enough milk. Be happy that your breasts have become so efficient at predicting and producing just what your baby needs, when he needs it.

At this age many babies start to pull off the breast during a feed to look around. This is not because you are not producing enough milk or necessarily because your baby is full. It can simply be because he has discovered how interesting the world is. Covering your baby and your breast with a breastfeeding shawl or simply a muslin or blanket may be enough to shield him from the world for the feed. Alternatively, give him time and space to look around and then resume feeding.

Since breasts are not calibrated and you cannot tell how much your baby is drinking, you need to rely on other signs that he is getting enough milk. If your baby seems unsettled in the evenings and wakes frequently before midnight, you could try to cluster feed (give him feeds frequently in the period between bath time and bedtime) or offer him a top-up bottle of expressed breast milk when you put him down in the evening. If he wakes within an hour of going to sleep at night, offer him another feed to see if he settles. Keep this interaction very calm: don't change his nappy (unless it is really necessary) or stimulate him, and limit burping to five minutes (see p.133). He should settle quickly if he needs the feed. If he doesn't settle and appears to be more restless, you may have over-fed him, causing him to feel uncomfortable. With a little trial and error you will soon determine whether your baby is more settled with a cluster feed.

growth spurts and milk supply

Provided your baby is lasting three to four hours between feeds during the day, and has a long six- to seven-hour stretch of sleep at night, is happy and content, gaining weight, and having six wet nappies a day, there is no reason to worry about your milk supply.

If your baby becomes unsettled or demands more frequent feeds, he may be having a growth spurt. Expect growth spurts at around six weeks of age, and again at around four months of age, when you will have to feed more frequently for 24 to 48 hours. Growth spurts are nature's way of ensuring that your milk supply increases to meet your growing baby's nutritional needs.

complementary or supplementary feeds

If you are keen to keep breastfeeding for a good length of time, there is no need to supplement your baby's diet by offering a bottle of formula at this stage. Rather, breastfeed your baby more frequently if he appears to be unsettled and needing more milk. If you have been advised by your doctor or health visitor that your baby needs to have additional milk, or you are returning to work, there are two options:

● **Supplementary feeding** This means giving a bottle of milk immediately after your baby has finished a breastfeed. This is also often called "top-up" feeding. You can top up with expressed breast milk or formula milk. Top-up feeds should not be necessary if your baby is gaining weight and is generally happy and content between feeds.

● **Complementary feeding** This is the term for giving a bottle as a full feed on its own, but when breastfeeding is the norm at other feeds. This might be the case if you are returning to work or are unable to breastfeed your baby for a certain feed.

formula feeding

If you choose to bottle feed, it is important to make the right choice of formula. Be guided by your health visitor, bearing in mind these few simple guidelines, which can save a great deal of time and anxiety:

● If you or your baby's father suffer from allergies, it may be wise to start on a hypo-allergenic formula. If there is no history of allergies in your family, choose any of the cow's milk-based starter formulas. These are especially formulated for a baby under six months of age.

● If your baby was big at birth and is hungry, he may need a more satisfying feed, such as one that contains more casein, so-called "hungry-baby formula". (Casein is the main protein present in milk.)

● If your baby is suffering from reflux (see p.141), the formula of choice may be one that is specifically "anti-reflux". If this is the case, discuss the appropriate choice of formula with your doctor.

increasing milk supply

Many mums begin to think their milk supply is dwindling at around four months due to increased demand from their baby. The easiest way to increase your milk supply is to feed more frequently when your baby indicates he is hungry. If he remains hungry and unsettled for longer than the usual growth spurt (24 to 48 hours), there may be a problem with your milk supply. If you plan to continue breastfeeding, it is worth taking a bit of time to increase your milk supply with the following tips:

● Drink plenty of extra fluids, such as water, Redbush tea (rooibos) or diluted fruit juice.

● Avoid caffeine and alcohol altogether – not only are they passed to your baby in your milk, they are also dehydrating and will affect your milk supply.

● Remember to eat. As life gets busy again you may forget about what you are eating. Make sure you eat frequent regular meals containing protein, fats and carbohydrates, as well as plenty of vitamins and minerals.

● Try to sleep as much as possible when your baby sleeps. Sleep and rest assist in the production of breast milk.

● Ask your health visitor about vitamin supplements for yourself.

● Mix up some "jungle juice" (see recipe, p.121) and drink it throughout the day.

● Don't over-schedule your life and get too busy; your milk supply may suffer on the days when you take on too much.

feeling close Feeding your baby is a sensory experience, whichever method you choose. If you bottle feed, try to imitate the sensory experience of breastfeeding, to provide your baby with the same closeness.

- Prepare and use the formula as directed by your health visitor. Using formula incorrectly may be dangerous to your baby's health.
- Always sterilize all feeding equipment thoroughly.
- Don't substitute cow's milk. It is unsuitable for babies under one year of age since it contains too little iron and vitamins A, C and D, and is difficult to digest. It is also too high in protein and sodium.
- Try a formula for at least 48 hours before swapping to another formula and beware of listening to too much conflicting advice from friends or family over which formula to choose.
- Give your bottle-fed baby a similar sensory experience to breastfeeding (holding him in your arms so he can feel your warmth and skin).
- If you can hear your baby gulping his milk, he is likely to be drinking too fast and may end up with excess gas. Adjust the flow by selecting a smaller teat and adjusting the angle of the bottle. You will soon find out whether he likes to drink rapidly, or if he prefers to take his time.

the sensory experience of bottle feeding

The sensory experiences a baby is exposed to during breastfeeding, such as your smell and the warmth of your body while he is eating (see also p.98) are vital for bonding. If you have chosen to bottle feed, do try to recreate this sensory world by using the following techniques:

- Always hold your baby close while feeding, so that he experiences your touch and other sensory experiences, such as your smell. Hold your baby in your arms to give him a bottle, don't just prop it in his mouth.
- Just as you would move your baby from one breast to the other while breastfeeding, alternate the side he feeds on when you bottle feed – from left to right. This will ensure that your baby receives sensory input equally on both sides of his body.

guilt over bottle feeding Parents find that guilt is ever-present in their lives, but one of the factors that seem to increase it most is the decision not to breastfeed, or to stop breastfeeding because it is simply too painful, or because you feel you are not able to produce enough milk for your baby. If you have battled with breastfeeding and have made the decision to switch to bottle feeding, either with expressed breast milk or formula milk, or if you cannot feed due to anatomical or health reasons, you may be feeling down, and as if a critical piece of mothering is no longer within your reach.

The vital part of being a mum is being emotionally present for your baby – not having the perfect birth or the perfect feeding experience. If you are meeting your baby's emotional needs in ways other than breastfeeding, do not allow guilt, sadness, or anger to be part of your emotional response to this decision.

sense-able secret
If it is not feed time, don't assume your baby is communicating hunger when he niggles or sucks his hands. Consider whether he is over-tired or has had enough stimulation. Read his signals and allow him the opportunity to learn to calm himself.

the **babysense** secret

reflux

If your baby is very unsettled during feeds and is a poor sleeper at this stage, you may want to ask your doctor to rule out gastro-oesophageal reflux (GOR), known as reflux. It is caused by an underdeveloped valve between your baby's stomach and his oesophagus (the pipe that carries food from his mouth to his stomach). This valve will strengthen with age, but until it does the acidic content of his stomach is repeatedly being regurgitated into his oesophagus. This may cause him discomfort, and in some cases excessive posseting of curdled milk or even projectile vomiting. It may even interfere with your baby's ability to feed well, which can have an impact on his growth and development. If you suspect that your baby has reflux, speak to your doctor about medication to neutralize the acid levels in his stomach. Occasionally surgery is required, but fortunately this is uncommon. Generally though, reflux is nothing to worry about, provided your baby is thriving and gaining weight.

raise it up If your baby has reflux, raising the level of his cot mattress with a wedge may help. The upright angle will help prevent the acidic contents of his stomach from being regurgitated.

how to spot reflux This condition can be alleviated somewhat, so look for the common signs. Your baby may have reflux if he:

- Resists lying flat to go to sleep, especially after a feed.
- Is happiest when held upright.
- Swallows and gags very frequently.
- Is a fussy feeder.
- Sleeps better if held upright, or when he lies on his tummy.
- Possets frequently and/or has frequent projectile vomiting.

how to manage Reflux can be tricky to manage while it lasts, but take comfort in the knowledge that it will pass with time. Follow these tips to make this period feel less disrupted:

- Feed your baby in a quiet environment with minimal sensory input. Over-stimulation leads to an increased likelihood of posseting.
- Keep your baby upright after a feed, and handle him gently (avoid vigorous winding).
- Raise your baby's cot mattress with a wedge (see Resources, pp.214–15).
- Feed your baby smaller amounts more frequently.
- Play white noise to help him sleep a little deeper once he is asleep.
- Try using probiotic medication to help your baby's gut process his feeds. Ask your pharmacist for a suitable probiotic medication.
- If you are breastfeeding, cut out dairy in your diet for a week and see if that helps. Try replacing the dairy with nuts and seeds.
- If you are bottle feeding with formula, ask your health visitor about specialized anti-reflux formulas. She might recommend one for you to try, or she may suggest ways to thicken your baby's milk to prevent regurgitation, or she might offer a lactose-free formula.

visual development

Your baby can now follow an object moving in an arc 15cm (6in) from his face and begins to follow you around the room with his eyes. During this period he will suddenly notice his hands. You will find him gazing at them and moving his fingers to see the results. This is the first active step in hand–eye coordination. He begins to explore his hands by putting them in his mouth. Since there are more sensory receptors in your baby's mouth than anywhere else on his body, he will derive great pleasure from sucking his hands and will also learn about the shape and size of his hands – essential for fine motor control later.

getting to know your baby

Your baby's movements become more organized and less random at this stage. His back and tummy muscles strengthen and he starts to explore the world with his eyes and hands. He becomes really smiley and social and starts trying to communicate by making gurgles and squeals.

moving, swiping, and reaching These form part of his developing fine motor skills. At six weeks of age, your baby's movements may appear very disorganized because the security he enjoyed in the curled-up position of the womb has decreased as his neck and back muscles develop and he uncurled. Your baby's primitive reflexes are diminishing since he has less need for them, but he does not yet have control over his movements, which is why his arms swipe aimlessly and his legs kick out a lot. As he approaches four months old, you will notice that your baby's movements become voluntary and he begins to act with intention. He will soon be able to control his arms and swipe at objects, trying to touch or reach out for them. Swiping is important for hand–eye coordination and also helps develop the arm muscles. Your baby may even begin to reach for objects hanging from his play gym if they are near enough. Encourage his attempts even though he will rarely be successful.

head control: get ready to roll The two-month-old baby works very hard to control his head, which is part of his gross motor skills. When lying on his back, he can now hold his head in the midline of his body so he can look at a mobile hung above him. If you give your baby the opportunity to develop his back muscles by lifting his head while lying on his tummy, he will develop strength (extension) down his whole body. Then by three months old he will be able to hold his head up at 45 degrees for a while when placed on his stomach. He will also hold his head erect when sitting on your lap. He will start to work hard on developing the strength of his tummy muscles. It is important that the back and stomach muscles develop in a balanced way because this is essential for rolling over, which will happen around four to six months of age.

smiles and communication Your baby responds to your voice now and makes throaty gurgles. By 12 weeks he will start to coo, squeal, and even babble. He recognizes mum and dad and responds to your attention. Your baby can link sounds with the object that makes them and will look to see where the sound is coming from. By three months, he will recognize a bottle or the position and movements you make before breastfeeding, and will make eager, welcoming movements as he prepares to feed. He also now really enjoys bath time.

target milestones

Your baby is developing his back muscles as well as his tummy muscles in preparation for rolling. Being able to tolerate and explore the world from his tummy equips him to begin crawling later. Critical elements at this stage include becoming visually aware and being able to control where his eyes look, and exploring his body with his hands. Expect these milestones to be achieved by four months.

look and see At this stage, your baby will notice her hands. You may see her gazing intently at them while moving her fingers. This is the first step towards hand–eye coordination.

area of development	target milestones
Gross motor	Lying on his back and starting to lift his knees and feet in the air as he strengthens his tummy muscles, vital for crawling later. Rolling from his back to his side. Holding his head up for a few minutes and resting his weight on his forearms when on his tummy.
Fine motor	Beginning to explore his knees and other body parts with his hands. Bringing his hands to each other in midline (the centre of his body). Keeping his hands in his mouth voluntarily.
Hand–eye coordination	Tracking objects that move across his line of vision with his eyes. Bringing his hands towards his mouth so he can explore them.
Language	Starting to make sounds as he learns to control his larynx to make noises.
Social/emotional	Smiling, becoming more sociable, and associating people with fun and playtime. Beginning to remain calm when faced with higher levels of stimulation.
Regulation	Developing state-regulation, the ability to keep himself calm by soothing himself in the face of high levels of stimulation.

"Your baby becomes really smiley and social and even starts trying to communicate with gurgles and squeals."

sensible stimulation: TEAT

your individual baby

The settled baby and social butterfly thrive when faced with the novelty of a stimulating space. But a sensitive baby is more affected by sensory stimuli, especially things he can see, so be careful not to overdo it. The slow-to-warm up baby may also initially fuss and be overwhelmed with a very busy or new sensory environment.

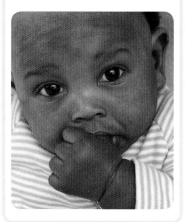

Stimulating your baby is critical to his development, and providing enriched experiences is a big part of parenting. Your baby is still very dependent on you to control when he is stimulated and the amount of stimulation he gets. You can start to create opportunities for stimulation, as outlined in the activities box (see opposite) in his daily routine. But do make sure that he does not become over-stimulated.

Your baby starts to be able to calm himself at this stage; do encourage this. If he is showing signs of soothing himself by sucking his hands or bringing them in to the midline of his body, don't intervene by feeding him (unless it is time for a feed) or popping his dummy into his mouth immediately. Rather, let him explore sucking so that he learns to calm himself independently.

timing

As he grows older, your baby will spend longer periods in the calm-alert state. By now you can expect a good 10 minutes in each period of awake time when your baby will be very receptive to stimulation (calm-alert). A certain time of day will emerge as the one when he enjoys a long period in this state. It is often mid-morning (after his first daytime sleep). This is the time to play with him and give him a new toy or a massage, or to go on a short outing.

environment

Your baby now spends time in a variety of environments and learns from each new space and stimulus.
visual Geometric patterns, bright contrasting colours and faces are still what your baby loves to watch most. They will enhance his development. Nature's mobiles – trees, butterflies, and clouds – make a wonderful sensory experience for your baby. Take him outdoors in a pram or a sling whenever the weather permits.
hearing Your baby loves the sound of human voices, so speak to him as much as you can, using varied tones and interesting facial expressions.

Don't forget to copy your baby's noises and coos, and pause when he is "talking" (cooing or squealing) so he learns that language is a two-way activity – this is the start of speech!
touch Applying deep pressure during massage and stroking his back is calming and at this stage your baby will really benefit from baby massage. Tickle and touch your baby lightly to stimulate him and have fun with him during playtime. Watch for your baby's reaction – sensitive babies tend to be irritated by light and unpredictable touch.

movement Slow rhythmical movements calm your baby – rock and pace with him in a sling before sleep times. Quick, irregular movements make your baby feel alert and should only be used during play. Always watch your baby's reaction and only use the stimulating movements if he enjoys them.
motor development To develop his back and tummy muscles, your baby needs to spend plenty of time on his tummy. Try putting him on a soft blanket on the floor. Get down to his level – lie on the floor with him – to encourage him to lift his head.

activities

sleep time

A quiet, calm sleeping environment is essential if your baby is to develop good sleep patterns.

visual Keep what he can see very calming around sleep time by dimming the lights, drawing the curtains or black-out blinds, and not putting brightly coloured toys in or near the cot.

hearing The soothing sound of lullabies or white noise (see p.26) will calm your baby. Sing quietly to your baby before bedtime as a lovely part of his winding-down routine.

touch Continue to swaddle your baby at night for as long as he likes it. If he seems to be resisting and is unsettled when fully swaddled, try swaddling him under his arms.

motor development If your baby sleeps on his side with wedges (see p.125), alternate the side on which he sleeps, so that each side of his body gets the chance to develop equally.

on the changing mat

This is a good time for visual stimulation, since your baby is lying on his back in a fixed position and is awake, ready to look around.

visual Keep a black-and-white or brightly coloured mobile hanging above the changing mat. Position it directly over your baby's head since he can now keep his head in the midline of his body to look at it. Introduce interest and variety by changing the mobile above the mat. To make a simple mobile, hang a coat hanger over the changing mat and alternate the objects you hang on it each day. Try tinsel, a baby-safe mirror, a red-and-white pom-pom, a string of cotton reels and any other interesting shapes or textures.

hearing Talk to your baby while changing his nappy, so that he learns about language. Hearing your voice will calm him if he does not enjoy the experience or will not keep still.

touch While he is undressed on the changing mat, place your hands on different parts of his body, and name them. For example, when you touch his knees, bring his hands towards them as well, so that he starts to link the names of his body parts with their location.

motor development When you pick up your baby from the changing mat, don't just lift him – make him do some work too. This will develop his stomach muscles. Place your hands on his shoulders and pull him gently into a sitting position so that he must hold his head up, strengthening his neck muscles. This will also help him learn the movement for sitting.

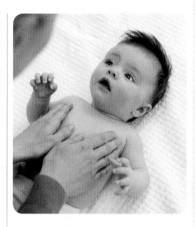

bath time

Don't over-excite your baby at bath time since it marks the start of the bedtime routine. Encourage dad to share in the bath-time activities, but alert him to the fact that this needs to be a calm time.

visual You are your baby's favourite bath toy. Make eye contact with him and show him colourful bath toys.

hearing Nursery rhymes with an element of surprise, such as "Pop goes the weasel" are very popular with babies of this age. Try them out while he enjoys his bath. Watch as your baby learns to anticipate the word or action to come.

touch Use massage and apply deep, still touch as part of your bedtime routine. Massage your baby's limbs and stretch them out before bath time, then massage his tummy lightly in the bath. Fill a sponge with water and squeeze it out over his tummy – this allows him to get used to the different sensations of water.

motor development Encourage your baby to kick and reach for toys or your face while he is in the bath.

activities continued ...

awake time

As your baby spends more time awake, play quietly with him, especially when he is in the calm-alert state. Do watch for signs that he's had enough.

visual Making facial expressions at your baby teaches him about his face and encourages him to mimic your face. This process of copying and planning a skilled movement is the start of motor planning. When your baby is in the calm-alert state, show him a book containing faces to help his eyes focus. Show your baby his hands. These are the first body parts a baby learns he has. Watch with delight as he stares at these appendages in amazement, realizing for the first time that these wiggly things are his! Towards the end of this period (four months), he begins to need more stimulation. Set up a play gym in your living room and put him under it for ten minutes each day. Prop him up on some cushions – this gives him a different view of the world.

hearing Talk to your baby as much as possible while he is awake. He will recognize your voice, and begin to learn about your home language and the norms of interacting. He will smile in response to a friendly tone of voice, so vary your tone when you talk to him.

touch You will eventually notice a time of day when your baby remains in the calm-alert state for a longer stretch. Massage your baby then. Aim to massage him at least twice a week. See p.105 for massage techniques.

movement Gently swing your baby round and up and down. Go at his pace and if he's not enjoying it, wait a few days before trying again.

motor development Continue to place your baby on his tummy each day for as long as he will tolerate it. If at first he doesn't enjoy it, lie him on your tummy while you recline at an angle. Each day lie further back until he's horizontal and really exercising his neck muscles. Alternatively, sit on the floor and support him over your leg or with a rolled blanket or towel under his chest. When he's in the tummy-down position, place toys or a mirror in front of your baby to entice him to reach out from this position. To develop his tummy muscles when he is lying on his back, hang a kick ball with bells near his feet. He'll be rewarded with its movement and sound each time he kicks it, encouraging him to do it again. Give your baby rattles and toys of various textures by placing them into his hands. Although he can't manipulate them yet and will probably drop them very shortly, it

does encourage the development of an active grasp. It also gives him an experience of cause and effect – "If I move my hand, I hear the toy make a noise or see it move." Play with his fingers so that he develops awareness of his hands.

travelling time

As your baby approaches three months, you'll find that he can shut out certain stimuli himself and so you need not regulate his environment as much as before. This means that you can start to socialize and get out much more than before. Use your travel time as a learning environment.

visual When out and about with your baby, continue to cover the front of the pram or pushchair with a blanket to keep bright lights and excessive visual stimulation to a minimum. However, as your baby approaches the three-month mark, you won't need to do this so much, since he is now less bothered by the bright, noisy world around him. Put a mobile or mirror over or inside his pram for him to look at. Give your baby something to look at during car travel when he is in a rear-facing car seat. Attach a mirror or draw a bold face on a paper plate and hang it from the head rest on the back of the seat that he faces. This will distract him if he gets bored or unsettled.

hearing Play a recording of children's singing voices or nursery rhymes when in the car. You will find that your baby loves the music you played frequently during your pregnancy and finds it calming.

movement Carry your baby in a sling or a baby carrier. This way he gets to see the world at your level and you can talk to him about what he sees. He will enjoy the movement of your walking rhythm. If you use a sling, sit him upright so he can see out. If you use a carrier, sit him facing outwards, encouraging him to socialize and take in the world visually.

Some babies have difficulty tolerating the movement of a car and become distressed. If your baby cries in the car seat, try the following:

• Keep a cotton wool swab with lavender essential oil in the car as this scent is soothing.

• Play calming music; lullabies or the soothing music you enjoyed during pregnancy, which is familiar to him.

• Place a heavy weight, such as a heavy teddy or weighted blanket over his lap while he is in the car seat, to help him feel contained.

motor development Immobilized in a baby seat is not ideal for developing a baby's muscles, so make it a priority to take him out of his car seat as soon as you arrive at your destination.

feed time

Having been a sleepy feeder, your baby becomes increasingly alert during feeds at this stage. If he becomes distracted, reduce stimulation to a minimum.

visual Tie a red or white ribbon to your clothes for your baby to focus on and fiddle with while he feeds.

hearing If your baby loses focus and does not feed well if he is in a noisy or interesting environment, don't talk to him during feeds and remove stimuli from around him (for example, switch off the television). Cover him with a feeding shawl to block out distractions. If he is able to continue feeding well regardless of what is going on around him, do talk or read to him.

motor development Changing the side on which you feed your baby, even if you're bottle feeding, helps him develop listening, seeing, and body movements on both sides.

toys and tools

You are still the most important toy in your child's life. It's your interaction with him, rather than any fancy toy, that provides the happiest moments and best learning experiences.

visual Play gyms or mobiles provide your baby with excellent visual and hand–eye coordination stimulation. Keep the objects on the mobile as interesting and colourful as possible, to encourage him to look and even to start reaching out. Try attaching the following items to a hanger to make your own mobile: a tinfoil spiral (cut out of a tinfoil plate or pie dish); a soft toy hanging face-down on string so that your baby can see the face; a baby-safe mirror; colourful rattles; a string of shells or pine cones and other natural objects; inflatable toys; fabric balls and blocks.

hearing To make a rattle, fill small empty bottles or pill containers with rice, pasta or seeds. Make sure that the lids fit well, or tape or glue them down so that your baby can't open them.

touch Textured toys provide tactile interest, developing the sense of touch. You can either buy textured soft animals or make your own by filling a sock with a plastic bag or beans for your baby to scrunch. To make a textured play mat, sew together fabric of varying textures and buttons to make picture or a design. Make sure there are no loose ends or loops to catch little fingers. Use this mat during tummy time.

chapter 11

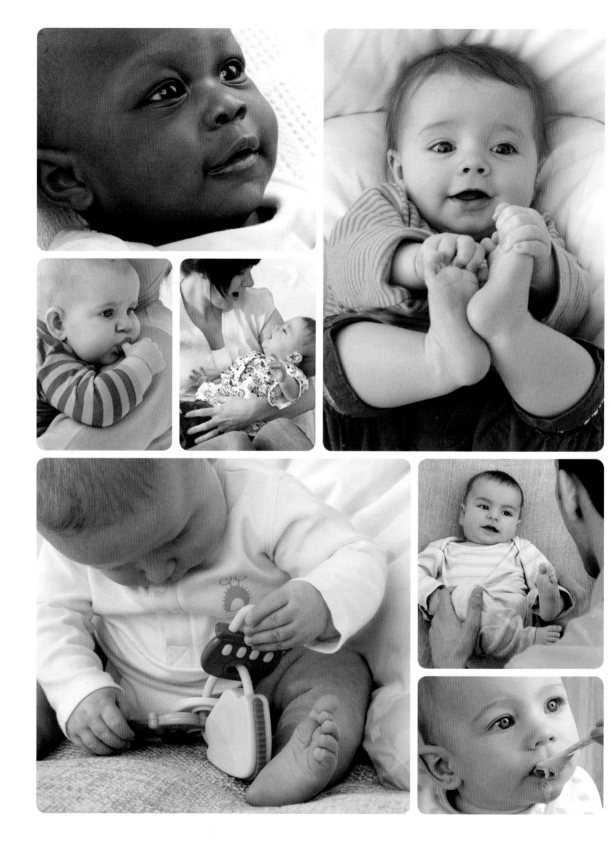

your baby at four to six months

As your baby approaches four months of age, you should congratulate yourself on passing the first "trimester of parenthood". Everything gets easier from here on. Your baby's face lights up when she sees or hears you and you should not be getting up so often during the night. Your baby's days are settling into a definite pattern with predictable times for feeding, sleeping, and playing. Just as you become more familiar with your baby's signals and her routines, new challenges present themselves. You will be faced with big decisions, such as when to introduce solids and what the best childcare for your baby might be if you're returning to work. The information in this chapter will help to quell any fears and equip you with the knowledge to make these big decisions.

baby-centric routine

● Try to limit your baby's awake time to between one-and-a-half to two hours and plan this time for changing, feeding, and playtime.

● Your baby will probably be sleeping for three to five hours during the day, divided into three or four naps and for 10 to 12 hours at night with one night waking. This will amount to a total of 14 to 18 hours in a 24-hour cycle.

● Your baby will be feeding every three to four hours during the day.

● Expect a growth spurt around four months of age, when you will need to feed your baby more frequently for 24 to 48 hours.

all worth it Although you may be struggling with the difficult task of mothering, seeing your baby's delighted response to your presence can make everything seem worthwhile.

a day in the life of your baby

Your baby's day should follow a predictable pattern by now. If you are still struggling to understand when to feed her and when she should sleep, you need to start guiding her towards consistently spaced feeds and regular sleeps (see pp.130–31). Getting her settled into a routine will make your life much more stress-free. By watching her signals you will soon learn when she is ready to be settled to sleep and when she is hungry.

mum sense: highs and lows

Your baby is now so cute and you delight in watching her development. If she has settled into a routine and your life is predictable you may well feel a sense of mastery over the tough task of mothering.

On the other hand, there will still be days when your emotions wobble and insecurities raise their heads. This is particularly evident at times of transition, for example when you realize that your baby is no longer a newborn: helpless and dependent on you. Your baby's life is now characterized by change and there are many new decisions to make. There will be the challenge of knowing when your baby is ready for solids or if milk is still meeting her nutritional needs. If you introduce bottles during this stage, you may experience mixed emotions. All these events are signs that your baby is getting older. You will find yourself oscillating between wishing the challenging early days away and aching as you realize that you can't stop time and control your baby growing up.

If you return to work at the end of this stage, you may be amazed at the conflicting emotions you feel. Firstly, the extreme sadness of realizing that you will miss your baby and may not be the first one to see her crawl or hear her first word. Then, of course, you may have that fleeting feeling of "Thank goodness I can do something for me and have a little time away from the mundane task of mothering." This of course gives rise to that ever-present feeling of maternal guilt.

It is understandable if there are days when you feel quite blue, particularly if your baby is not yet sleeping through the night. Your baby may start waking again earlier at night because she is hungry, so you may find yourself tired and despondent at the prolonged lack of sleep.

Just keep an eye on your mood, and if you feel overwhelming sadness, anxiety or feel you simply can't go on, seek help from your doctor, health visitor, or an accredited counsellor for postnatal depression (PND), also known as perinatal distress (see p.59). It is a fairly common condition: one or two women in ten will be diagnosed with PND up to two years after their baby's birth.

baby sense: time for routine

Over the past four months you may have been craving a bit of predictability to your day. If you were advised to start a routine early, you may have found it a challenge to get your baby settled into a set day. But by four to six months old, your baby is now ready for a routine.

establishing a sleep routine

Establishing a sleep routine is as easy as one-two-three:

1 Watch the time Note the time your baby wakes from her last nap and prepare to put her down to sleep again one-and-a-half to two hours later.

2 Notice the signals As her awake time (see p.51) ends, watch her for signals of tiredness and point them out to your partner and other caregivers so that they too can learn to recognize her tiredness not just by the clock but by her signals. Common sleepy signals include: rubbing eyes, tugging ears, yawning, hiccups, sucking her fist, thumb or hand, and pulling fabric or clothing towards her face (see pp.52–53).

3 Put her down Take your baby to her sleep space and help her become drowsy by holding her and rocking her gently and perhaps humming a lullaby, and then put her down when she is drowsy but awake.

establishing a feeding routine

Up till now your baby's feeds have been quite flexible since you have been following your baby's lead. Now is the time to start create a feeding routine by spacing feeds more regularly. By the end of this stage you can be introducing solids. Introduce a milk-feeding routine using the following strategy:

1 Watch the time At four months, your baby's feeds will consist of four or five milk feeds during the day, with the first at around 6am or 7am. Three hours after this (around 9am or 10am), be prepared to feed her again if she seems hungry, and so on throughout the day.

2 Notice the signals To make this process easier, watch her signals for when she is ready to learn to eat. These include sucking on her hands, rooting for a nipple or teat, or becoming unsettled.

3 Feed your baby Offer her the next milk feed three to four hours after the previous one.

As your baby approaches six months, you can begin to think about starting her on solids. Your feeding routine will adjust once you do this. At four months, your baby's feeds will consist of four or five milk feeds during the day. By the time she is six months old, you can reduce this to four milk feeds interspersed with solids. You can offer milk and solids at regular times so that she is fed at predictable times each day. See p.161 for a suggested feeding routine once solid feeds are established.

establishing a sleep routine

1 As well as noting the timing of your baby's sleeps, watch for her signals of tiredness, such as yawning.

2 Hold your baby if she needs help settling before sleep times.

3 Settle her in her cot while she is drowsy but still awake so that she learns to fall asleep on her own.

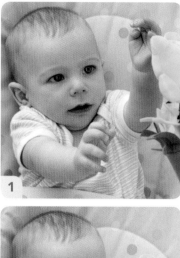

from calm to crying

❶ In a calm-alert state your baby has an open expression and calm, interested features. This is the time to stimulate him.

❷ As he gets tired or hungry, or has just had too much stimulation, he becomes fractious – the active-alert state.

❸ If he is not soothed by sucking, a cuddle, or sleep, your baby will cry.

when to stimulate?

Although the signals of alertness, tiredness, and over-stimulation are common to most babies (see pp.38–41), the reality is that every baby is different. By now your baby will have established her own set of signals that indicate how she is interacting with her sensory world, and you should be well practised at reading them. Stimulate your baby when she is in the calm-alert state – well-rested and not too hungry.

the calm-alert state: time to stimulate By the time she is four months old, your baby will spend longer periods between naps in the calm-alert state. In this magic state, she really enjoys interaction. She has attentive expressions, displays minimal movement and is focused on specific stimulation. This is the state in which your baby responds best to her world, and learns well from her encounters with people and her environment. When your baby makes eye contact, calls out to you, and starts to reach for toys, give her new activities (see pp.164–67) to encourage her brain to develop and to make connections between synapses (junctions between the brain cells), leading to learning.

less is more: time for chilling Knowing the positive effect of stimulation on your baby's brain, it is tempting to try and stimulate her as much as possible in an attempt to enhance her intelligence or development. Just remember that yet more stimulation or interaction when your baby has had enough will be counterproductive.

Watch your baby for signals that she is over-stimulated – she will kick and move her body excitedly and energetically or look away and suck her hands vigorously. These warning signals say that she is in an active-alert state. This state is not ideal for learning since your baby is receiving too much input from her busily moving muscles and expending energy trying to stay calm. When you see these signals, change the sensory environment (see pp.32–33) and help your baby to soothe herself (see p.45) by sucking her hands or a dummy. If you miss or ignore these signals and she continues to take in sensory information, she may end up crying.

crying: time for calming and sleep Although the colicky weeks are over now, your baby may spend extended periods crying if she becomes over-stimulated or tired. Crying is a very clear signal that she has had enough. In this state your baby feels distressed and overwhelmed. You will need to use sensory soothing strategies (see p.45) to help her calm down. Crying often indicates that it is time for a nap and if you are watching your baby's awake times (see p.51) and starting to establish a routine, you will know when to put her down to sleep.

helping your baby sleep

By the time your baby is four months old, you might expect her to be waking only once at night. However, between four and six months you may be surprised when just as you think you are getting it right, your baby starts to shorten that stretch at night again and demand a feed in the middle of the night to settle. Even if you are expecting this, you may feel as though you are moving backwards. Sleep disruptions are common at this time and all for good reasons.

sensory secrets to good sleep habits

Paying attention to your baby's signals that she is tired and making sure that her sleeping environment is dim and calming will help you to set up a daytime-sleep routine. This will ensure good sleep habits at night.

daytime-sleep secrets Daytime sleeps are essential and are linked to how well your baby sleeps at night. An overtired baby will wake more often at night. If your baby resists falling asleep during the day, the chances are that you are not keeping an eye on her awake times (see p.51). If you allow your baby to be awake for more than two hours at a stretch, she goes into her second wind and can't fall asleep naturally. You will find that you have an overtired baby who can't switch off and you will have to resort to any method to put her down, such as driving round the block or rocking her to sleep. This is a classic pitfall in the four- to seven-month-old and can be the cause of bad sleep habits.

evening settling secrets At this age, a regular bath and bedtime routine every evening becomes essential. This sets the stage for sleep and, if done regularly from now onwards, will become your baby's bedtime cue for sleep because it acts as a signal to the brain to begin to shift down from a calm-alert (and wakeful) state to the all-important drowsy state before settling to sleep. The magic of a bedtime routine is that from about two months until well into the toddler years, it can remain unchanged. If you are travelling and your baby is out of her comfort zone, she will settle to sleep much more easily if her bedtime routine remains unaltered. The key factors in a good bedtime routine that support sleep are: a calming bath, a darkened room, a consistent space for sleep (the same place at the same time for every sleep, whether a nap during the day or the night sleep) and soothing interactions.

sleep: what to expect at this stage

- Your baby now stays awake for longer during the day, but after one-and-a-half to two hours of awake time, you should prepare her for bed. Bad habits are more likely to arise if you stretch her awake time and your baby goes to sleep overtired. A daytime-sleep routine is essential at this stage.
- Daytime sleeps may remain at 45 minutes long (the length of a sleep cycle) or your baby may start to stretch one sleep longer.
- You are probably no longer swaddling your baby at sleep times and can progress into a baby sleeping bag for the night sleep.
- If you are giving your baby a chance to find ways to calm herself such as by sucking on her hands or holding her hands together, she should be able to soothe herself back to sleep if she stirs at night and is not hungry.
- Babies who soothe themselves usually "sleep through" the night (10 hours) at around four months of age. The first night feed (1am to 2am) will fall away. If you are getting your baby down by 6pm or 7pm, she will sleep until between 4am and 6am before needing a feed.
- Sometime between four and six months of age your baby will start to wake more frequently at night, indicating that she is hungry and in need of more nutrition to get her through the night.

"Daytime sleeps are essential and are linked to how well your baby sleeps at night."

bedtime routine

Predetermine a bedtime appropriate for your baby's age – usually between 6pm and 7pm depending on afternoon naps and on what you've been doing during the day.

Bathe your baby about an hour before bedtime is due. In the early days, use fragrance-free bath products especially designed for babies since new babies may be sensitive to smells at this time of day. Keep everything relatively calm and quiet. Even if dad comes home during bath time, his interactions must be soothing as opposed to exciting (easier said than done!). Wrap your baby in a warm, soft towel when you take her out of the bath. Towels with hoods are cosy.

Go directly to her sleep space (already prepared to be a calming sensory environment with dimmed lights). Do not take your baby out of this sleep space until the next morning. Play soft soothing lullabies, white noise, or sing to your baby. If she enjoys massage and finds it calming, massage her with soothing fragrance-free carrier oils such as olive, avocado, or grapeseed oil. When she is older than five months, use scented organic baby massage products, if desired. Dress her in soft night clothes and use a good quality night-time nappy and a sleeping bag.

Turn off or dim the light. Give her the last feed of the evening in the dark room in your arms. After her feed, burp her for no longer than five minutes. If she is not yet drowsy, stand and rock her, or sing a lullaby to

sense-able secret

Putting your baby to bed at the roughly same time every evening, in the same place, in a soft sleeping bag, will help you to establish a routine.

misreading your baby's signals

Your response to your baby's signals can affect her ability to settle into sleep. It is easy to misread or miss your baby's signals of sleepiness. If so, she may become overtired and you will find it harder to get her to sleep.

your baby's state	signals	your response
Tired baby reaches end of awake time	Fatigue signals: rubbing eyes, sucking hands, looking away	Ignore or miss signals of fatigue
Baby goes into second wind and seems alert	Over-stimulation signals: kicking, screeching, panting	Cannot settle overtired baby to sleep
Has been awake for a long time now and becomes fractious	Fussing signals: grizzling, rubbing eyes, moaning	Rock or feed baby to sleep

baby expects same treatment every night

the **babysense** secret

help her become drowsy. When she is drowsy but not asleep, put her into her cot. Repeat this routine every night from now on.

By keeping your baby's bedtime routine as consistent as possible, it will become a very important sleep cue that will really ease her to sleep. A consistent bedtime routine is especially important if your day has been busy or your baby's sleep space changes, for instance when you are on holiday or if you move house.

sensory soothing tools

Use the tools in this chart, listed by sensory area, and sensory soothing strategies (see p.45) to settle your baby into a drowsy state. But be sure to stop them before your baby is asleep, or they might become habits.

sensory component	how to include in bedtime routine
Touch	● Warm bath ● Soft, warm towel ● Soft, warm clothes ● Soothing massage after bath
Movement	● Rocking your baby gently in your arms ● Pushing your baby in a pram to induce drowsiness ● Walking with your baby in a carrier or sling
Sucking	● Dummy ● Thumb ● Breast- or bottle feed
Visual	● Read or show a bedtime story ● Dark/dimmed room ● Night light for toddlers
Smell	● Lavender ● Chamomile ● Vanilla ● Familiar smell of her sleep object
Sound	● White noise ● Lullaby ● Gentle classical music
Body position	● Holding your baby in your arms ● Putting your baby in the same position in her cot

sleep habits

To avoid bad sleep habits developing, follow a regular daytime-sleep routine.
● Watch her awake times (see p.51) and put her down after one-and-a-half to two hours.
● Read her signals of tiredness.
● Take her to her room 10 minutes ahead of sleep time.
● Soothe her to drowsy (see table opposite for soothing methods).
● Let her fall asleep independently.
● Let her wake on her own.

sleep expectations

At four to six months of age, your baby begins to develop memory and expectations about where she is put to sleep. Where she falls asleep will be where she expects to go back to sleep if she wakes at night. If that is in your arms, bed, or room, your baby will wake at night expecting the same situation. So ensure that you are comfortable with what she needs in order to fall asleep.

solving sleep problems

You may have a really good sleeper who has slept well from an early age. If this is the case, you may find that your baby continues to sleep well and falls happily asleep and resettles herself at night. However, between four to six months of age some babies develop disrupted sleep patterns. Your previously good sleeper may start to wake in the early hours of the morning. Or maybe your baby has never slept through and now things suddenly get worse, not better. There are four key reasons for sleep disruptions at the four- to six-month stage. This advice should help you to feel more in control:

changing nutritional needs Towards this stage, milk will satisfy your baby's nutritional needs and she should be able to stretch happily for 10 hours at night before needing a feed. After four months of age, however, many babies start to wake more frequently because milk no longer fills them for the entire night. At this point you may begin to consider solids. Advice on when to start solids may be conflicting, and it is important to note that introducing solids at this age is not a magic wand resulting in sleep. To determine whether your baby is ready for solids, see box, p.160. Until your baby is on solids, give her a feed if she wakes more than four hours since her last feed. Feed her quietly in the dark, do not change her nappy unless it is soiled, and then resettle her to sleep. If she will not resettle after the feed, sit with her in your arms until she is drowsy and still, perhaps rocking her gently, then put her down and place your hand on her tummy, applying gentle pressure.

health issues If your baby has been a good sleeper and is suddenly waking more often, you may wonder whether she is teething or ill.
● **Teething** Most babies teethe after six months of age, very rarely before (see p.171). However, if your baby is unsettled in the day, has acrid smelling poo, is waking often and seems uncomfortable, she may be teething. If she has all the signs of teething, including a little white tooth in her gums, help her to feel comfortable by using teething powders (a natural remedy to rub on your baby's gums, available from your pharmacist) or pain relief as suggested by your health visitor or doctor.
● **Ear infection** If your baby has recently started crèche or if she has older siblings at play group, she may start to catch colds and germs at this stage. If she does not settle after a cold has passed, ask your doctor to check whether her ears are clear. Congested ear canals causes pressure on the ear drums and may result in night waking. If your doctor checks her ears and finds a problem, he might recommend a safe nasal decongestant for infants.

short daytime sleeps It is common for babies of this age not to sleep longer than 45 minutes at a stretch during the day. This is because they do not link sleep cycles and wake during light sleep (see p.30). As your baby gets older she will naturally start to link sleep cycles and start to have one longer daytime sleep. Help her to learn to link sleep cycles:

1 When your baby wakes after 45 minutes, if you can hear her moaning, listen and don't go to her for a few minutes unless she is really crying.

2 Go in and keeping the room dark, re-swaddle your baby, give her a blanky or dummy, and pat her gently for five minutes.

3 If she will not resettle with this assistance, abandon the sleep and pick her up, but be sure to watch her closely during her awake time (see p.51) to pick up the signals that she's ready for her next sleep and put her down as soon as she is drowsy.

sleep habits If your baby is waking needing to be fed, rocked or patted to sleep, she has a bad sleep habit and now needs to learn how to fall asleep without your assistance. Then, when she wakes, she'll be better able to get back to sleep by herself. Sleep soothers, such as a thumb, dummy, or sleep blanket, muslin, or soft toy, can help her to fall asleep and get back to sleep.

To introduce one whenever she is unsettled or going to sleep, give her a small sleep blanket or soft toy consistently over the next few weeks. Whenever your baby cries when she is awake, whether it is for pain, tiredness or just for a cuddle, pick up the sleep soother and put it on your shoulder and then cuddle your baby on your shoulder. Before long she will associate this object with comfort and happy feelings. In the middle of the night, give her this comfort object in place of the crutch (for example, being fed or rocked to sleep) she has been using.

sleep blanket safety

Due to the risk of suffocation, babies should not sleep with duvets in their bed for warmth. However, a sleep object in the form of a toy or blanket is important for healthy sleep habits. Make sure the toys or blanket your baby uses is small so that even if it is near her face there is no risk of suffocation.

Q&A is my baby hungry?

My five-month-old has been a very good sleeper and has slept through the night from eight weeks old. Recently, though, she has started waking earlier and earlier in the morning and it's really hard to get her back to sleep. Last night she woke at 1am and every hour thereafter. I keep giving her a dummy, but am exhausted. When will she sleep through again?

Your baby was a good sleeper and so the fact that she is waking at night reflects a real issue that needs to be addressed. Between four and six months of age, your baby's nutritional needs change and she has started to wake because she is hungry. By giving her a dummy when she wakes, you are not solving her problem and this is why she continues to wake hourly thereafter. You should feed her when she wakes at night. Once your baby is fed, she is likely to fall asleep and sleep for a long stretch, since her nutritional need has been met. It is time to start speaking to your health visitor about introducing solids because your baby is giving you clear signals that her milk feeds are not as satisfying as they were before.

feeding: what to expect at this stage

- If you have been exclusively breastfeeding, your milk supply will have increased to meet the growing demands of your baby. Your supply will be well established at this stage.
- Expect to give four to six milk feeds in 24 hours. Aim to feed your baby every three-and-a-half to four hours during the day.
- Expect a growth spurt at four months and respond by feeding your baby more frequently for 24 to 48 hours. Your breast-milk supply will increase on demand.
- A bottle-fed baby may start to feed less often now and may drink larger volumes (120–240ml/4–8½fl oz) four to five times in 24 hours.
- At some point during this stage, your baby will appear hungrier, not stretch for as long between feeds, and wake more frequently at night. To meet her growing appetite, you will need to breastfeed her for longer, consider introducing a supplementary feed, increase the amount of formula you make up, change her formula to a more filling one, or introduce solids.

expressing breast milk

❶ By hand: you can express with a manual pump (shown here) or an electric one. Place the nozzle over your nipple and areola and squeeze the handle repeatedly to draw out the milk.

❷ Someone else can feed your baby with your expressed breast milk when you are out, or you can use it to supplement a breastfeed.

feeding your baby

Your little one is growing up. Until this point all her nutritional needs have been met by milk, either breast or formula. In this four- to six-month stage, she may require additional nutrition and you will be faced with whether and how to introduce solids. You may also return to work around this time, so if you would like to continue breastfeeding, it is a good idea to start expressing. This will ensure that your milk supply remains undiminished, and means that someone else can feed your baby with your expressed breast milk.

expressing breast milk

If you are successfully breastfeeding your baby and want to occasionally offer a bottle, it is a good idea to start expressing milk. You may want to have your partner do a night feed for you, use expressed breast milk to supplement a breastfeed (such as after the evening feed), or be returning to work. Expressing does not always come easily and to begin with you will find that you express very little. But over time your breasts will adjust to the machine's suction and the milk will flow more easily.

guidelines

- Try to express milk after a feed when you are at home. This is when the richer hindmilk will be released.
- If you are at work, try to express milk whenever your baby would have a feed. This will ensure that you continue to make enough milk.
- If this schedule is difficult to manage, try to express at least once during your working day. Lunch time is usually good – put your feet up, have a bite to eat and read a magazine.

- Allow the freshly expressed breast milk to cool before refrigerating it (if you have an office fridge), or placing it in a sealed cool box.
- If you have no refrigeration facilities at work, or you are on the road, consider investing in a good-quality cooler box. Some top-of-the-range breast pumps come complete with accessories such as specialized cooler bags to store the expressed milk.
- Breast milk can be stored in the fridge for 24 hours, and frozen for up to three months. Freeze expressed milk in washed and sterilized ice trays or small plastic containers – specialized plastic bags are also available.
- Thaw frozen milk by standing the plastic container in a jug of warm water. Don't microwave to defrost or warm it – this may destroy some of the breast milk's nutritional value.
- Thoroughly sterilize all the parts of the pump and the container.
- Discard any unused milk stored in the fridge after 24 hours.

feeding guidelines

The general rule of thumb for how much expressed breast milk (EBM) or formula to offer is as follows: 150ml (5fl oz) of milk (EBM or formula) per kilogram of your baby's body weight, divided into however many feeds you are giving in 24 hours.

For example: Weight of baby = 5kg (11lb)

5 x 150ml (5fl oz) = 750ml (26fl oz) in 24 hours

750ml (26fl oz) divided by six feeds (if you are feeding four hourly) = 125ml (4½fl oz) per feed. This is a guide only – some really hungry babies demand more, while others may be happy with less. Let your baby guide you – if she constantly finishes the bottle you offer her, and still looks hungry, add a bit more (try 25ml/¾fl oz to start), and see what she does with it. If she has had enough, she will refuse more – if she is still hungry, she will drink eagerly!

changing nutritional needs

Between four and six months your baby's nutritional needs will change. Whereas before milk met all her calorie needs, now she needs a bit more of everything, especially iron. Deciding when to introduce solids is depends on your baby's age and signals of readiness. The Department of Health and the World Health Organisation say it is best to exclusively breastfeed your baby until she is six months old. There is also recent research (since 2009) indicating that any time from four months may be a suitable time to introduce solids. This conflicting advice reinforces the need for you to consider your individual baby. If you think your baby is ready before the age of six months, talk to your health visitor, especially if your baby was premature. Remember that you should not rush into solids until your baby is ready.

sense-able secret

Provided your baby is gaining weight and is not ill, don't feed her if less than three hours have passed since the last feed. If she is fractious, help her to soothe herself by encouraging her to suck her hands, or by rocking her. You can also try offering 50–80ml (2–3fl oz) of cooled, boiled water from a spoon, bottle, or cup, as she may be thirsty.

when to introduce solids

- Your baby is between four and six months.
- She can no longer go for three-and-a-half to four hours between daytime milk feeds.
- She has begun waking more frequently at night.
- She sits supported in a chair and holds her head up well.
- She is very interested in your food and reaches for a spoon.

Important note: Solid food must not take the place of the three milk feeds a day, which are more important at this stage.

introducing solids

It is important to be absolutely sure that your baby is ready before you start her on solids. See the box (left) for signs that she is ready and discuss it with your health visitor. Watch your baby's signals and feed her when she is in the calm-alert state and not too hungry. As a rule of thumb, offer the solids feed two hours after milk feeds (around two hours before her next milk feed). Do not wake your baby for a solids feed – delay the feed or drop it altogether. Follow these steps:

step one Begin with a single grain (rice or maize) cereal. If your baby is younger than five months, this extra fuel will be all she needs.
- Take one heaped teaspoon of dry cereal and mix it with either expressed breast milk, formula, or cooled boiled water to make a sloppy mixture. It will make about three teaspoons.
- Offer a small amount to your baby at her lunch time, between 11am and 1pm. Use a small plastic scoop spoon or the tip of your clean finger.
- Gradually increase the amount you give her each day, and adjust the consistency of the mixture according to her demands.
- If your baby is older than five months, continue for two weeks before moving onto step two.

step two Begin this step only if your baby is older than five months, has been enjoying step one for the past two weeks, and is not managing to stretch from her early morning feed until the next one in four hours' time. If she is younger than five months, continue with step one and wait for her to show you that she is hungry first.
- Offer your baby "breakfast" two hours after her early morning feed (at about 8am). Give her the same amount of cereal as she has for lunch.
- Continue giving the same amount of cereal, in the morning and at lunch, for the next few days before moving onto step three.

step three From now on, substitute the cereal in your baby's lunch-time meal with vegetables, and give her fruit with her meals.
- Choose vegetables that are yellow or pale green inside (carrot, courgette, sweet potato). Boil or steam them, then finely mash them with a mouli or the back of a fork.
- Choose some fresh, raw fruit (banana, ripe pear, apple – steam first – papaya, avocado pear, mango or melon) and mash them through a mouli for the first feeds. Later, try chopping them into bite-sized chunks. Offer this in her cereal at breakfast and after her vegetables at lunch.
- Offer your baby as much as she will eat – usually a few teaspoons. Continue with cereal and fruit in the morning and vegetables at lunch,

until she shows signs of needing a third meal, then move onto step four.
- If your baby is older than five months, continue step three for a week, then move onto step four.

step four Introduce a dinner-time meal, consisting of the same foods as for lunch, before her bath.
- Offer your baby the same quantity of fruit and vegetables at dinner as she eats for lunch. Although she is now having three meals a day, don't alter her milk feeds – give her milk every four hours.
- Continue these three meals a day, plus her milk, for a further two weeks, then move onto step five.

step five Start this once your baby is six months old, or has been on step four for two weeks.
- Introduce one tablespoon of natural yoghurt into one meal of the day. Either mix it into her cereal, or stir it into fresh fruit, or give it separately after her vegetables.
- Continue this fruit and vegetable-based diet until your baby is more than six months old. Do not give your baby anything else, such as meat, chicken, cheese, eggs, or fish yet.

beginning solids When beginning to introduce solids, start with one heaped teaspoon of cereal, mixing it with breast or formula milk.

day plan when feeding is established

Once your baby is eating three meals a day – and remember this may take anything from two weeks to three months from when you start her on solids – her feeding routine may look like this:

time	suggested menu
6am	Breast / bottle
7–8am	Breakfast: cereal / fruit / yoghurt
10am	Breast / bottle (if she starts to drop this feed, reduce the quantity of breakfast you are giving her)
12 noon	Lunch: vegetables / fruit / yoghurt
2pm	Breast / bottle (if she starts to drop this feed, reduce the quantity of lunch you are giving her)
4pm	Dinner: vegetables / fruit
6pm	Breast / bottle
6.30pm	Bedtime – she should last for eight to ten hours without needing any further milk feeds

first feeds Offer your baby her first taste of the rice cereal mixture when she is calm and not too hungry. You could try giving her half a milk feed first to make sure she is not desperately hungry, but not too full to refuse more food.

baby's developing skills

① Look and feel: your baby will begin to be able to reach out for and grasp objects, and by six months may be able to turn a toy around in her hands.

② To and fro: rolling is an important milestone at this stage. Your baby will roll from her tummy to her back first.

the **babysense** secret

getting to know your baby

Between four and six months of age, your baby gains good control of her head, becomes proficient at grasping and reaching, and will begin to learn to sit. She will probably reach the important milestone of rolling over by the end of this period. She'll also discover what fun her mouth is and, at some point, will start taking weight on her legs if you support her.

hands and mouth As your baby's primitive reflexes disappear altogether, she starts to be able to control some of her body movements and even reach out for objects. She can already hold her head in the midline of her body when lying on her back and will now start to manipulate objects with two hands. At this stage, her grasp of objects is crude but she can get all manner of things to her mouth! Don't mistake this as a sign of hunger or early teething. Since the touch receptors in her mouth are more finely tuned than anywhere else on her body, she learns about her world through her mouth using her gums and lips to explore objects and learn about their shape and texture.

rolling over When on her tummy your baby will push up on her elbows and may start to push up on her palms, straightening her arms. She may also start to reach for objects in this position and then collapse over her supporting arm, causing her to roll over onto her back accidentally. When lying on her back she will have such fun grasping her toes that she may lose her balance, rolling over halfway to the side. This accidental rolling is the start of a very important milestone: rolling, which will emerge towards the six-month mark. By six months your baby should be rolling one way (usually from her tummy to her back), and maybe even both ways. Playing with her feet is important for other reasons too – it's how she develops her tummy muscles. Similarly, when lying and playing on her tummy, she will lift her head and thereby develop her back muscles. The development of both tummy and back muscles is vital for rolling and crawling, which are among the most important milestones of the first year.

sitting and exploring Your baby will learn to sit towards six months, making your life much easier. At first she'll need support – she will often lean forward on her hands – but by the end of this stage she will be able to sit almost unsupported for brief moments. At around the same time, she will begin reaching intentionally and her hands will become useful tools. She will be able to manipulate toys – holding and turning them. She will hold objects in her whole hand (known as the palmer grasp) and start to bang them and maybe start to use her thumb and index finger to pinch and poke things. She cannot yet let go voluntarily.

mouths are fun During these weeks your baby will find her mouth. Now she'll realize it's not just good for exploring toys, but also as a playmate. She'll play with her saliva, blow bubbles, and play with sounds. She'll discover that she can imitate some of your sounds and will start to make vowel sounds. This is the start of babbling. Even deaf babies babble – this shows us that our brains are pre-programmed for early speech. Your baby really loves to laugh and will squeal and chuckle with delight when you tickle her or swing her round.

target milestones

Your baby starts to master her world and gets very excited by the effect she has on her environment. Her major movement milestone is mastering rolling, but she will also start to sit supported. Rolling helps her to balance her tummy muscles and is critical for all areas of development. Also, your baby should now start to use her hands intentionally to manipulate objects. She will develop the ability to grasp objects voluntarily and eventually to let go intentionally. Now your baby moves into a more alert, sensory-seeking phase. She loves engaging with you by babbling and socializing and will delight in the effect she has on people. Expect these milestones to be achieved by six months of age.

area of development	target milestones
Gross motor	Actively rolling from tummy to back. When on her tummy pushing up on straight arms. Sitting upright with support and reaching from this position.
Fine motor	Reaching for toys with one or both hands. Playing with her feet.
Hand–eye coordination	Holding her head still while her eyes track a toy. Exploring the properties of toys with her mouth.
Language	Beginning to hold a babbling conversation and imitate sounds. Babbling, including the sounds: "ka" and "da".
Social/emotional	Showing a preference for people she knows and beginning to be shy with strangers.
Regulation	Settling herself back to sleep in the middle of the night if she is comfortable. Giving warning signals before she starts to cry.

ready to move Until three months of age, your baby probably could not bear any weight on her legs. Now she will love to stand supported on your lap. As she nears six months she'll love to bounce in this position, too. This is her way of exercising the muscles needed for pulling herself up to stand. Your baby will love movement games. It is important that you stimulate this sense because the vestibular system is important for the development of muscle tone and movement coordination. See overleaf for some good movement games.

social awareness Your baby is now very visually alert – she is interested in anything new. Suddenly she will be easily distracted during feed times and milk feeds may have to be given in the peace and quiet of a bedroom, or at least a place with no interesting people or conversations around. You can try using a feeding shawl to shield her from the world when out and about. Your baby will now recognize and thrive on familiarity. She understands and enjoys routine. Her concentration span is increasing too, and she can spend more time examining and playing with an object.

regulation Your baby is growing up and has developed the ability to stay calm when faced with a good deal of stimulation. She will also have the capacity now to regulate her sleep and wake states and can fall asleep independently if you allow her to do so.

encouraging new skills By placing a toy just out of reach, you will encourage your inquisitive baby to begin to display new skills, such as reaching over her shoulder for an interesting object when lying on her back.

sensible stimulation: TEAT

Your baby is like a sponge, soaking up all sorts of stimuli and the new sights and sounds you expose her to will encourage brain development. Her eye muscles are more developed now and she focuses with interest. Start to encourage these developing eye movements by providing your baby with opportunities to track a moving object. She will also start to fine-tune her auditory skills, listening to sounds and attaching meaning to them. As she approaches six months, she'll love to be rocked, rolled over, swung, and generally moved about. All this movement is vital for her muscles and also increases her sense of spatial awareness. Lots of movement is vital for the development of later skills such as crawling.

timing

Your baby now spends more time awake and in the calm-alert state (see p.31). In the mornings, try the activities on these pages and let her spend time under a play gym or with toys. In the afternoon, when she spends more time awake, take your baby on an outing or spend time doing movement-related activities, such as rocking her, rolling her over, and swinging her around. Movement in the late afternoon has been found to improve the length and quality of a baby's sleep at night.

environment

At four months your baby is suddenly able to cope with more stimulation. If she was suffering from colic, it will have abated now and she finds it easier to stay calm.

visual Start introducing your baby to more visually interesting places and objects, but watch her for signs of over-stimulation. Place her where she can watch a moving mobile or brightly coloured image; put one in each room. Remember to keep her sleep environment visually calming. Do not let her watch television yet – it does nothing for her development.

hearing Talk to your baby about what you are doing or what you see in as much detail as possible, using parentese – a slightly higher-pitched, sing-song tone of voice. Use her name over and over so that she learns it. She'll start to recognize and love the sound of her name. Share jokes and laughter with your baby – she won't understand language jokes, but will laugh when surprised.

touch Let your baby continue to mouth objects as it is an important learning process. Introduce a "treasure basket"; a small basket or container in each room filled with different objects with various textures and sounds. Try putting in some kitchen objects such as wooden spoons, textured fabrics, different-sized blocks and small toys.

Make sure everything is safe and non-toxic as your baby will put it all in her mouth.

motor development Let your baby spend time on a soft blanket or sheepskin rug on the floor, especially time on her stomach ("tummy time"). This will encourage motor development and helps her to achieve milestones such as sitting and rolling, and moving between these positions. Take your baby out of her car seat or pram as soon as you reach a destination so that she can stretch and exercise her muscles. Take a mat with you if you are worried about dirt when you put her on the floor.

activities

sleep time

Your baby can now cope with more stimulation during the day, but she may still need help to calm down and reach a relaxed, drowsy state before sleep.

visual Keep her sleep space dim and calming and avoid visual stimulation just before her sleeps (both day and night). Do not put mobiles or bright or interesting things over her cot.

hearing Sing quiet lullabies and play soft, soothing music while she is falling asleep. White noise, such as a fan, a humidifier, or a white noise recording will help your baby to settle to sleep.

touch Choose soft blankets, bedding and sleepwear without scratchy seams. A rough seam on a sleepsuit may be all it takes to wake

your baby between sleep cycles. Cover the bottom sheet with a soft receiving blanket, well tucked in.

movement Continue to use slow, rhythmical movements before sleep times and to calm your baby, such as rocking her gently. Put her down when she is drowsy, but still awake.

on the changing mat

Your baby will really enjoy looking at objects and touching them when lying on her back for a nappy change.

visual Put a mobile that you can alter over the changing mat (see p.125). When your baby nears five months old, encourage her hands to move to the midline of her body and reach out by attaching interesting objects to the mobile with elastic so that she can reach out, grasp and pull the object towards her.

hearing Describe what you are doing at the changing mat, for example, "I am putting on your top, now your trousers…"

motor development To encourage rolling, use components of the movement while dressing her. Bend her leg slightly and roll her onto her side, place the nappy under her and roll her back again. Build neck control and tummy strength by holding her arms and gently pulling her into a sitting position when finished.

bath time

The bedtime routine starts with bath time, so don't over-excite your baby. Instead, play quietly and then be very calm after the bath.

hearing Talk to your baby and tell her about her day. Use this time when you cannot leave her unattended to chat and interact together.

touch While your baby is naked or just wearing a nappy, touch various parts of her body with different textures, for example, brushes, various fabrics, gloves, sponges. Choose textured bath toys, such as different sponges, loofahs, and plastic toys. Toys designed for pets often have an interesting texture – for example, a plastic fish with soft rubber spikes. After her bath, rub her down well, and give her a baby massage (see p.105).

movement The tactile sensation and warmth of the bathwater create a containing environment ideal for introducing movement. Sway your baby to and fro in the bath.

smell Use baby bath products with a calming scent, such as lavender.

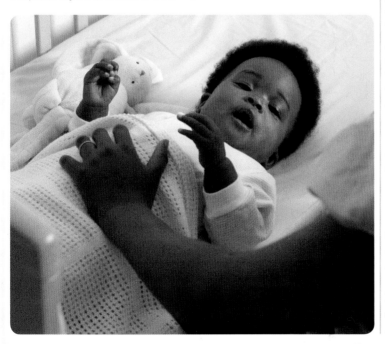

activities continued ...

awake time

As your baby gets older she will enjoy longer stretches of calm-alert time and you can start to stimulate her a little more. Be sure to tune in to her signals and follow her lead – slow down if she shows you that she is stressed or over-stimulated.

visual Play games to encourage visual tracking, such as bobbing a ball across her field of vision, rolling a ball past or away from her, shining a torch on the wall, and blowing bubbles. Also point out interesting objects around the house or garden, or moving cars and animals. Play peek-a-boo: briefly cover a toy or her face and then uncover it. Vary the texture of fabric you use.

hearing Ring bells, shake rattles, and use your voice, moving around the source of the sound, to help fine-tune her listening skills. Recite rhymes and sing songs with an element of surprise. Copy your baby's babbles as she explores new sounds. When she says "da" or "ka", imitate her so that she is encouraged to repeat it.

touch Let your baby play and roll on different surfaces, for instance on grass, a sheepskin mat, or a fleece. Keep up your baby massage. In the next stage of development she won't enjoy being on her back anymore so use these weeks for massage.

movement Carry your baby in various positions – facing towards or away from you or over your arm. Rock her about, dance around the room with her, and play aeroplanes by manoeuvring her around in the air (slowly at first). Play plenty of bouncing games with her standing

or sitting on your lap. Combine this with action rhymes (such as "This is the way the lady rides"). Gently rock her over a large physio ball, or roll her in a blanket and unroll her slowly. In the late afternoon, give your baby at least 5–10 minutes of movement, such as pulling her around in a box, swinging her in a hammock or sitting on a swing with her.

motor development Once your baby can sit supported, encourage her to reach for toys by placing them just beyond her reach. Help her practise sitting by propping her up with pillows, removing some as her balance improves. Let your baby play on the floor often to encourage her muscles to develop, and place her on her tummy to strengthen her back and neck muscles in preparation for crawling. Put a mobile, rattle, baby mirror or ball in front of her. If she dislikes this position, place a rolled-up towel under her chest at first. Play another version of aeroplanes: lie on

your back with your knees pulled towards your chest and place her, tummy down, on your shins, holding her arms. Move her towards and away from you. Sit on the floor and lie her over your legs in a crawling position, then rock her to and fro. Play give-and-take games to improve her ability to grasp and release objects.

travelling time

You may be feeling cooped up after four months of mothering and will be pleased to know that your baby is now ready for more interactions with the outside world. She will enjoy trips out and visits to new places, although her tolerance for new and exciting experiences will be limited if she is tired or is a sensitive baby.

visual When your baby is awake, let her watch the world and follow moving objects to develop her eye muscles. If you are out and about at sleep time, cover the pram with a blanket or turn her to face you in the carrier or baby sling, to shut out the world so she can sleep.

hearing Play a recording of children's songs or soothing classical music in the car.

touch In the car, tie textured toys to a coat hanger and suspend it from the grab handle above the car window, so that your baby can play with them while sitting in her car seat.

movement Use a sling or baby carrier for outings whenever possible. Interacting at your height is great for your baby's language development and the stimulation of your body's movement is good for her movement system, helping to build balance.

motor development When you carry or hold your baby, offer less support by holding her lower down on her body so that her stomach and neck muscles have to work to keep her upright. Don't leave your baby in a baby seat for long periods. This position is too passive and does not encourage her tummy and back muscles to work.

feed time

Your baby will become quite distracted during milk feeds. Limit distracting sensory input so it doesn't take too long. Now she will start exploring new textures as solids become part of her diet.

visual If visual input distracts your baby, feed her in a dull, non-stimulating environment for a while. Show her how you eat with delight on your face. This will encourage her to start to take an interest in eating since you will be introducing solids at the end of this stage.

touch The sensation of solids in her mouth may make your baby gag initially, so start by offering smooth textured cereal. As she progresses onto other foods, try to purée vegetables and fruit yourself so that she does not become accustomed to the smooth texture of bottled food.

motor development Once your baby is on solids, encourage her ability to grip small items by giving her a variety of finger foods such as carrots and apple slices. She probably won't eat them but will enjoy gnawing at them. Watch her closely in case she gags or manages to bite off a small piece that she could choke on.

toys and tools

Research has shown that playing with a wide variety of toys with different textures and functions enhances development. This does not mean that you must rush out and spend a fortune on toys. What it means is that you must offer your baby a wide variety of sensory experiences – especially in terms of touch.

visual Encourage your baby to look at books with simple, brightly coloured pictures. Board and waterproof books are practical as your baby is likely to want to mouth them. Pictures of faces in books and magazines will still fascinate her. Your baby will start to smile at her own face in mirrors, which encourages self-awareness. Use puppets in conversation to develop visual and language skills. Baby gyms with dangling toys encourage focus, reach, and grasp.

hearing Read books to your baby and let her listen to songs to aid language development. Give her rattles to hold and shake.

touch Use play mats with different textures, such as a sheepskin rug. Make a "sensory snake" by filling a long sock with items that feel and sound different: a scrunched-up plastic bag, pasta shapes, cotton wool and so on. Sew up the end to ensure that she can't get any of the contents out – she may choke on them. Stitch patches of different textured fabrics on the outside.

movement Give your baby a large ball to play with and roll over. Put up a swing in the garden or in the house. Make a hammock of lycra fabric for its soothing feel and rocking motion. Play baby go-carting by sitting your baby in an open box lined with cushions and pulling the box along.

motor development Place your baby on her tummy on a textured floor mat. Offer objects of different shapes, sizes, weights, and textures so she develops a wide variety of grasps. The type of grasp needed for a large, soft block is very different from that for a pea.

chapter 12

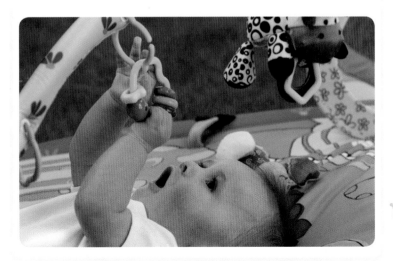

your baby at six to nine months

By now you've survived half a year of parenthood and your carefree "BC" (before children) days seem very long ago! This stage of your baby's life is one of the most rewarding. No one knows your baby better than you do. You know his every cry, facial expression, and idiosyncrasy intimately. Your baby strongly prefers you to all others in return and during these months he will develop separation anxiety, protesting every time you leave the room. This can be hugely frustrating for you. On the other hand, try to think of this stage as the last of the easy days – the calm before the storm. As your baby approaches nine months and beyond, he will become mobile and this adds new meaning to the word "hectic"!

baby-centric routine

- Try to limit your baby's awake time between sleeps during the day to two to two-and-a-half hours.
- He will still need two or three naps and may sleep for close to 12 hours at night. This amounts to around 14 to 16 hours' sleep in 24 hours.
- Your baby needs three to four milk feeds and three solid meals a day. You do not need to give him milk at night anymore.

sense-able secret
Spending time with other mothers and their babies, such as at coffee mornings or parent-and-baby groups, can provide the companionship and support you need at the moment.

a day in the life of your baby

Your baby should be in a settled routine now that does change as he grows, but on the whole is the same from day to day. Help to maintain his routine by ensuring his naps and bedtime are at consistent times and in the same sleeping environment.

mum sense: have I lost myself completely?

Six months in is possibly the most rewarding time for mothering so far. For the first time your relationship will feel reciprocal – you are getting something back for all the hard work. Many mothers feel as though they have found a New Best Friend, a little mate to do things with and take on outings. And you will be thoroughly delighted by your baby's development and emerging personality. Some of the best friends you will have in your life will be the ones you make now, the mums of other babies your baby's age. You never seem to run out of things to say and it mostly revolves around sleep and what comes out of your baby's nose, mouth or bottom! However, when you have a quiet moment or a day without interacting with other adults, you may find yourself contemplating your existence. Common personal challenges at this stage may include:

- **Loneliness** Being a mum can be lonely, especially if you live far from extended family and your baby's routine causes you to miss seeing friends.
- **Not my own day** Gone are the days of popping off to the shops or a spontaneous drink after work. You now need to consider a little life at every waking (and sleeping) moment and this can hamper you.
- **Not what I planned** Just as you think you have got some predictability into your day, your baby will throw a curve ball, whether it's an extra long sleep or a mild fever, and you will have to shuffle around your plans many times a week.
- **Carrying the load** A shocking reality of parenting is the "chore wars" – the debate over which parent is carrying more of the load. You know in your sane moments that it is the most ridiculous thing to quarrel over, but there are times when you feel the need to compare who is doing more as a parent: you or your partner.
- **Work or home** Be reassured what whichever route you take, you will find meaning – be that as a "stay-at-home" mum who is fulfilled most of the time by being the centre of her baby's world and making an impact on a future generation, or as a working mum who is fulfilled with her career, but faces the challenge of balancing all the demands in and out of the home.

baby sense: reasons for crying

By this stage your baby will be reasonably well settled and his previous episodes of crying caused by colic or too much stimulation should have abated. However, new challenges present themselves as your baby gets older, and he will begin to be distressed by different issues.

baby's teeth

Some of the joys of having a baby this age come from the predictability of his routine and watching him eat solid foods. When disruptions throw his routine out of sync, he eats poorly and his sleep is disrupted, your first thought may be that he is teething. The reality is that teething is not the cause of all ills. It is useful to be aware of the signs of teething (see box, right) so that you don't put every disruption down to teeth. Once you understand the nature of teething, it's easy to manage it.

Teething is considered to occur when a tooth actually cuts through the gum and appears in your baby's mouth. When your baby is born, his primary teeth are already formed, except for the roots, hidden in the jaw. On average, most babies cut their first tooth at around seven months of age. However, babies have been known to start teething before six months and as late as a year and a half old. Genetic factors play a role and very early or very late teething usually follows a familial pattern. Ask your baby's grannies when you and his father cut your first tooth. It is likely that your baby's first tooth will appear at around the same time.

When your baby starts sucking on his hands and chewing everything in sight, don't assume that he is teething. Normal milestones in this stage involve chewing on his fingers and hands and blowing bubbles. Mouthing and drooling prior to six months of age is very unlikely to be teething. There are other reasons for your baby to mouth his hands:

● **From nine weeks** Your baby may just be soothing himself. We know that at around this time your baby's reflexes disappear and for the first time he can keep his hands in his mouth and derive some self-soothing pleasure from sucking on them.

● **From three months old** Your baby may simply be learning about his body. During this stage, he will begin to put everything to his mouth, chew excessively on his hands, and create plenty of drool and bubbles. This is a vital stage when your baby is learning about the size, shape, and texture of new objects. When you see something new, you use your eyes and hands to explore the object's qualities, but because your baby's eyes and hands do not interpret the qualities of objects well yet, your baby learns more about something by putting it in his mouth than by looking at it.

● **From six months old** Your baby will probably start to teethe now. Every baby responds differently to the emergence of teeth. You (and your

---

signs your baby is ready to cut his first tooth

If your baby is gnawing at and biting down on objects in combination with any of the following symptoms, ask your doctor to rule out any other illness before assuming he is teething:

● Excessive drooling that leads to a red and spotty rash around his mouth.

● Resisting having a spoon put in his mouth at mealtimes.

● Frequent, loose stools that have a distinctive acrid smell.

● Nappy rash.

● Low-grade fever not accompanied by illness.

● Runny nose.

● Tugging at his ears.

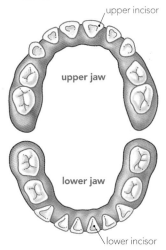

first teeth The first teeth to make their appearance are generally the bottom middle two incisors, followed by the two top, middle teeth.

traditional teething remedies

There are many teething remedies available. Consider some of these if medication or commercial teething rings don't seem to help:

● Homeopathy (a form of alternative medicine) offers remedies that may ease discomfort, and can be highly effective. Seek a diagnosis from a qualified homeopath before using any homeopathic teething remedies.

● Essential oil of cloves is known to be a natural local anaesthetic. Mix one drop of clove oil in two tablespoons of organic sunflower oil and rub the mixture onto your baby's gums. Before you give it to your baby, try the mixture on your own gums to make sure it's not too strong. If you feel any irritation, add more sunflower oil.

● Cold food can help relieve gum pain. Cut up a bagel, put the pieces in a sandwich bag, and store it in the freezer. When your baby is uncomfortable, give him a piece to gnaw on. The coldness helps numb the gums, and the edge of the bagel will massage your baby's gums as he chews on it. You could also try vegetables such as carrots and cucumbers – cut them into chunks and put them in the fridge beforehand.

● Make a natural teething ring: wet the corner of a flannel with water and freeze it. Once frozen, give the flannel to your baby who will love the tactile sensation of holding the cloth and enjoy the relief of the cool cloth against the gums.

baby) may be lucky and sail through the teething stage, or there may be some seriously wobbly days (and nights). In general, sensitive babies respond unhappily to emerging teeth as they are affected much more by the discomfort and more disturbed by change. Settled babies, on the other hand, barely notice that anything has changed, until one day you will notice that a tooth has emerged as he grins at you.

managing teething It is important to ascertain whether your baby is teething during daylight hours – it is tempting to blame every night waking or daytime grumble on teething.

In addition to the criteria on the previous page, look for extra evidence just below the gums in the form of a tooth (a hard white bump in the gum). If you have decided that a tooth is about to erupt, try the following suggestions:

● If your child is niggly or irritable, use teething medication recommended by your health visitor: teething powders, gels or paracetamol. He may have a headache (he won't be able to tell you this, but may be generally fractious and you may see him grabbing at his head or rubbing it) and or a sore mouth (it may look red or

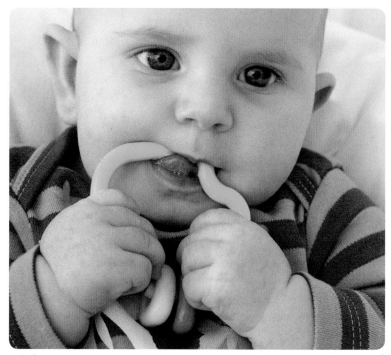

relief Chewing on a teething ring may help to soothe your baby during teething. There are many brightly coloured rings available that your baby will enjoy playing with, as well as using for sucking and chewing comfort for a sore mouth.

inflamed), especially while eating. You may also want to consult your doctor before giving him medication.

● Store your baby's dummies and teethers in the fridge – the coolness helps to soothe inflamed gums.

● Your baby may enjoy gnawing at your finger in preference to a teething ring (don't worry; your finger is tough and this won't hurt you). This is also handy if a ring is not available. Try pressing down on the inflamed gum with a clean finger to alleviate the soreness.

separation anxiety

Between the ages of seven and eight months, babies start to develop separation anxiety. This ranges from mild upset to intense distress when you leave them, if only for a moment. This is completely normal and a common feature of the first year. All children experience some degree of separation anxiety, but it can be significantly worse in slow-to-warm-up and sensitive babies. The reason your baby will become anxious when separated from you and thus become clingier is that he has not fully developed "object permanence", the knowledge that an object or person still exists when you can't see it. At this age your baby fears that you may disappear and not return to him if he loses sight of you. He may want to be in your arms all the time and cry inconsolably if you try to leave him, even if it is just to go into another room. He may also react with distress to strangers, even extended family members. It can be very frustrating to parent a baby who is unsettled unless you are holding him, and you may be feeling trapped. It is common for separation anxiety to worsen between eight and nine months and it only really resolves when your baby gets closer to a year, when object permanence is fully established.

The best way to deal with this anxiety is to spend special or quality time with your baby. Hold him, speak to him and cuddle him. When you have to put him down to do something, continue to talk to him. Mirror his emotions and reflect how he is feeling by saying, "I know you want mummy and I am right here. But I have to ... and then I will pick you up again". At the same time, give your baby a toy to distract him from needing you for a few minutes and encourage his attempts to play while you get on with your task.

Whenever you leave your baby, always say goodbye – never sneak out of the room. Once you have left to go to another room, continue to talk to him from the other room, so that he learns that you still exist even when he can't see you. When you come back, always greet him happily and with lots of cuddles.

To speed up the development of object permanence, play hide-and-seek games and peek-a-boo with your baby to help him grasp the concept that something still exists when he can't see it.

don't leave me! Your baby may develop separation anxiety around six to nine months, because she doesn't understand that you will return when you leave her.

helping your baby sleep

After six months of parenting, you probably felt sure you'd be having a full night's sleep, so you may be feeling disillusioned if your baby is still waking at night. Sleep issues may occur at this stage due to separation anxiety, disruptions in sleep habits due to teething, and nutritional changes. Any of these hiccups may result in habit-forming night waking.

sensory secrets to good sleep habits

Your baby's sensory world holds the key to sleep. See pp.18–27 and p.35 for a reminder on how to keep his sensory world calm.

movement stimulation We know that an active day filled with movement helps us sleep well. Babies are no different and need good doses of movement during the day if they are to sleep well at night. To ensure your baby has enough stimulation, introduce some intense movement by rocking him in a hammock or swinging him in a baby swing. Do this twice in the afternoon, for at least five minutes at a time. You can do it for longer if your baby tolerates the movement well.

sensory sleep space The environment your baby sleeps in should enhance sleep and ensure that he is not over-stimulated:
● Keep his sleep space consistent (put him to bed in the same place each time) so that the sensory qualities of the environment trigger sleep.
● Use black-out lining on the curtains or blinds to create a dark space so he is unlikely to be woken by daylight, especially if he is an early riser.
● Remove toys, other than his comfort object, from the cot.
● Switch off the baby monitor at night if your room is close to your baby's room to prevent you from over-responding if he stirs at night. This will allow him opportunity to soothe himself.
● Make sure he has his long midday sleep in this normal sleep space.

sensory overload Avoid sensory overload before sleep times as this will trigger the release of hormones that keep your baby awake and he is less likely to settle without assistance. Watch for signals that tell you that your baby is becoming overloaded, such as becoming irritable or rubbing his eyes and ears (see p.40). Limit his awake time (see p.51) to two to two-and-a-half hours to avoid overtiredness. Try to schedule baby groups and outings around his sleeps.

introduce a sleep soother All babies need a soothing method to resettle independently at night. Some soothers your baby might use are on his own body, such as his thumb or his hair. Your baby might suck

---

sleep: what to expect at this stage

● During the day, take your baby to his sleeping environment and prepare to get him down to sleep after he's been awake for two to two-and-a-half hours.
● Your baby's sleep routine could include: a morning nap at approximately 9am; a midday sleep for between an hour and two hours; and a late afternoon catnap of between 15 and 45 minutes (this catnap disappears as your baby nears nine months of age or if his other daytime sleeps are both long).
● Wake your baby by 4.30pm in the afternoon if he is still sleeping so that he will settle with ease in the evening. As a rule of thumb this is the only time you should wake a sleeping baby of this age. Do not wake your baby from any other daytime or night sleeps.
● Aim for a bedtime of not later than 6pm to 7pm. Your baby may wake for the day anywhere between 5am and 7am.
● Your baby can be expected to sleep through the night from 7am to 5am or even to 7am.
● If your baby wakes at night, give him the opportunity to soothe himself before responding to him.

self-soothing

Try to find something your baby can use to soothe himself when he wakes at night, rather than something he will depend on you to provide.

sensory component	dependent on you	independent soothers
Touch	• Stroking your hair • Being patted to sleep	• Stroking a piece of satin or silk or fleece • Touching his face • Stroking his own hair
Movement	• Car • Pram	• Rocking his head • Moving his hands
Sucking	• Rocking to sleep • Your breast • Your finger • Bottle	• Thumb • Dummy (can be an independent soother by nine months)
Body position	• In your arms • Being held in a certain position	• Wedging himself against the top of the cot • Sleeping in a certain position
Sounds	• Mum singing	• Humming or moaning • Singing to himself • White noise CD

night terrors

Babies who scream and cry at night and appear to be awake, but seem to be unaware of your presence are said to be having "night terrors". These differ from nightmares because your baby is actually in deep sleep, while a nightmare will wake him. Night terrors are directly related to overtiredness and are usually seen in toddlers and babies who are not getting enough daytime sleep or are going to bed too late.

his thumb, sing to himself, or stroke his own hair. It is important that you allow and even encourage your baby to develop independent calming strategies, so that he can settle himself back to sleep at night without having to call for you. If your baby doesn't appear to do so, try guiding his hands to his mouth or hair when he is upset. He can also use these methods during the day to calm himself if he gets upset – without you having to provide comfort for him every time. Other soothers you could introduce to your baby are items such as a security blanket or a dummy.

sucking

Non-nutritive sucking really helps to calm young babies. Some babies learn to suck their own hands from very early on, and some even manage to find their thumbs, while others need a dummy to suck on. All of these are excellent soothers for babies at night. Do not stop your baby from sucking, but guide him towards a method that works for you both (see overleaf).

sleep objects

A security blanket or other sleep object is the best sleep association for your baby and something that most babies take to quite easily. Choose something your baby is taking a liking to. It should be something soft, small enough to put into a nappy bag and small enough not to have a risk of suffocation. Most importantly, it should be something you can replace a year down the line if your toddler loses it. Examples of good sleep objects are: a small teddy, a small fleece blanket, a muslin, or a blanket with satin tags.

to introduce a security object

Give it to your baby whenever he fusses, whether for pain, irritation, or tiredness during the day, when he gets a hug. Put it on your shoulder (if it's a blanket or soft toy) and let him cuddle against it.

After a week or two of consistently offering the sleep object with your comfort, your baby will find comfort day and night in this security object.

thumb sucking This self-soothing strategy is the first very clever, independent skill your baby learns. Your life will be easier if your baby can calm himself, especially at sleep time. If he is dependent on you to calm him (for example if he was discouraged from sucking, and therefore did not develop that skill), he will call for you and need your comfort every time he wakes at night or becomes upset during the day.

The advantages of thumb or hand sucking are that your baby can do this independently from very early on. The negative is that thumb suckers do have a higher risk of needing orthodontic treatment at a later stage. Whether thumb sucking will result in bucked teeth however, depends on your family's predisposition to dental problems and how long your child sucks his thumb. It is harder to get rid of a thumb-sucking habit as you can't conveniently "lose" a thumb (in the same way you can lose a dummy).

dummies On a sensory level, your baby needs to suck in order to be calm, and if he is not doing it himself (by sucking his hands or thumb), a dummy is a very effective tool. Getting rid of the dummy is a bridge you can cross later. It will depend on your baby – some just reject the dummy naturally in the first year, others need to be rewarded for giving it up in the toddler years. You can limit dummies to sleep times from six months onwards if you don't want her to use it during the day.

teaching your baby to use a dummy At around six to nine months, many babies start to wake for you to replace the dummy in the middle of the night. They are not yet able to use the dummy independently. By about nine months old however, you can expect your baby to be using his dummy independently at night. So, if your baby is older than eight months and still waking you to give him his dummy at night, try these three steps to help him use his dummy independently:

❶ In the first few days, keep putting in his dummy when he cries at night, but during the day, don't put the dummy in his mouth. When he asks for it, place the dummy in his hand so that he learns to pop it in himself during daylight hours.

❷ Once he has achieved daytime independence, do the same at night – don't place the dummy back in his mouth, rather put it into his hand or attach it to a small sleep blanket and put that in his hand so he must do the final step of putting the dummy into his mouth on his own.

❸ When he has advanced to that stage (usually within a few days if he is older than eight months), stop putting the dummy in his hand and guide his hand to the dummy in the dark. The next night put every dummy in the house into his cot, giving him maximum chance of finding one of them at night, even if he has thrown some of them out of the cot earlier.

sleeping well during the day

Your baby's busy sensory world still has the potential to overwhelm him. If he becomes over-stimulated, he will become overtired very quickly, and be grumpy and difficult, especially around sleep time. Avoid over-tiredness and over-stimulation by putting a daytime-sleep routine in place (see p.151). If you already have a routine, but are struggling to get your baby to sleep and keep him asleep it may be because he is overtired or has developed a bad sleep habit.

overtired baby If your baby is overtired because he has missed a sleep you may struggle to settle him. Try these tips to make him drowsy:
● Set aside 20 minutes to settle your baby and take him to a darkened room. Change his nappy, and put on a recording of white noise.
● Hold your baby in your arms and rock him until he is very drowsy. Then, put him down, placing your hand on his tummy and applying deep pressure. Continue to hold your hand on him gently if he niggles.
● If he is distressed and you end up rocking your baby to sleep, don't blame yourself, just remember next time to watch the amount of time he spends awake (see p.51) so he doesn't get overtired.

breaking sleep habits If you have been having a run of busy days and your baby has been sleeping when you are out, predominantly in his buggy or the car seat, you may find that he will only fall asleep if he is in these places. To help him make the transition from falling asleep in the car or buggy back to falling asleep in the cot, follow these steps:
● Stop going out in the car at sleep times for a few days. Rather, put him in his car seat or buggy and rock him to sleep in his sleep space. This keeps the movement consistent but changes the sleeping environment.
● If your baby has only ever fallen asleep in his buggy, begin to rock the buggy only until he is drowsy, then stop rocking it, and let him fall asleep by himself. Decrease the period of rocking each day.
● Once your baby is falling asleep with no movement, put him straight into his cot at sleep time. Don't forget to help him to become drowsy first. He may need some help – maybe a little patting, stroking or shushing – for the first few days that you put him directly into his cot.

settling in the evening

Your baby's bedtime routine must be calming and consistent because it acts as a cue for his brain to start shifting down into the drowsy state for bedtime. Aim for a bedtime of between 6pm and 7pm. Watch for signals of sensory overload at this time of day, and be sure to be home, in a calming space, not socializing. A calm bath time can be hard to achieve if your baby loves the excitement of the water, but try to keep your

lengthening the midday sleep

By six months of age, most babies have begun to link sleep cycles during one nap (a sleep cycle is 45 minutes, see p.30). This will probably be for the midday sleep. For the two short naps, your baby can still be expected to wake 45 minutes after falling asleep. To help your baby have one longer nap, try the following:
● Give your baby his lunch before this nap as he will sleep better with a full tummy. This midday sleep may happen any time between 11am and 1pm, depending on what time he woke from his morning nap. If this sleep time is as early as 11am, move lunch before the sleep or offer a hearty snack at this time, and another one when he wakes.
● If your baby stirs after 45 minutes, either listen for five minutes to see if he will resettle, or go into the dark room, offer him his comfort object and pat him back to sleep.
● If these methods don't work that day get your baby up, but persist each day to encourage a longer midday sleep. Keep an eye on the amount of time your baby spends awake so you know when it is time for his next nap.

separation anxiety at night

Around eight months of age, your baby's sleep may be interrupted because of separation anxiety. At around six to eight months of age, your baby will begin to question whether you still exist when you leave him. This upsets him as he has formed a strong attachment to you and may protest at the separation and cry as you leave. Your baby may wake during light sleep states seeking reassurance that you will return to him. This is linked to your baby's developing object permanence (the understanding that things still exist when we can't see them).

● If you feel his night wakings are caused by separation anxiety, go to your baby and tell him gently to go back to sleep, give him his sleep object (blanket or soft toy) and leave the room. Do not start a habit at this stage, such as feeding him to sleep or rocking him, but do demonstrate that you will return to him after a separation.

● A comfort object, such as a blanket, is vital at this stage so your baby can use it to soothe himself when he wakes at night and whenever you are not in the room.

● During the day, always say goodbye when you leave your baby, even if it's just to have a shower, and always greet him happily on your return, so that he learns that separations are accompanied by happy reunions.

● Manage this stage with lots of hugs and cuddles and remember that it won't last for long.

interactions with each other muted. Follow bath time with a soothing massage (see p.105) and then feed him in the dark of his room. Do not take your baby out of his room between 6pm and 6am – in this way he will think the world ceases to exist while he is asleep.

If he is wakeful after the last feed, rock him to a drowsy state, but be sure that you do not rock him to sleep. Once he is drowsy, place him in his cot, say good night and leave the room. Do not hang around to see what he does. Many babies chatter, move about, and may even play for a bit before dropping off to sleep.

sleep coaching If your baby is not settling at sleep times, and you have followed all the steps so far, it is now time to try using some sleep-coaching strategies (see also pp.198–99). These will teach your baby to fall asleep independently. This is healthy for his emotional development and quite appropriate for this age group.

If your baby begins to fuss when you put him down, either the second you leave the room or after a bit of time alone, return to him. To sleep coach him successfully, you may need to sit with him for a few nights until he learns to soothe himself to sleep. Help him by patting and soothing him for the first night, then gradually decrease your assistance over subsequent nights by simply sitting alongside his cot without talking to him. Do not look worried or concerned; rather just close your eyes. Give him his sleep object and help him to lie down if he stands up, but other than that just sit with him. He may cry if he is expecting to be rocked or fed to sleep, but be consistent and unwavering. Keep this up until he falls asleep, which can take up to a few hours. You will have to repeat this procedure when he wakes in the night. He should learn the art of soothing himself in about a week.

night-time sleep solutions

Babies do have the capacity to sleep through the night at this stage. So, if you are still being woken at night, it's worth considering the common reasons why and finding solutions for them.

your sensory baby The sensitive baby can be a very poor sleeper from the start and this stage is no different. Your sensitive baby feels and hears every little sensory impression intensely. To help him sleep:

● Play white noise in his room to mask noises from outside.

● Do not have your baby in your bed or bedroom because he may sleep better if undisturbed by your movements and noises.

● Unpick or cut the labels out of vests and sleepsuits as they may be scratchy. You could also turn vests inside out. You may even want to look for seamless vests that have no irritating sensory ridges.

- Do not lift your baby up at night, which may wake him further. Instead, put your hand on him and apply deep pressure to soothe him back to sleep.

The social butterfly may wake simply to check that you are there or to seek sensory input. If you find your baby rocking on all fours in his cot at night or even pulling himself up to stand in his cot, he may be restless because he is not tired enough to sleep. To help him sleep:
- Engage in a lot of movement in the late afternoon: go to the park and swing him; invest in a hammock or baby swing; go for a walk with him in a sling before supper.
- You may want to limit television to very little or none at all; the sedentary time in front of a screen does him no good.

A slow-to-warm-up baby is generally a good sleeper, as long as his routine is consistent. However, if you move house, go on holiday, or move him into his own room, all good habits go out the window while he finds his comfort zone again. To help him sleep:
- Keep his room in exactly the same configuration with the same smells and bedding.
- When travelling take his travel cot, bedding, and sleep object with you to ensure as much consistency as possible.

changing nutritional needs Milk alone will not sufficient for your baby now. If he is still waking frequently to drink milk during the night, it is important to check that he is getting enough to eat before starting any sleep-coaching strategies.

At this age protein in your baby's diet, or lack thereof, can have a profound impact on sleep. Protein is vital for two reasons. Firstly, it takes longer to digest and keeps the tummy feeling fuller for longer. Secondly, protein builds the body and provides the building blocks for brain development. Along with fat, proteins contain the fatty acids essential for brain growth that our bodies do not produce. At night, when your baby sleeps and his brain processes information, these essential fatty acids are critical. Very often, if a baby is waking hungry at night, it is because he is not getting enough protein, particularly in the meal before bed, so ensure that his evening meal contains it (see p.181).

teething This is often the first thought that pops into your mind if your baby is unsettled at night. See p.172 for ways to manage teething during the day and at night. Don't panic – act appropriately:
- If he has many signs of teething and there's a little tooth just under the gums, prepare for sleep disruptions for about three nights.
- Give him his sleep object and resettle him, but do not feed him. This will not solve teething irritation and is likely to result in poor habits.

Q&A
restless sleeper

My baby started crawling at seven months old and since then, wakes frequently at night, trying to crawl in his sleep and even stand in his cot. Should I be worried?

This is a common sleep hiccup that accompanies the learning of new skills. As your baby learns something new, his brain spends time while he is asleep processing the new skill and the synapses used fire to reinforce the connection. This happens when your baby is in the light sleep state. Most babies can sleep through this, but some wake to rehearse the crawling or learning to stand. There is nothing you can do for your baby and you can leave him to play unless he is really crying. If he does start crying, go to him and settle him by patting or rocking him. Many babies will rehearse a skill and settle themselves back to sleep with no problem.

feeding: what to expect at this stage

- Milk become secondary to solids. Your baby needs four milk feeds a day (on waking, mid-morning, after lunch, and again at bedtime), but will drop the mid-morning milk feed by nine months.
- If you have not yet started your baby on solid food, it is essential that you do so now.
- Provided he is thriving and not ill, there is no need for milk at night once your baby is on three solid meals a day, including protein.
- If you are bottle feeding, ensure that your baby's formula is appropriate for his age.
- He should be eating solid food three times a day (at breakfast, lunch and dinner).
- Try introducing a small finger-food snack in the mid-morning and mid-afternoon.
- It is important to introduce protein into your baby's diet, including dairy produce, poultry, red meat and legumes. He needs protein for healthy growth and development and the constituent amino acids for good brain development. Protein should be included with each meal.

CAUTION If you or your baby's father have allergies, or if your child has already started to show signs of allergies, certain proteins such as nuts, fish, soya, and eggs are best avoided until your baby is older. Do seek advice regarding his diet from your doctor, health visitor, or a dietician.

feeding your baby

Now is the time to start introducing your baby to solid food if you haven't already. After a few weeks he will be enjoying these new tastes and exploring new textures. Once your baby is older than six months, he requires protein in his solid food.

milk feeds

Your breast milk changes to meet your growing baby's needs, but if he is on an infant formula, now is the time to move on to one specifically for babies aged six months and older. This milk contains more protein. Do not offer your baby cow's milk, but use infant formula mixed according to instructions. Your baby's minimum milk requirement (breast or formula) is approximately 600ml (21fl oz) per day. If he does not drink his breast or formula milk with enthusiasm, remember to include milk in his solid meals, in the form of white sauce, yoghurt, or other dairy foods.

solids

Although breast or formula milk still play an important role and must not be excluded from your baby's diet, now that he is six months old, milk alone cannot meet his increasing nutritional needs. If you have not yet introduced solids, follow the five-stage plan laid out in chapter 11

new foods Introducing solids provides the opportunity for your baby to try different textures, which will help to develop mouth muscle control.

(see pp.160–61). Complete the stages over a period of two to three weeks, starting with one meal of a single grain such as rice, working up to three meals a day before starting to add animal protein. If your six-month-old is already eating solid food, move straight on to the diet plan below (see p.182).

solids for variety Your baby is wired to delight in his sensory world. Eating provides yet another opportunity to explore and broaden his experiences. Introduce a single food at a time, about three times in a row, before moving on to another new food.

Try not to let food become an "issue" between you and your baby. Respect his moods and feelings – just as we have days when we don't feel madly hungry, so does your baby. If he seems to have finished eating, just remove the food and don't try to force him to eat it. Cook different foods together to introduce different taste combinations, for example lasagne provides pasta, meat or vegetables, and sauce. Expand your baby's eating world by introducing:

● **Textures** The introduction of more textured food will encourage and develop your baby's chewing and mashing skills. This helps him to develop muscle control of his tongue, lips and cheeks, which is a vital part of language development. Do not limit your baby to jars or stage-one baby food as this can contribute to fussy eating later. Babies need to experience texture, such as lumps and crunches in food, which is why babies who eat homemade food from the start are less fussy eaters as toddlers.

● **Finger foods** These help to develop fine motor control in little fingers, as well as developing the taste receptors in his mouth so he can manage more tasty and textured foods. Good ideas for finger foods include unsalted rice cakes or bread sticks, toast, peeled soft fruit, small chunks of cooked vegetable, and dried fruit. Be sure to watch him carefully while he is eating to ensure no bits break off that he can choke on.

protein Foods high in protein are necessary at this stage of your baby's growth and development. Protein is the bodybuilding foodstuff vital for optimal growth and development. From six to nine months of age, your baby needs seven to nine teaspoons (one heaped teaspoon = one serving) of protein per day, mixed with a variety of carbohydrates, fats, fruit, and vegetables, and spread out over three meals.

Don't give protein derived from foodstuffs other than breast or formula milk to babies younger than six months of age. This is because certain proteins may be allergenic and the digestive system of a young baby is unable to handle allergens. Once your baby is over six months of age, he will need extra protein to be included in his diet. See the box above right (protein for babies), for some good options.

protein for babies

vegetable protein
● Legumes: kidney beans, butter beans, lentils, chick peas
● Ground nuts and nut butters: peanut, cashew, almond
● Avocado pear, broccoli
● Seeds: sesame, sunflower, pumpkin
● Brown rice, barley, quinoa

animal protein
● Dairy products: yoghurt, cottage cheese, cream cheese, hard white cheese, unsalted butter
● Eggs (well-cooked)
● Fish: tuna, pilchards, sardines, salmon, mackerel, hake
● Poultry: chicken, chicken liver, turkey, ostrich
● Pork and ham (but check for salt content)
● Red meat: beef, lamb, rabbit

foods to avoid

Be aware that your baby does not need salt in his food. Never add any to food that you make and be sure to check labels of any products you buy to ensure that it does not contain salt. Be especially careful with preserved meats (such as bacon), and ready meals. Even those designed for babies may contain high levels of salt, which can damage your baby's kidneys. Avoid adding any additional sugar to his food. Get into the habit of reading labels and avoid foods with sweeteners, colourants and preservatives. Avoid processed foods, packaged sauces and spices.

getting enough? Your baby needs three teaspoons of protein at each of her three main meals a day. Yoghurt is a good source of protein.

finger foods Giving your baby whole steamed foods from this age is a wonderful way to encourage variety and good eating habits.

the **babysense** secret

diet plan for six to nine months of age

Use this table for ideas on what and when to feed your baby at this stage. He will still need three or four milk feeds a day.

time	meal	food and amounts
6am	Milk feed	150–240ml (5–8½fl oz)
8am	Breakfast	Offer a carbohydrate-rich breakfast to supply your baby with energy to start the day: ● Infant cereal (6–12 months) or porridge made of cooked oats, maize meal, or semolina ● Two to three teaspoons of protein, for example cottage cheese, yoghurt, egg, ground almonds or formula milk ● French toast ● Fresh fruit, ground almonds or puréed dates
10am	Milk feed	150–240ml (5–8½fl oz). This feed may fall away as your baby nears nine months of age
12 noon	Lunch	Offer one of these options of carbohydrates and/or vegetables with protein, followed by fruit and yoghurt: ● Avocado pear and cottage or cream cheese ● French toast ● Vegetable soup with crumbled bread ● Mashed potato with cheese sauce ● Macaroni cheese, mince, or fish bake ● White rice with creamed spinach or cheese sauce ● Chicken, lamb, or vegetable stew ● Fresh fruit with yoghurt or almonds or pumpkin or sesame seeds
2pm	Milk feed	150–240ml (5–8½fl oz)
3pm	Snack	Diluted juice or water, and finger foods, such as rice cakes or steamed vegetables
5pm	Dinner	Offer the same as for lunch
6–7pm	Milk feed	150–240ml (5–8½fl oz)

supplements

Your baby should be able to get all his nutrients from the food he eats. If your baby is a good eater then he does not need added vitamins unless others in the family come down with an illness. If, on the other hand, he is a fussy eater, it is worth speaking to your doctor or health visitor, who may recommend a specific supplement:

● **Plant proteins** If your baby has an insufficient intake of plant proteins you might like to try liquid supplements, for example wheatgrass juice. They have been shown to improve growth, development, and sleep.

● **Vitamins** If your baby is drinking breast milk or 500ml (17½fl oz) or more formula per day and eating an average diet, he does not need additional supplements. However, if you have concerns, ask your doctor or health visitor about vitamin supplements.

● **Iron** Babies are born with iron stores that run out by the time they reach four to six months of age. Iron is essential for the functioning of the central nervous system and plays a key role in the transport of oxygen to the brain. Iron deficiency has been associated with decreased immune function leading to more infections, fatigue, loss of appetite, and sleep disorders. Sources of iron include green leafy vegetables, egg yolks, and red meat, such as beef, liver, and kidneys. Infant cereals are fortified with iron, as are some varieties of fruit and vegetable juices. If your baby is a fussy feeder and does not get enough of these foods in his diet you might like to consider giving him a plant-based iron supplement, but do consult your doctor or health visitor first, as given in incorrect doses, iron supplements can be toxic.

Q&A
refusing to eat solids

I have a seven-month-old and I am struggling to get him to eat solids. I have been trying since he was five-and-a-half months old, yet he still does not want to eat. I have tried home cooking, jar food, infant cereals, yoghurt, fruit ... everything! Fortunately he is not underweight as he still insists on his bottle five times a day. He is waking at night and I know he is hungry. What should I do?

Your baby needs to eat solid food now, as milk does not supply all the nutrition he needs as a growing baby. The reason that your baby is not taking to solids is that he does not have an appetite because of all the milk he is consuming. You need to limit his bottles to only three per day and just one at night until he is eating. This will give him an appetite for solids. Start with infant cereal and then move onto fruit and vegetables. Once he is eating well, drop the night bottle too. Try to feed him home-cooked food. If he still will not eat and is gagging on solids, speak to an occupational therapist or speech therapist to see if he is hypersensitive to textures in his mouth.

fussy? If your baby is a fussy feeder and will not eat a varied diet, you may want to consider supplements. Check with your doctor or health visitor.

your social baby

Your baby is developing into a real chatterbox. A singsong babble, chuckles and irritated screams are all part of his new verbal repertoire. Your sociable little baby may even begin to imitate conversations. He knows his name and understands what "No" means. He also starts to understand social situations and waves goodbye.

Your baby may now have a strong attachment to a transitional object such as a blanket or soft toy. This is a sign of his growing independence: he now has an independent source of security other than you.

getting to know your baby

Your baby becomes more and more social during these special months. He tries to get everyone's attention and really interacts with his world. This is an exciting time for him as he learns to sit, "stand" (when supported), and finally crawl while also learning to manipulate objects and develop "object permanence" (see opposite).

rolling and sitting When your six-month-old baby is placed on his back he will work hard at developing his tummy muscles to help him sit and crawl. He will not only love to lift his legs and hold on to his feet, but also to lift his head to look at his feet. All these challenging tummy and back muscle exercises will now pay off, as your baby rolls both from tummy to back and back to tummy. During this stage he will begin actively to protest about having his nappy changed because the position you put him in is much too passive for this active stage. Nappy changing becomes a real challenge when he tries to roll over onto his tummy.

Your baby can now sit unsupported and, by the end of this stage, manage to sit up from lying down and vice versa. This newfound freedom will delight him. And because your baby is content to sit and play for a while, many mums report life becoming more normal for the first time since their babies were born – at last you get some personal space.

crawling Your baby will soon move in and out of a sitting position with ease. He will start to reach to get a toy, and even to turn to the side and retrieve a toy a little distance away. This is how he'll one day find himself in the crawling position – he'll reach too far and end up on all fours. In this position, he may spend a bit of time rocking before collapsing on to his tummy. After a few more days of rocking on all fours he'll just set off, usually backwards at first.

The way your baby reaches the crawling position does not matter; he may belly-creep first or "leopard creep": go from tummy-lying into a crawling position. What is important is that he does crawl, or at least initiates some form of forward motion. If he is slow learning to crawl, you can assist him by giving him lots of tummy time.

movement and manipulation When held in a standing position, your baby can now support his weight fully and loves to bounce on his feet. In fact, any movement becomes a fun game for most babies. You will find that he loves to bounce, move and sway.

Now that he can pass toys from hand to hand and manipulate objects, he also loves to hold anything. As well as exploring objects with his mouth, he examines them more purposefully with his hands.

developing "object permanence" As he nears eight months, your baby starts to experience stranger anxiety and notices as soon as you are out of sight (see p.173). By nine months, he will develop "object permanence", which is the awareness that something still exists when it is out of sight. So now he'll look around for a dropped toy and will love peek-a-boo games. He also really enjoys nursery rhymes and other body games such as "This little piggy".

pulling along As your baby tries to crawl, she may "leopard creep": push up on her arms and attempt to pull herself along.

target milestones

Your baby really loves to interact with people and to engage with his world. The increased stability in the centre of his body means that his arms and hands are free to manipulate and explore and learn. He is developing emotionally, and a real personality emerges. Expect these target milestones to be achieved by nine months.

area of development	target milestone
Gross motor	Sitting stably and exploring while in this position. Moving into a kneeling position. Crawling is primary means of locomotion. Climbing to explore the environment. Taking full weight when standing supported.
Fine motor	Voluntarily releasing objects he is holding. Banging objects and tearing paper. Picking up tiny things such as peas with his forefinger and thumb (pincer grip).
Hand–eye coordination	Transferring objects between hands. Visually examining objects in his hands carefully.
Language	Combining sounds such as "ba-ba" and "da-da". Understanding what "No" and "bye bye" mean.
Social/emotional	Using movements, such as pointing and reaching, to communicate. Decreasing fear of strangers by the end of this stage.
Regulation	Self-soothing is well-developed – he should be able to settle to sleep given the opportunity. Self-regulating his appetite and giving clear signals of hunger or fullness.

holding on Now that his manipulation skills are better developed, your baby will use his hands more than his mouth to explore objects.

CAUTION baby walkers

You may wonder whether a baby walker is a suitable toy for your baby. In fact, there are two important reasons why you should not use a baby walker:

● They contribute to falls: the top-heavy distribution of your baby's weight in a baby walker means that they tip over easily. In the USA, tipping over of baby walkers is one of the biggest causes of head injuries in babies in the first year of life.

● They hamper development: baby walkers are most often used at a time when a baby should be practising the skills needed for crawling. They not only hamper the development of crawling on a motor level, but also diminish the motivation to crawl, because the baby can get where he wants to using the walker. In addition, the supported standing position has a negative effect on the development of the hips, legs, and feet as weight-bearing limbs for walking.

If you would really like to use a baby walker, don't use it as a babysitter. Use it in moderation: no more than 10 minutes a day, and with constant supervision. A better option is a push-along trolley or a stationary activity centre.

sensible stimulation: TEAT

Not content to sit and watch the world go by, your baby works hard now at becoming more mobile. His motivation to move around is the catalyst for an explosion of motor skills: he begins to pivot on his tummy and creep and crawl. He also starts to develop bilateral hand use: using both hands together. As he can handle more and more sensory input, you can begin to stimulate him more using the ideas given here. Always watch him closely for warning signals that he's feeling over-stimulated or insecure. Keeping to a routine is important now as your baby thrives when he has a familiar structure to his day. Encourage him as he strives to achieve vital milestones such as rolling and crawling, which lay important foundations for later development.

timing

Include both stimulating activities and calming strategies in your day. But for the first time, stimulating activities now begin to feature more prominently. Your baby's awake time lasts two to two-and-a-half hours now and during this time he will be able to cope with stimulation for close to an hour at a stretch. This is the time to look for a swimming, baby gym or music class – he will manage the interaction with delight.

For 10 minutes before daytime sleeps and an hour before bedtime in the evening, limit stimulation and make sure you play calmly.

environment

As your baby becomes older, try to make his environment more stimulating than calming, except around sleep times.

visual Your baby really learns through his sense of sight now and will visually explore objects. Limit the number of toys you present at one time so that he can explore each one properly. Constantly providing too many toys may hinder a good attention span. Don't put the television on in the background – the combination of mindless visual and auditory information is not beneficial for your baby.

hearing Talk to your baby constantly about his world and what you are doing. It's good to play music and songs in the background.

touch Play areas and the outdoor world offer great opportunities to explore his environment through touch. Take your baby to a farmyard or beach to experience the tactile elements there.

motor development Parks and play areas are wonderful places to encourage your baby's motor development. You can show him the grass and leaves in the park or help him to explore the play equipment.

activities

sleep time

Even though your baby can cope with more sensory input now and remain in a calm-alert state for longer, limit stimulation before bedtime, especially if he is a social butterfly or sensitive baby, who will struggle to settle to sleep if over-stimulated.

visual Early morning waking is typical at this stage. Keep the room darkened by using black-out blinds or linings on the curtains to encourage later sleep. Limit bright or interesting items in or too near the cot.

hearing Soft lullaby music can still have a calming effect, but if your baby is not used to it, it may stimulate him rather than calm him. White noise still works well to settle babies into a deeper state of sleep.

touch Use soft blankets, bedding, and clothing. Find a soft toy or blanket to serve as a comfort object to which he can become attached and so use to calm himself (see p.176). If your baby has the odd really bad night's sleep and after going through the process of elimination (see p.112), you still have no clue as to why, try to keep a record of what he was wearing that night. Sometimes an irritating label or scratchy fabric disturbs babies at night. This is especially true for sensitive babies.

movement Calming movement is now less necessary at sleep time. In fact, rocking may rouse your baby more than lull him to sleep.

on the changing mat

Towards the end of this stage your baby will start to resist being placed on his back for nappy changes.

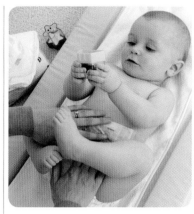

visual Fun mobiles with changeable pieces that are within arm's reach are still great for this age. Your baby will love looking at them, and coordinating what he sees with reaching will be rewarding. Use manipulation toys, such as bricks and blocks, and bright books to keep him busy while you get the task done.

hearing If you have a music mobile over the changing mat, play it for him when you change his nappy.

motor development To teach your baby to sit up from lying down, after a nappy change hold one of his arms and roll him to the other side and up into a sitting position. This teaches his muscles the feeling of the movement.

bath time

This is still the start of your baby's bedtime routine, so be careful not to over-excite him at this time of day; instead play quietly and then be very calm after his bath.

visual Place bath toys in the bath so that he can watch them floating towards and away from him to develop his eye muscles for tracking.

hearing Sing and talk to your baby. Use other senses to add to his picture of his body – for example, start naming his body parts as you wash them in the bath.

visual Use touch to draw your baby's attention to a body part – rub his tummy firmly with a flannel or put bubbles on it and encourage him to reach for them, or scrub his toes gently with a soft scrubbing brush and say "These are your toes". Add some baby bubble bath to give your baby a new texture to explore.

motor development Your baby will be ready to sit in the bath now. Use a bath support or non-slip mat to ensure he does not slip and fall under the water and never leave him alone while he's in the bath, not even for a second. Give him pouring toys. This action is excellent for developing muscles in the shoulder. Plastic beakers should be small enough to handle and tip.

smell Use baby-safe lavender or chamomile scented bath products for a calming effect before bedtime.

activities continued ...

awake time

This is the prime time for learning and development. Your baby is now ready to deal with more sensory input and, if he is in the calm-alert state, will learn a lot about his world.

visual As he now loves outings, take your baby out in his buggy and point out interesting things while you describe them to him. To encourage eye tracking and strengthen his eye muscles, play games where he can watch a ball roll away or point out a moving aeroplane or car. Your baby will enjoy hiding games. To help him grasp the idea of object permanence, partially or fully hide objects for him to find.

hearing Show your baby where sounds are coming from so that he attaches meaning to the sounds he hears. When talking to your baby, use exaggerated language and gestures and copy the sounds he makes. Read books to him, showing him their bright pictures. In the kitchen, while you're cooking, sit your baby on the floor with pots and pans to bang on. Give him other objects that make interesting noises. Use puppets to encourage communication. Give him soft toys that play music or squeak. Recite rhymes that actively involve him. Try "Pat-a-cake" with gestures, "Incy-wincy spider", "Sing a song of sixpence" and others that encourage the anticipation of actions.

touch Turn a walk into a feely tour, letting your baby feel the various textures in the natural environment such as leaves, bark, and so on. Use the feely tour to illustrate the qualities of things, for example soft leaf, rough sand, wet grass. Sing finger and toe songs such as "Round and round the garden" and "This little piggy". Keep a variety of touchy-feely objects, such as rubber pet toys, differently textured fabrics, wooden blocks, and small squashy balls, for him to play with in each room of the house.

movement Sit on a swing with your baby and move it in all directions. Use entertaining moving toys such as a large push-along truck, holding your baby on the back. Help him to pull himself up to stand on your lap and let him bounce if he enjoys this. Baby bouncers are controversial because they encourage bad patterns of standing and bearing weight in some children. If in doubt, don't use them. If you put your baby in a door bouncer for some movement stimulation, do so for no more than 10 minutes each day, and never leave him unsupervised.

motor development Sit your baby on the grass or carpet and let him reach for toys around him. This promotes sitting and balance and

entices him to crawl. Now is the time to start swimming lessons if you wish to. Time spent with you in a warm pool is wonderfully stimulating for all the senses and also for his motor development. To improve his sitting balance, sit your baby on your lap and slowly raise one of your legs fractionally, just enough to elicit a balance reaction from him without making him fall over. Encourage your baby to crawl by placing toys just out of reach. Let him spend time on his tummy, or place him on all fours over your leg and rock him in this position, giving him a sense of the movement. Encourage him to crawl over obstacles such as pillows, blankets, and you. Develop hand function by giving him items with interesting shapes to handle. Play clapping rhymes such as "Pat-a-cake". Encourage the use of both hands together by tearing paper, such as old newspapers. You could also give him different types of paper to scrunch up. Put stickers on your baby's hands for him to pull off. Place an object in each of his hands, or give him one big object that he will only be able to hold using both hands.

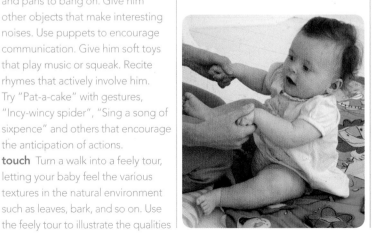

travelling time

Use music and toys to make journeys interesting for your baby. He will love outings in the buggy or baby carrier.

visual Your baby may start to resist being put in the car seat. Distract him visually with a mobile made of natural objects that make interesting noises or feel unusual, such as seedpods and feathers. Hang this from the grab handle above the window.

hearing Invest in a good quality CD or recording of children's songs.

movement If your baby gets car sick or dislikes being in the car, it could be that he is hypersensitive to the movement. Help him cope by using calming strategies such as sucking (on a dummy or give him diluted juice in a bottle or sippy cup). Very cold liquids help motion sickness.

feed time

This is a great opportunity for exploration and learning. It's also an advantage that the object he puts to his mouth actually tastes nice!

touch Allow your baby to enjoy texture play with foodstuffs such as spaghetti, soft pasta shapes, lumpy custard, jelly, watermelon, coloured ice, chocolate pudding, and cereal. Describe the qualities of the food.

motor development Handling finger food is one of the first things your baby can do for himself and he'll love it. Encourage fine motor control by giving him small pieces, but watch him in case he chokes. In the highchair watch how your baby starts to practise releasing toys by dropping them. Attach a short string to the toy so he can pull it up again.

toys

There is such a vast market for toys for this age group that it would be impossible to mention all the wonderful items out there. You don't need a great number of toys at once. Let your baby become familiar with a few toys and then rotate them. Only put out a few toys at a time, or your baby will become overwhelmed. He will forget toys that have been put away and then rediscover them. This is an especially good idea after holidays and birthdays when children get many gifts. You might also like to explore what the local toy library has to offer.

visual Look for books with bright, clear pictures, preferably board books or plastic books that will survive chewing. Make personalized books using photos of "his things" (cup, mum and dad, phone, bed). Books with plastic cords that tie on to the buggy are excellent for travel time as they won't get lost or dropped out of the buggy. To help him grasp object permanence, make or buy toys that disappear and reappear, such as a pop-up toy. Draw a face on a wooden spoon and slip it inside an empty toilet roll. Push the spoon up to make the face appear at the top of the roll, then pull it back so that it disappears.

hearing Provide rattles and bells, demonstrating how to use them. Play CDs with songs and music and show him pictures of animals, making their sounds.

touch Any objects of different textures will fascinate your baby. Try stacking blocks covered in interesting textures. Give him teething rings and tactile books so he can explore the different textures with both his hands and mouth.

movement Swings and hammocks are good for stimulating movement. Never leave your baby unsupervised in a swing or hammock.

motor development Buggy toys are fun for travel time and encourage a variety of fine motor functions. Don't forget about traditional, long-lasting toys, such as simple wooden cubes and balls.

 your baby at six to nine months

189

chapter 13

your baby at nine to twelve months

The first year is almost over. You have welcomed a brand new little person into your life, who has changed, moulded, and enriched your world. Your parenting skills seem to improve day by day, although self-doubt and maternal guilt may still trouble you. Over the past nine months, you have become an expert on topics such as baby feeding, sleeping, and development – and a mine of information on which brands make the most nutritious foods for babies and which restaurants are buggy friendly. Your baby is entering the most exciting (and, for you, most exhausting) phase of her first year of development. She is becoming mobile and will finally be able to discover for herself what an exciting place her world is.

baby-centric routine

● Try to limit your baby's awake time to two-and-a-half to three hours between sleeps and plan your feeding, changing, outings, and playtime within this time.
● Your baby will probably be having between one and three naps during the day, varying from 45 minutes to two hours in length and should sleep for 11 to 12 hours at night without needing a feed.
● She will probably be sleeping for 14 to 15 hours in a 24-hour cycle.
● You will be down to two or three milk feeds in 24 hours and three good solid meals a day.

choosing individual care

● If your baby is cared for in your home, will the carer stick to your baby's routine?
● If your baby is cared for by a family member or friend, are they up to date with all the latest child-rearing principles? You may like to recommend that they read a recent babycare book and do a first-aid course.
● Will the carer respect your wishes on your baby's care, such as limiting television and no smoking in the same house as your baby?
● If your baby is cared for out of your home, is that place safe, clean, and properly child-proofed?
● How is a distressed child treated?
● Will the carer feed your baby according to your schedule?
● Does the carer have the necessary child protection policies in place?

a day in the life of your baby

Your life seems to be returning to order and now you can predict your days and make plans more confidently. If your baby's routine is up-ended, she is much better able to cope with the disruption. It also helps you with planning your day if her routine is reasonably settled.

mum sense: childcare worries

At this stage of your baby's life you may be faced with the reality of returning to the workplace. The decision to be a stay-at-home mum or a working mum is not made lightly, and you must base your decision on your personal and economic needs. Some mothers are fulfilled by their mothering and nurturing role, while others need extra challenges and stimulation outside the home in order to feel balanced. Some women return to work full-time, others manage to find part-time work that allows fulfilment in both the personal and professional sides of life.

When you look for childcare and leave your baby with someone else, a barrage of new emotions arise. There is not a mother on this earth who is not torn as she walks out the door for the first time, leaving her baby in the care of someone else. The secret to making these separations manageable is in the childcare you choose.

choosing the right childcare

As hard as it is to leave your baby with someone else, you can be assured that much research has been conducted that shows that babies in good, consistent care with a loving caregiver are in no way emotionally hampered. In addition, although she may form a close relationship with her childminder, this does not affect the emotional bond between you and her. As long as she has a safe, caring environment, she will learn about relationships and have her basic needs met.

You may be fortunate enough to have the option of having your baby cared for in your home by one person consistently. This could be a nanny or au pair or a caring friend or family member. If you choose childcare away from your home, wonderful caring nurseries and childminders can create a consistent and happy place for your baby. All childminders must have insurance, be first-aid trained, and have a CRB (criminal records bureau) check, and staff in nurseries should have a CRB check and the nursery be registered with Ofsted, so do ask for these credentials. Take your time and consider all options carefully. Do some research. Find addresses of local nurseries online or from your local classified ads, and pop in, unannounced, to get a feel for the place. Trust your instincts!

making the relationship work The person or place you choose to look after your baby becomes a central relationship in your life. You need to develop trust and respect just as with any other relationship. In order to do this, consider these tips:

❶ Find someone who respects and supports you. Feeling constantly undermined, judged, or second-guessed will not work well in the long run.

❷ Choose someone who or a facility that is welcoming and delighted when you drop in unannounced.

❸ Respect your baby's carer and treat her as a valued employee: don't underpay her, pay her late, or expect favours and services for free.

❹ Don't micromanage the carer. You have chosen her because she has the credentials to do the job. Spend time introducing her to your baby's signals, routine, and feeding and then give her room to care for your baby.

baby sense: in the home and out and about

Whether at home or out and about, you may need to consider new challenges and possibilities now that your baby is mobile. Two of these are child-proofing and whether to stimulate your baby with classes.

child-proofing

Your mobile baby is a dangerous little person to have around the home. She is exploring but has limited understanding of safety and boundaries; this will have you on your toes day and night if your home is not baby-proof. Spend some time child-proofing your home and garden.

not through there Stair gates are an essential to prevent accidents.

out of reach Store medication high up, where your baby cannot see it.

choosing a nursery or childminder

- Are you made to feel welcome by all the staff?
- Is there a relaxed atmosphere, and a sense of happiness around?
- Is the nursery clean, bright and airy, with no smells of dirty nappies or cooking?
- Are the toys and play equipment in a good state of repair?
- Are babies in a separate section from toddlers and older children?
- Do the staff know all the children by name?
- What is the staff/child ratio? For young babies and even toddlers, it should be one carer to a maximum of three to four children.
- Do the children seem to be content, happy, and stimulated?
- How is a distressed child treated?
- Do they offer a healthy diet?
- Are the staff suitably qualified – and do they have the opportunity for continuing education?
- Is there a daily activity programme appropriate for each age group?
- Is the nursery or childminder's location convenient for you? Consider traffic and rush hour – what time will you have to leave work to pick up your baby?
- How will the nursery communicate with you?
- Is there an outdoor space and if so, are you satisfied with the equipment on offer? Is there enough space for the number of children in the nursery?
- Does the nursery have the necessary child protection policies in place? Do ask to see certificates.

caring for new teeth

At this stage dental care is more about what you must not do than what you must do to prevent decay. Here are the tips for preserving your baby's teeth:

● Never allow your baby to fall asleep while drinking a bottle of milk or juice. The sugars in milk and juice cause tooth decay over time.

● Avoid sugary snacks completely at this age.

● Offer your baby healthy food that requires her to chew; this stimulates the flow of saliva which helps to clean out food particles.

● Put a small amount of baby toothpaste on your clean finger, or a silicone finger brush and rub gently onto your baby's new teeth. There is no need to rinse.

● **Water** Your baby can drown in just a few centimetres of water, in less than a minute, so be very careful about leaving water in buckets, basins, and of course supervise her at all times when she is in the bath. Cover or fence off any ornamental ponds or bird baths in the garden.

● **Breakables** Place all precious objects and anything that can break out of reach. Your life will be less stressful if the objects on your coffee table are unbreakable.

● **Electrical equipment** Keep electrical cords, such as from irons and kettles, out of reach so that she cannot pull boiling water or a hot iron onto herself. Cover all accessible plug points with socket covers.

● **Bathrooms** Close bathroom doors at all times as there are many hazards in this room. Your baby may end up playing with toilet water or disposing of entire rolls of toilet paper into the toilet. Store medication high up, out of reach, and where your baby cannot see it.

● **Kitchens** Keep all cleaning substances out of reach in high cupboards as most are toxic. Fix child-proof locks to kitchen cabinets containing items that may be dangerous, such as knives or heavy pans.

● **Furniture** Affix bookshelves and cabinets securely to the walls and get rid of wobbly furniture and tables – cruising babies are bound to pull themselves up on them and could pull heavy items over.

● **Stairs** Fit stair gates top and bottom and keep them closed.

baby-stimulation classes

As a new mum, you may feel quite overwhelmed at times by all the opportunities out there for developing your baby's learning. If so, you might like to consider baby-stimulation classes, which enhance some areas of development, give you ideas for games to play with your baby, the chance to meet other mums and babies, and most importantly, to spend focused one-on-one time with your baby. These classes are also an excellent way of making new friends, if you are new to an area.

You need to be sensible about when you schedule these classes and whether your baby will benefit from what they offer, such as music or swimming or baby yoga. Firstly, choose a good time and convenient location. Your baby will not benefit from the class if she is being stimulated when she is hungry or tired. Furthermore, some babies, especially very alert and somewhat fussy babies, become over-stimulated by the experience so there is little or no benefit derived from the class.

Weigh up the pros and cons of the baby-stimulation classes in your area. Don't feel pressurized by maternal guilt to take part in extra activities if you see no direct value in them. However, if you have the time and means and can be sensible about how it fits into your baby's life, these classes can provide great opportunities for enjoying individual, uninterrupted time with your baby.

helping your baby sleep

If you thought you could expect a full night's sleep a year into parenting and your baby is not yet sleeping through, you will probably be feeling disillusioned and exhausted. Actually, your expectations were correct and if your baby is not sleeping through the night, you can try these steps to ensure that she does soon.

sensory secrets to good sleep habits

Your baby's sensory world affects how well she sleeps. Refresh your memory and rule out sensory reasons for sleep problems, see below. If you answered "no" to any of these questions, revisit the sensory keys for sleep (see pp.174–79).

- Do you play lots of movement games in the late afternoon?
- Does she always sleep in the same place and is it calm?
- Do you make sure she is not over-stimulated in the late afternoon?
- Does your baby have something to suck (her thumb or a dummy)?
- Does she have a sleep soother, such as a blanket or soft toy?

busy body As your baby explores her world and develops new motor skills each day, her muscles give her brain lots of sensory feedback. This helps her to develop proprioception: an awareness of how her body moves in space. This has a wonderful impact on sleep. Like the effect of going for a long hike or spending the day swimming in the sea, exercise of muscles helps to improve your mood and promotes good sleep. Many parents find that as soon as their baby starts moving – crawling and walking – their sleep improves. There is one exception to this and it occurs at the onset of most milestones: around the time your baby learns to crawl, stand and walk she may be a little restless and start practising her newfound skill at night (see p.179).

head banging and body rocking Some babies will bang or roll their heads or rock their bodies before falling asleep. This can be very distressing to watch, but if your baby is not hurting herself, she is probably just using this movement to calm herself. If you feel concerned, it may be worth asking your doctor for a check-up.

This rhythmic behaviour is often caused by a sensory need, such as the need for movement or proprioception. Some babies use the movement to organize themselves when they feel over-stimulated and overtired. By moving her body rhythmically, she balances her arousal system, feels calmer and eventually falls asleep. Head rocking and banging generally disappears by four years of age. Overtiredness and over-stimulation can contribute to it, so encourage a daytime nap or some regular quiet time,

sleep: what to expect at this stage

- Your baby will settle with ease if you aim to have her back to sleep a maximum of two-and-a-half to three hours since she last woke.
- During this stage, your baby will drop her late afternoon nap and only need two daytime sleeps: a mid-morning nap at approximately 9am; and a midday sleep for more than an hour or two.
- Wake your baby if she is asleep after 4pm so that she settles with ease in the evening.
- It's best if you try for a bedtime not later than 7pm. Your baby may wake for the day anywhere between 5am and 7am.
- Your baby can be expected to sleep through the night for 11 to 12 hours without requiring a feed.

195

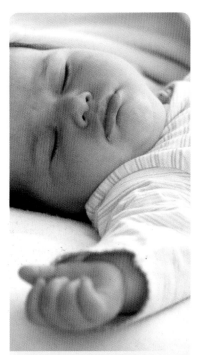

sense-able secret

During a "cusp age", it may be tricky to get your baby's bedtime and nap times sorted out so that she sleeps peacefully, but be reassured that it should only be a couple of weeks until she adjusts.

and move bedtime earlier if your baby has dropped her afternoon nap. Encourage her to participate in more intensive movement during the day. This could include going on a swing, pushing a little trolley loaded with blocks or books, and lots of outdoor play. Take her to a park if you don't have a garden. Very rarely, head banging and body rocking are associated with neurological disorders. A paediatrician will be able to diagnose these uncommon conditions, so if you are worried, consult your doctor.

helping your baby sleep well during the day

Your baby should have a happy daytime-sleep routine and will settle into it with ease if you are consistent about it. Remember your baby is more likely to settle independently if:
● You watch her awake time – keep an eye on the amount of time she has been awake for (see p.51) and make sure she sleeps every three hours. If she is overtired she is more likely to fight sleep.
● She is allowed to – if you consistently interfere and stand over her cot while she settles or consistently rock her to sleep, she will never learn to fall asleep on her own.

cusp ages Your baby should be awake for a maximum of two-and-a-half to three hours at this age. Keeping an eye on how long she has been awake will help you to get her to sleep quickly and happily. But at certain times in your baby's life, she may begin to protest about going to sleep during the day. This often happens because she is on the cusp of being able to do without a certain nap. When this happens, you will need to stretch the length of time she spends awake in the afternoon to accommodate bedtime, which you can bring forward to an earlier time.

These tricky stages are age appropriate. Called "cusp ages", the first one occurs between the age of nine months and her first birthday:
● Between six and nine months, most babies have two to three short naps, which may be as short as 45 minutes, and one longer daytime sleep (depending on the length of their naps).
● Between nine months and a year, you may need to drop the late afternoon nap or shorten it if it interferes with your baby's settling in the evening. Some babies still need a catnap to see them through the evening rituals of bathing, feeding, and so on. Be sure to wake your baby by 4pm if she is having an afternoon nap so that you can keep bedtime between 6pm and 7pm.
● Towards the end of her first year, her late-afternoon nap will fall away entirely and your baby will have a longer stretch of awake time in the afternoon. Of course, this means that your baby will be awake for up to four hours in the afternoon and may be overtired. When this happens, change to an earlier bedtime for a few weeks to help your baby adjust.

helping your baby settle in the evening

A bedtime routine acts as a signal for your baby's brain to release hormones that induce sleep and therefore is an essential part of every evening. In the early evening, a young baby is very susceptible to sensory overload and meltdown. This is especially true if she is at a daytime-sleep cusp age (see opposite) and has dropped her afternoon nap. Be sure to keep stimulation to a minimum and avoid rough play or exciting activities. You might like to try a routine like this:

● Plan a time for bed that's related to when your baby woke from her afternoon sleep, but between 6pm and 7pm. Occasionally, you might need to keep her awake for slightly longer in the late afternoon to coincide with the bedtime routine. Most babies can handle this if they are good sleepers, but if your baby is particularly unsettled in the early evening, let her have a short catnap for 30 minutes before 4pm. After this, wake her up and start your bedtime routine a bit later.

● Start the evening routine with a soothing warm bath followed by a calming massage (see p.105). Keep bath time quiet.

● When you take your baby out of the bath, wrap her snugly in a warmed towel and handle her firmly and confidently. Take her into her sleeping environment, put her nappy on and dress her and put her in a sleeping bag for the night if she has started to kick off her bedclothes. Keep all interactions in the room calming. Try not to handle her too much or over-stimulate her.

● Encourage her to hold her sleep object (such as her blanket or soft toy) to soothe herself, dim the lights, and give the last feed of the day in the dark. Keep your baby in your arms for this feed, so that she does not associate her bed with a feed. Hold and rock her (if necessary) to make her drowsy. Take time, slow down and relish these quiet moments.

● When your baby is relaxed and drowsy but not asleep, put her gently into her bed, kiss her goodnight, and leave the room.

if she won't settle If your baby will not settle for her daytime or evening sleeps and the bedtime routine is turning into a battleground, now is the time to help her to learn to fall asleep independently.

You may be concerned that sleep training will be traumatic for your baby, or even emotionally damaging. After all, some methods of sleep training involve separation from you, hours of crying, and may even result in a baby vomiting after a long period of crying. However, if you use the gentle, "sense-able" approach to sleep coaching, as suggested overleaf, you will not encounter this problem. The reason is that with this method of sleep coaching, you do not leave your baby alone. As a result, you give your baby a message of consistency and confidence so she will feel secure and not abandoned.

time for bed As part of your baby's bedtime routine, dim the lights and calmly put her into a sleeping bag in her sleeping environment.

confident coaching If your baby won't sleep, you can coach her gently. Stay calm and try to appear confident, so that your baby does not experience the coaching as traumatic.

the three C's of sleep coaching

If you are having trouble getting your baby to settle herself to sleep or to sleep through the night, you can gently coach her to do so over a week or so. Consider these points before starting.

confidence Babies under three years of age experience events as traumatic and attach feelings of fear to similar circumstances if her parent communicates fear during the event. Sleep coaching is no different. If you stand over your baby's cot with a look of fear in your eyes when she cries or with tears streaming down your face, she will experience the event as traumatic. It is vital to communicate confidence and calmness to your baby. As she looks up when you start to teach her a new way of calming herself to sleep, she should see an emotion that makes her feel secure that you know what you are doing. Inside you may be feeling very anxious as you embark on sleep coaching, especially if you have tried methods such as "controlled crying" unsuccessfully. However, this is not controlled crying and you will be sufficiently prepared before you start to teach your baby a new and developmentally appropriate skill – that of going to sleep independently. This method has been tried and tested over many years of professional practice. However, if you do not feel confident in this method of solving your baby's sleep problem, don't do it, as it will not work and it will be hard for you and your baby.

consistency Essential to teaching your baby the new skill of soothing herself to sleep is consistency. It is no good to start teaching the skill at bedtime and sit through an hour of crying only to revert to giving your baby her crutch by feeding or rocking her to sleep eventually. The message that your baby receives is that she must cry long and hard to have the old method reintroduced. If you are inconsistent the sleep-coaching process will take significantly longer. If you do not feel you can follow sleep coaching consistently until the end, do not embark on it. It will be confusing and unfair for your baby.

collaboration This means working together. Sleep coaching is an act of teamwork between you, your partner, and your baby. It is essential that you work together and do not undermine the process for each other. This is important especially because it has an impact on consistency: no matter which parent responds at night, you both need to do it the same way. It may be better for one parent do the sleep coaching to get 100 percent consistency. But even if only one parent carries the load of actually doing the sleep coaching, both parents must agree to the process and support each other. You must also both be prepared for a whole week, perhaps more, with little sleep.

how to sleep coach your baby

After checking that your baby's basic needs have been met (see box, right) and agreeing to be confident, consistent and to collaborate, you are ready to embark on sleep coaching. When starting the programme, be rigid with the steps and follow the advice strictly. As soon as your baby or toddler's sleep improves you can become more flexible. If your baby or toddler has learned to be dependent on you to get to sleep, she will probably protest within minutes of you leaving the room.

1 Follow the bedtime routine on p.197, then leave the room. First listen to her cry. If she is simply moaning or chatting, do not go in – give your baby the opportunity to soothe herself to sleep. This goes for when she cries in the middle of the night too – don't go in until she really cries. If she is crying, go in to her with a chair. Give her her sleep object, such as her blanket or soft toy, and help her lie down if she is standing, but other than that, just sit with her. Sit down next to her and put your hand on her, don't move your hand and don't talk, except to say "shshsh". You are giving her three sensory inputs to support her sleep: she can see you, she can feel you, and she can hear you. Sit with her until she goes to sleep. Do not look worried or concerned; just close your eyes. She may cry if she is expecting to be fed or rocked to sleep, but be unwavering and just sit with her. Even if she cries for a while, just sit appearing calm and confident. Do this each time she wakes throughout the night, always giving her the sleep object first.

2 The next night start the routine in the same way, walking out of the room. When she cries, go in to her, just sit next to your baby but this time just shshsh her; don't touch her. She experiences two sensory inputs: seeing you and hearing you. The second night may be difficult if you are tired, but your baby will be getting the idea of putting herself to sleep if you are consistent. Do the same during the night each time she wakes up.

3 On the third night start bedtime in exactly the same way, walking out of the room. When she cries, return and this time just sit quietly until she falls asleep. You have removed the tactile and auditory crutches you were giving your baby. She only experiences one sensory input: seeing you. Do this every time she wakes at night.

4 On the fourth night, when she starts crying, return to the room, give her the sleep object and then stand near the door until she falls asleep.

5 Finally on the fifth night, listen to see if she can put herself to sleep independently. If not, return to her, give her the sleep object and then stand outside the room where she can see you, occasionally saying "shshsh" as she cries. Usually by this stage your baby has learnt the new technique of falling asleep independently. One week down the line, expect a protest night – where she will wake several times. Expect it and handle it the same way as the coaching week.

see box, right

ruling out basic needs

Before embarking on sleep coaching, do rule out any basic needs your baby may have. Make sure these issues have settled before you begin.

health Make sure your baby is well. Do not embark on sleep coaching if your baby:
● has had a cold within the past month that has not fully cleared; this may result in congestion in the ear (different to an ear infection) which creates pressure on the ear drum during sleep.
● is on medication for a chest infection or asthma as it may have stimulant qualities that work against sleep.
● is acutely ill, for example with a fever, gastroenteritis, a urinary tract infection, and so on.
● has severe nappy rash or is teething.
● has a chronic disorder such as eczema or anaemia that affects sleep.

daytime sleep Establish a daytime-sleep schedule. This is essential to ensure that your baby will settle in the evening and not wake frequently at night. An overtired baby will experience disrupted sleep at night.

diet Ensure your baby's diet is adequate for her age, with sufficient milk and solids that include protein if she is over six months old (see p.181).

bedroom Put your baby down to sleep in the same place and keep it calming by playing white noise or lullabies.

play separation games

To help with separation anxiety, play games with your baby during the day such as:

● Peek-a-boo: place a flannel over your face or in front of your baby's face briefly and say "Peek-a-boo" as you drop the fabric to reveal yourself to your baby.

● Find the toy: place any interesting or loved object such as a dummy or teddy under a blanket or sheet and say "Where's teddy?" then pull the fabric back, revealing the item.

● Hide and seek: hide around the corner of the sofa or bed and call your baby. If she looks towards the sound of your voice or crawls towards you, respond by showing yourself with a big smile and laugh. This teaches your baby that you still exist when she can't see you, and that a happy reunion accompanies any brief separation.

night-time sleep solutions

If your baby is managing to settle herself to sleep at bedtime, 90 percent of your job is done. Most babies who can settle themselves to sleep in the evening independently will do so in the middle of the night. If your baby does not settle herself at bedtime, the first step is to sleep coach her (see p.198) to make sure she can. If your baby settles at bedtime but is still expecting some help to fall back asleep when she wakes in the night, consider these reasons for her waking, and the accompanying strategies:

separation anxiety Your baby may still be going through some separation anxiety at this age (see p.173). To resolve her anxiety, try to deal with her separation issues during the day:

● **Watch, wait, and wonder** Spending one-to-one time with your baby has been proven to decrease separation anxiety and will enhance your relationship with your child. This method has amazing effects not only on sleep, but also on your child's well being, all the way through into the toddler years. Just try to have 30 minutes of totally undisturbed time with your baby or toddler three times a week. Turn off the phone, do not attend to others, just focus on being with your baby. **Watch** her play, uncritically, without intervening – just watching her and following her lead as she plays. Use age-appropriate toys and sit on the floor with her. **Wait** for your baby to include you in one of her tasks. When she does, play on her level, not directing what she is doing. **Wonder** out loud about what your baby's play means to her. This will help you to connect with your baby, which helps her to feel more secure.

● **Handle separations positively** When you leave your baby, you may feel anxious, sad, or guilty, but it is vital that you do not communicate this to her. Do not be tempted to sneak out and disappear to avoid the tears. Try to handle separations matter-of-factly and always say goodbye. This is very important as it helps your baby learn to trust that you will always let her know when you are leaving for any period of time.

● **Happy reunions** Just as you need to be consistent with your goodbyes, you must always return with a happy greeting and spend time reuniting with your baby. You may find that she is a little clingy after you return. If you expect this and put aside a bit of time to re-bond, your baby will manage better the next time you separate.

● **Help her adopt a security object** Take time to help your baby find a "security object" such as a blanket or soft toy. Choose one object and offer it to your baby along with comfort whenever she cries. If your baby is tired or over-stimulated or has hurt herself, place the blanket or soft toy on your shoulder so that as she cuddles in to you, she receives comfort from the object too. Give her the object at bedtime – she'll be less likely to wake you when she wakes in the night seeking comfort. If your baby wakes and you are certain she is just looking for comfort, go to her, pat her, make sure she has her security object, and leave the room. Be sure that during this phase you don't create any habits that will be hard to break.

nutrition Your baby is now on a full diet of solid food, eating everything you eat mashed up or as finger food. However, if you eat takeaways or ready meals, do not give her any of these because they contain too much salt, sugar and preservatives for a baby. A diet that includes fruit and vegetables as well as carbohydrates and proteins plus two milk bottles a day will be good enough to ensure that she sleeps well. If she is waking at night, especially if she demands a bottle when she wakes, you may wonder if hunger is the root of the problem. There are three circumstances when food may affect her sleep:
● **Protein** This is essential for growth of your baby's body and brain, which is significant at night when she sleeps. Make sure her diet has at least one teaspoon of protein per kilogram (2.2lb) of body weight in 24 hours (for sources, see p.181). By nine months of age your baby will weigh around 8–10kg (18–22lb), so will need a minimum eight to ten teaspoons of protein per day, divided into three meals, on average three teaspoons of protein per meal. Another simple way of estimating her protein need for each meal is to make it the size of the palm of her hand.
● **Iron** This mineral is necessary to make the red cells that help carry the oxygen in the blood, and is also essential for cell growth. If your baby doesn't get enough iron, her blood won't transport oxygen efficiently, making her tired and more susceptible to illness. A serious lack of iron can lead to anaemia, which could mean her brain development is impaired. For sources of iron, see p.183.
● **Feeding your baby milk at night** This decreases her appetite during the day. She may become a fussy eater and not eat the nutritious food that contains the protein and iron. In this case she will wake more often at night and need to be fed milk so the cycle repeats itself. The only way to break this negative cycle and increase her appetite for food during the day is to break the habit of night feeds.

habits Undesirable sleep habits become entrenched so easily, especially if your baby has not yet learnt to calm herself effectively or use a sleep soother. If she is used to being helped to sleep, and cannot settle herself, she will expect you to help her every time she wakes up. The good news is that your baby is old enough now to learn new skills and break past habits. Some are hard to break and if your baby has been crying a lot, she may need to sip on some cooled boiled water to quench her thirst. Be sure to meet your baby's need for comfort during the day and give her lots of love and cuddles.

breaking the feed-to-sleep habit

The comfort of sucking on the breast or bottle can lead to sleep problems if your baby has learnt to fall asleep only when sucking, whether this is when she goes to sleep or when she wakes at night. You can break this habit by not feeding her to sleep. Make sure your baby's diet is adequate for her age; she no longer needs milk feeds during the night. However, a feed after 4am may be appropriate if your baby has been asleep for 10 hours. If it is close to sleep time when you feed her milk during the day, ensure that she has finished feeding before she falls asleep. Follow these simple guidelines:
● When the feed is finished, or when she wakes in the night expecting a feed, pick her up and hold her close to you. Rock her gently and soothe her until she is asleep, no matter how much she protests (nor how long it takes). It may be easier to simply sit next to her cot and pat her.
● Stay in the sleep space with your baby and keep the environment quiet and calm.
● When she is asleep, place her back in her cot. If she wakes up, repeat the procedure until she is asleep. This may take a few days to perfect, so don't give up.
● When she is used to falling asleep without feeding, and is happy to fall asleep in your arms, move to the next step, which is to teach her to go to sleep independently in her bed. Use the sleep coaching strategy on p.199.

bad dreams?

If your baby wakes screaming at night, you may assume that she is having a bad dream. The reality is that before she becomes a toddler, your baby is probably not having a nightmare. Under one year of age she does not have language with which to label the visual images in her mind. For this reason, imagination is thought to only really develop after 18 months, when language is exploding. If your baby wakes screaming at night it is more likely to be a night terror.

night terrors While nightmares wake a child, your baby will probably not wake up from a night terror, she just screams. She may also show physical signs of distress, such as sweating, rapid heart rate, or bulging eyes. The worst part is that she may not respond to you, or be aware of anything else in her environment. This can be very disturbing, since a night terror may last a long time – up to 30 minutes – and your child may even strike out at you when you seek to comfort her. Night terrors can be experienced by young babies (although the most common age of occurrence is between two and five years old).

Night terrors, unlike dreams, occur when a baby is sleeping deeply, usually within the first part of the night, within one to three hours of falling asleep. At the end of her deep sleep cycle (as she enters REM sleep), one part of her brain wakes up, but another stays in a deep sleep state (due to an immaturity of the nervous system). So she is seemingly awake, but actually in a deep sleep. The brain is likely to associate the physical symptoms of the night terror such as rapid heart rate and sweating with fear, which is why your child may cry and scream during an episode. In some cases, high fevers can cause night terrors by disrupting the sleep cycle. They are seldom caused by psychological trauma, and most children return to sleep easily once the episode is over, and have no recollection of it the next day.

coping with night terrors There is not much you can do for your baby when she is having a night terror, other than holding her tightly and reassuring her that you are there. Sometimes touching her may cause unnecessary stimulation, making it worse, so you may have to simply wait it out while keeping her safe.

Research has shown that night terrors are common in children with abnormal sleep schedules and who are fatigued. Overtiredness in particular is linked to these sleep disruptions. By keeping your baby's awake times in mind and sticking to a regular daytime-sleep and bedtime routine, you can avert night terrors. Make sure your baby has a daytime nap, move her bedtime earlier and avoid excessive stimulation and sensory overload during the day, particularly before bedtime.

coping with night terrors
1 During a night terror your baby may scream, but appear to be unaware of your presence, which can be very distressing.
2 The best thing you can do for your baby during a night terror is to hold her and reassure her that you're there.

feeding your baby

Your baby will now be eating three meals of solids a day and from here on her eating pattern progressively becomes more and more like yours. You can cook meals from scratch for the whole family to enjoy and feed your baby the same, as long as you haven't added salt or honey. Just make sure she can cope with the texture and consistency without choking.

milk feeds

Most babies now have one milk feed on waking and another at night before bedtime. Some babies still enjoy a milk bottle just before or after their lunchtime sleep. There is no need to rush to drop this feed, but be aware your baby may not want or finish this feed. Offer 250ml (9fl oz) of milk at each feed or breastfeed for as long as she wants for each of these two feeds. Since she is getting dairy in other forms in her solids meals (white sauce, cheese, yogurt), you do not need to worry if she does not finish her bottles or only has a small breastfeed. It is advisable to keep your baby on breast milk or formula milk, in addition to a full diet of solids, until she is a year old. Add formula milk to her cereal but when cooking you can start to use cow's milk. Cow's milk is low in vitamins A, D, and C, and especially in iron, so is not appropriate for milk feeds until your baby is twelve months old. It is important to remember that babies (even up to the age of two) need sufficient fats and cholesterol in their diet. This is to ensure both adequate calories and cholesterol for the growth and development of the brain. If you start your baby on cow's milk after her first birthday, give her full-fat milk, not semi-skimmed or skimmed milk.

moving onto a feeding cup Offer your baby her mid-morning and mid-afternoon water or juice in a feeding cup with a spout. Use a feeding cup with handles on both sides so that she can hold it herself. Don't worry if she doesn't appear to know how to actually use it – with time she will work it out. Invest in a non-spill cup to avoid hours of carpet-mopping. If you are not breastfeeding, continue to give your baby her morning and evening formula in a standard feeding bottle with a teat.

solids

If you have delayed introducing solids from any food group until this point, now is the time to increase variety in her diet. It is of the utmost importance that you include protein in your baby's diet and reduce the number of milk feeds offered. If you are following the feeding routine as recommended in the previous chapter (see p.182) keep going.

Increase portion size according to your baby's demands. She should be having around 225g (8oz) of solid food per meal. Bear in mind that

feeding: what to expect at this stage

● Your baby may drop her after-lunch milk feed and may only want milk when waking and again at bedtime.
● She does not need milk at night unless she is ill or not thriving.
● Your baby must be on a full solids diet now, which includes all the food groups and a good portion of protein in each meal (see pp.180–83).
● If your baby is eating solids and happy you do not need to worry if her growth curve levels out – she is using up a lot of energy with all the movement.
● Expect a hunger spurt when she starts crawling.

her appetite will vary from day to day, so don't worry if she eats less than this from time to time. Most of the time, she can eat what the rest of the family is eating, provided it's healthy home cooking and you avoid salt or honey. Introduce her to more texture by making it coarser. You no longer need to purée her food, except for certain fibrous textures such as cooked meat or chicken. Rather, mash her food with the back of a fork. Start experimenting with different tastes, for example adding a little garlic, tomato, or onion to her food. Don't worry if she spits out or gags when you introduce something new – it's normal. She will be very interested in finger foods and starting to feed herself. Don't despair when your baby plunges her entire fist into her bowl of food. These attempts to feed herself are a wonderful sensory experience and help develop her hand–eye coordination. Continue giving her finger food, but avoid anything that will break off into hard pieces and not soften once in the mouth.

sense-able secret

Once your baby becomes an independent feeder, stay sane by placing a plastic tablecloth under her feeding chair at mealtimes. Give your baby her own spoon, too – it will keep her busy so that you can get on with the process of feeding her.

meal plan for nine to twelve months of age

Your baby's feeding routine is now predictable and her meal plan should be consistent, but don't worry if she has days when she is less hungry.

time	meal	food and amounts
6am	Milk feed	200–240ml (7–8½fl oz)
8am	Breakfast	Carbohydrate such as cereal, porridge or white bread with a piece of fruit, plus protein such as yogurt, egg, or ham
10am	Snack	Diluted juice or water, and finger food, such as bread sticks or steamed vegetables
12 noon	Lunch	Vegetables with carbohydrate such as potatoes, rice or pasta, plus protein such as meat, dairy or fish, with some fruit for dessert
2pm	Milk feed	This feed may decrease or drop away entirely over this period
3pm	Snack	Diluted juice or water, and finger food, such as small chunks of fruit
5pm	Dinner	Offer food from the same options as lunchtime
6–7pm	Milk feed	250–300ml (9–11fl oz)

getting to know your baby

At this stage your baby will be focusing on locomotion. Whether she's a really fast crawler or a precocious walker, she will be all over the place and the term "war zone" takes on a whole new meaning. Being mobile is important for the development of spatial awareness and now your little one starts to map her world.

from sitting to walking Your baby has been enjoying extended periods of sitting unsupported on the floor. In this position she'll really start developing her fine motor skills, but as she gets closer to a year, sitting becomes too static and she'll only use it if exploring something interesting or as a transitory position before crawling off again or pulling herself up to stand. During this stage, she begins to pull herself to a standing position in earnest. Any person, animal, or piece of furniture will be a leaning post. She'll land with a bump on her backside in order to get back to the floor. Once she's standing, it isn't long before she starts to rock on her legs while holding onto something. One of those rockings will eventually become a step and soon thereafter she'll be cruising along at a rate of knots, holding onto the furniture. Cruising is the vital stage before walking and can continue into the second year. Walking is the most variable milestone and should not be used as a gauge of developmental success unless there are other indicators of giftedness or serious delay. Some babies start to walk at nine months and others don't walk until 16 months.

dexterity and language Your baby will start using her hands as tools now. She can give you a toy and will practise releasing it accurately. She can point her index finger and she pokes at small objects and holes. Mouthing decreases as she actively starts to manipulate and explore objects with her hands instead. She uses her fingers to feed herself, chewing on biscuits and holding her own bottle and sippy cup. She also starts to use language to communicate, she understands more than you'd believe. She loves to imitate noises, such as a cough. She will also babble loudly, doubling up syllables into "ga-ga" or "ba-ba", for example. She may even say a few real words by the time she is a year old. "Da-da" usually comes first – it's easier to say than "ma-ma". A deaf child's vocalizations will now differ from those of a hearing child, as they remain sparse and monotonous.

Your baby's sense of humour is developing rapidly and she becomes very affectionate towards you. She loves games such as clapping hands and waving bye-bye. But her mood will turn in a second if you try removing a favourite toy or taking her away from dangerous situations.

out and about This is an enjoyable stage, when your baby actively seeks stimulation and is also able to cope with it better. Outings and parent-and-baby playgroups become really worthwhile as she expands her world.

"Your baby is practising old skills such as sitting but working hard to prepare for her next major milestone – walking."

sense-able secret

To ensure your baby's continued wellbeing and development, stick to your routine (but be flexible enough to alter it as your child develops). Follow a sense-able feeding plan and establish good sleeping habits. Use the TEAT framework – stimulating or calming your baby at the right times – to enhance her development.

target milestones

Independence starts to develop by 12 months, when your baby will make decisions about where she wants to be. She'll practise old skills such as sitting, but is working hard to prepare for her next major milestone – walking. Expect these target milestones to be achieved by a year of age.

area of development	target milestones
Gross motor	Very fast crawling as her primary means of getting around, including going up stairs. Squatting to play. Climbing onto anything she can explore. Standing independently without support. Walking with support, holding your hand. May begin to walk independently.
Fine motor	Smoothly releasing large objects, but still a little clumsy with small ones. Beginning to use hands to work together, such as holding a jar while taking off the lid.
Hand–eye coordination	Carefully inspecting the qualities of objects; loves container play and turning pages. Beginning to throw toys. Stopped putting everything in her mouth as she can explore more effectively with her eyes and hands together.
Language	Saying one or two words with meaning.
Social/emotional	Socializing begins in earnest as your baby can express her emotions and interacts enthusiastically with others. Remembering social rituals such as saying "good bye" and kissing.
Regulation	Fully regulating basic functions such as hunger and sleep. Limited ability to control mood. Expect temper tantrums linked to frustration.

sensible stimulation: TEAT

Your baby is now able to move from a sitting position. Encourage her by placing interesting toys out of her reach. Help her to crawl and provide opportunities for her to explore by creating baby-safe areas in your home. To encourage cruising, position pieces of furniture at just the right distance apart. Your baby will be feeling more frustrated now. Try to understand this when you remove her from a potentially dangerous situation that she is happily exploring and offer an alternative source of entertainment that has the added advantage of safety. Tell her plenty of stories that teach her about her body and take her on lots of outings during her awake times as she now wants to learn about the world.

side by side Babies will play alongside each other in what is known as "parallel play". It won't be until the toddler years when your baby starts to actively play with another child.

timing

Your baby now has long stretches of time in the calm-alert state in which she will play and explore. Make time for stimulation by planning outings and activities for her awake time, such as going to the park or to baby gym classes. Introduce her to social situations. She will still play alongside her friend rather than with her – parallel play rather than cooperative play – but just being with another child will teach her about what to expect from little compatriots. Make sure she still has down time and calming activities just before bed, so that it is easy to settle her to sleep.

environment

Your baby actively explores her environment now. Because she can control her states well and does not become easily overloaded by different activities or new people, you can increase the amount of stimulation she receives. By now you will know her temperament and her threshold for sensory input. If she is a sensitive baby who is easily over-stimulated, make sure she has quiet times too.

Keep a baby-toy basket in each room. These toys will help to keep your baby occupied as you move from room to room during the day. Choose a sensory theme for each room, for instance living room – smell toys; kitchen – sound toys; bathroom – touch toys. Or each basket can have one toy to stimulate each sense, for instance a smelly toy, a noisy toy, a textured toy, and a bright visual toy.

visual A baby carrier is a wonderful place to explore the world when on a walk – you and your baby are seeing the world from the same height and can talk about what you see.

hearing Talk about everything you are doing. Your baby will then pick up on words and emotions.

touch Continue to give your baby lots of hugs and cuddles. Use baby massage if she still likes it (see p.105).

activities

sleep time

A calm environment for sleeping is still important – as your baby's senses take in more information, it becomes harder for her to switch off and go to sleep at bedtime.

visual If your baby sleeps well and is not fractious during the day, livening up the décor of her room should not affect her sleeping patterns.

motor development Your baby is now mobile enough to choose her own sleep position. If she chooses to sleep on her tummy, don't worry – the risk of SIDS has decreased. You will disturb her sleep if you turn her each time she rolls over onto her tummy.

on the changing mat

Nappy change time continues to be a challenge, as your baby hates being on her back. Provide toys to distract her, so that you can get the nappy change over with quickly.

visual Keep a variety of bright pictures, especially faces, to hand to her or place some above the changing mat. Photographs of family members or pets in plastic slip-in frames will keep her entertained while you complete the dreaded task.

hearing Talk to her about the pictures or the people or pets in the photographs while changing her.

bath time

This remains the start of the bedtime routine, so don't over-excite your baby. Be calm after her bath.

visual Waterproof books and bright bath toys are fun.

hearing Sing songs and recite nursery rhymes describing her body.

---

touch Enhance her body image by touching parts of the body, and naming them for your baby, "These are your toes" or "Let's wash your tummy". Teach your baby the qualities of toys: heavy and light, sink and float. Introduce a new texture at bath time – spray shaving-foam on to the tiles next to the bath or on to the wall of the bath itself.

motor development Let your baby stand at the bath to be undressed, which encourages cruising.

smell She will enjoy scented baby bubble bath and other bath products.

---

awake time

Most of your day is now spent with running around after an active, awake baby. Enjoy this time by stimulating her with various activities.

visual Show your baby moving things, such as birds flying and trees swaying in the wind to encourage visual tracking. Blowing bubbles for her to watch develops the same skill. Babies love to see themselves in the mirror. Point out her body parts as she gazes at her reflection.

hearing Talk about the things your baby shows an interest in. Speak to her all the time, labelling events, feelings, and objects. On outings talk about what you see for example, the animals and the noises they make.

touch Touch the things you see outdoors, such as flowers and animals. In the warm summer months, set up large tubs with variously textured substances for your baby to explore: water, jelly, sand, balls of all sizes, varying the substances each week. Try inviting your friends and their babies

– keep them supervised at all times. Sing and act out touch songs, such as "Round and round the garden." Keep several tactile objects in each room of the house for her to play with.

movement Rough-and-tumble games are fun with babies of this age. Go to the park and let your baby play on moving equipment such as roundabouts, swings, and slides.

motor development To encourage hand–eye coordination, hang a light ball in a stocking or a net in front of your baby so that she can catch it as it floats slowly by. This gives her time to plan the action. Give her a large ball to throw, gradually moving on to smaller ones. Let her throw toys into a basket. Play ring-on-a-stick games to encourage purposeful release. In the kitchen, keep pots or plastic containers that can be stacked up. She will do this enthusiastically now that her release skill is well-developed. Let her unpack the plastic-ware from your

cupboards and teach her how putting everything back can be fun. Make an obstacle course, with cushions, tables, and baskets for her to crawl in, out, and under from. Use old boxes to make tunnels and hidey holes that babies love to explore. Let your baby crawl up a slide or incline to develop her shoulder muscles. Teach her to go down steps backwards, on her hands and knees. This is important for her safety as well. To encourage standing and cruising, place safe, interesting objects on chest-height surfaces. Push furniture close together and progressively move it apart. Let your baby push a trolley to help her progress to walking. As she gets closer to a year, encourage walking with the "1, 2, 3, weee" game: she walks between mum and dad, holding your hands; each time she takes a step count "1, 2, 3" then swing her in the air on "weee!"

travelling time

Travelling can be a very frustrating time for your busy mover. She will protest at being strapped into a seat and stimulation is often essential to make a trip bearable.

visual Attach a toy-on-elastic to the grab handle so that your baby can pull it towards herself to play with. Alternate between squeaky toys, touch toys, and a book.

hearing Play recordings of children's songs. Teach your baby the actions in action songs at home and she will keep herself happily occupied by doing them in the car.

movement Carry your baby in a back-pack carrier on walks. She will love the movement and seeing the world from this new vantage point.

feed time

Mealtimes can be a challenge now, because your baby's new-found desire to feed herself coupled with inadequate motor skills will probably leave her covered in food. Place a plastic sheet under her highchair and provide her with her own spoon at mealtimes, then relax about the floor and feed her with another spoon.

visual Make food visually attractive to encourage a poor eater – try using brightly coloured foods, such as green broccoli and purple beetroot.

touch Even though it's messy, let your baby feed herself – experiencing different food textures is an important learning opportunity.

motor development Give your baby finger food in a variety of shapes and sizes to encourage her to develop her grip and finger dexterity.

toys and tools

The range of toys available for this age is staggering. Don't spoil your baby with loads of toys – she will get as much enjoyment and benefit from playing with safe household objects. If she has lots of toys, put some away and rotate the collection, so that there is always something new and interesting to catch her attention.

visual Lift-the-flap board books will fascinate and involve her.

hearing Your baby will love CDs of children's songs and nursery rhymes. Invest in musical toys: anything from tuned bells to a ring-stacker that plays a separate tune for each ring stacked.

touch Try books with touch components: different textures for different animals or objects, such as soft woolly material for a fluffy sheep, will help to develop her sense of touch.

movement Encourage lots of movement on playground equipment, such as swings and rolling horses.

motor development Sturdy push-along toys are great for helping her learn to walk. To encourage fine motor control, look for activity centres or toys with holes to encourage pointing and poking. Make her a fabric book and on each page sew an item that requires fine motor control (a Velcro strip, button, press stud and so on). Give your baby thick wax crayons and paper and show her how to scribble. Open-and-close toys are great for helping to improve hand–eye coordination.

afterword

A year down the line, you have mastered the art of soothing your baby, reading her signals and simply loving her. It may be hard in retrospect to recall the early days of parental insecurity – you really have come a long way. Now the toddler years loom on the horizon, bringing a whole new set of challenges and moments of elation.

Your toddler is her own person and over the next two years will develop her personality and the foundations for success in all areas of life. As the developmental explosion continues, it's worth becoming aware of the critical areas of development that your little one is working on.

The toddler years can be an emotionally fraught time. Your baby needs to develop autonomy and independence, and as she reaches milestones in these areas, such as the ability to say "no", she will flex her muscles and you may find yourself in a battle of wills. What's the best way to deal with this? To recognize that your baby has her own will and that this is essential to her development. She needs to gain a sense of herself as different and unique. For this reason, do not fight every battle; give your toddler opportunity to have her say and room to assert herself. But if an issue is important to her health or security, be firm and set boundaries.

Boundaries are especially important at bedtime. The toddler years are often a time when sleep challenges arise. The best way to avoid them is to set up patterns that make bedtime predictable, such as putting your child to bed in the same place and at the same time every night. The bedtime routines in this book will stand you in good stead during this new stage of development. Night waking, however, is not always a boundary issue. Many toddlers experience fears at night as their imagination emerges at around 18 months. Moving to a "big" bed at around two years of age is another common trigger for sleep disturbances. With the physical boundary of cot bars removed, many toddlers roam at night simply because they can. In tackling these night-time disturbances, you can choose to be firm and walk your toddler back to her room, allow her to creep into your bed, or establish a middle ground by tucking a "camping" mattress under your bed, which can be pulled out for her to sleep on when she is anxious at night.

Eating is another area in which toddlers can create havoc. "Toddlers exist on fresh air and love" goes the saying, and some days this will seem all too true. Toddlers are notoriously poor eaters partly because it's an easy arena in which to assert their new-found independence, but also because their appetites vary so much from meal to meal and from day to day. One very common cause of poor eating in toddlers is consumption of milk at night. It's best not to give your toddler milk feeds between bedtime and the early morning (4am at the earliest) unless she is ill.

Why? Milk does not contain all the nutrition your growing baby requires and yet it fills her up, spoiling her daytime appetite for food that does contain the essential fatty acids and iron she needs. To manage toddler feeding, it's important to create firm boundaries about where your toddler eats and what you offer her. Once you've done this, allow her to control how much she eats. Then you rid yourself of the responsibility and can relax. Your toddler will probably eat one meal a day very well and the other two much less well. She only really needs to eat a portion the size of her fist to survive, so offer more but don't enter into food battles.

Potty training, toddler tantrums and siblings may be part of the fun of the years ahead. Whatever issues you run up against, all the important principles you have learned in *The Babysense Secret* will stand you in good stead, but perhaps these are the most important to bear in mind:

● Read your child's signals of over-stimulation and tiredness and you will successfully avert most toddler tantrums.

● Protect your toddler from over-stimulation in busy social situations to prevent unwanted behaviour or misbehaviour.

● Keep a daytime sleep routine a priority as you move into the preschool years, since enough sleep will help to keep your child calm and content.

But most of all, enjoy this precious time with your toddler, and may you continue to have many happy days and peaceful nights.

glossary

Anaemia A lack of haemoglobin, or iron, in red blood cells, usually the result of insufficient iron-rich foods in the diet.

Antibodies Also called immunoglobulins, these are proteins made by white blood cells that neutralize foreign proteins (antigens) found in bacteria and viruses, so protecting the body from infection.

Autonomic nervous system The subconscious part of the nervous system, which controls vital body functions such as heartbeat, breathing rate, and temperature.

Awake time The amount of time a child can spend happily awake. This can be up to an hour in a newborn, and lengthens to about five to seven hours in a five-year-old.

Baby signing A system of sign language to assist communication with a person suffering from deafness or learning difficulty that can also be used with babies from about the age of six months.

Baby types The four sensory types on which the babysense approach is based: social butterfly baby, slow-to-warm-up baby, settled baby, and sensitive baby.

Bonding The development of a close, interpersonal relationship, especially between parents and their baby.

Chronic condition A condition or illness that persists for a long time, in some cases for life, for example asthma.

Colic Bouts of unexplained high-pitched crying in babies aged two to 14 weeks, commonly in the early evening. Typically the baby grimaces, her face becomes very red, and she draws her legs up to her abdomen.

Colostrum Thick, yellowish fluid produced by the breasts in the first days after birth, after which it is replaced by breast milk. It contains high levels of antibodies to protect a baby from infection. It has more minerals and proteins than breast milk.

Competition of skill A point in development where two different newly acquired skills compete for the brain's energy; consequently the brain's focus moves from the first to the second.

Complementary feed To give a baby bottle of formula or breast milk when breastfeeding is the norm.

Congenital abnormality An abnormality or deformity existing from birth, usually arising from a damaged gene, the adverse effect of certain drugs, or the effect of some diseases in pregnancy.

Controlled crying A method of teaching a baby to sleep on her own by leaving her to cry herself to sleep in her cot for controlled amounts of time, with a parent checking at intervals.

Co-sleeping Sleeping with your baby in the same bed. A co-sleeper cot is a special bed or cot that attaches to a parents' bed so that the baby can sleep alongside her parents.

Cot death see *Sudden infant death syndrome*

Counsellor A qualified therapist who gives advice and guidance to a person, for example with postnatal depression.

Demand feeding The practice of feeding a baby whenever she asks to be fed, rather than according to a set schedule.

Developmental delay A term used to indicate that a child has delayed achievement of one or more developmental milestones. Global delay implies that the child has delays in all areas of development.

Eczema An chronic inflammation of the skin that causes intense itching and a scaly rash or even blisters. It is often the result of allergy.

Gestation period The period of time (normally 40 weeks) in which a foetus develops, beginning with conception and ending in birth.

Habituation A decrease in the brain's response to a stimulus after repeated exposure to, for example, a particular sound. Once accustomed to it, habituation prevents excess sensory information from being registered.

Health visitor Healthcare professional, often attached to a GP's surgery, who provides advice and support to all parents of children under the age of five.

Hormones Chemical messengers released by certain body cells in one part of the body that affect cell function in other parts of the body.

Hypnagogic startle A sudden jerking of muscles that occurs as a person moves from light or REM sleep into deep sleep. It can be strong enough to wake a baby.

In utero In the womb.

Incubator Thermostatically controlled, closed cabinet, or cot, in which a premature or sick baby may be nursed.

Intelligence quotient (IQ) A score resulting from standard tests used to measure intelligence.

Interoception Sensory stimuli from the body's organs, for example, the digestive system (hunger) or the temperature control system (cold or warmth).

Kangaroo care A method of caring for a premature or very young baby to give her skin-to-skin contact with her parent, most commonly the mother, for several hours a day.

Midwife A healthcare professional who provides care for women during pregnancy, labour, and birth.

Milestones Key stages of development, such as head control or crawling, achieved as a child's nervous system develops, which always occur in a specific order.

Motor skills The physical skills that a baby acquires, normally divided into gross motor skills (such as crawling and walking) and fine motor skills (for example, palmer and pincer grips).

Nature–nurture debate Discussion as to whether physical and behavioural traits are formed by genetics (nature), experiences (nurture), or a combination.

Neonatologist A paediatrician who specializes in the care of newborn babies. A neonatal nurse is a nurse who specializes in the same area.

Nervous system Consisting of the brain, spinal cord, and nerves, this is the body system that coordinates conscious and subconscious bodily functions.

Neurodevelopmental disorder A disorder that results from impairment of the growth and development of any part of the nervous system.

Nurse specialist A nurse with an advanced degree in a particular aspect of patient care, for example, paediatrics.

Object permanence The point in a baby's development when she realizes that an object exists even when she cannot see it. It generally occurs when a baby is about eight or nine months old.

Occupational therapist A professional who works with children and adults to help overcome the physical effects of a disability so that they can participate in everyday activities.

Paediatrician Doctor who specializes in the care of children; paediatricians also specialize in different aspects of child health.

Palmer grasp A baby's ability to hold an object in the palm of her hand. This skill develops at three to four months old.

Parentese A form of speech used by parents when talking to their babies, that combines a high-pitched musical tone of voice with long vowel sounds and strong facial expressions.

Physiotherapist A therapist who identifies and helps to improve movement and function in any part of the body, often after illness or injury.

Pincer grip The ability to pick up an object between forefinger and thumb. Most babies can do this by the age of nine months.

Postnatal depression Also called PND or perinatal distress, this is a depressive illness that can develop after having a baby.

Premature baby A baby born before 37 weeks of pregnancy.

Proprioception This is one of the body's internal sensory systems. Proprioceptors in sensory nerves collect information about the body's position and the state of contraction of its muscles, and use it to maintain posture and balance.

Psychology Academic and medical studies concerned with the scientific investigation of mind and behaviour, including sleep and mental illness.

Reflexes An involuntary or instinctive response to a stimulus.

Reflux A condition that occurs when the valve between the oesophagus (gullet) and the stomach is underdeveloped, and results in excessive posseting, and sometimes projectile vomiting. Most babies grow out of this, but occasionally surgery is required.

Saccades A series of involuntary, abrupt, rapid, small movements or jerks of both eyes.

Sensory information This is a combination of information provided by the five external senses (touch, smell, sight, hearing, and taste), combined with input from our internal world (organs, muscles, and body position).

Sleep object A small object, for example a soft toy or blanket that a baby uses to soothe herself to sleep.

Sleep states Two different states during sleep: light sleep initially, when a baby moves and her eyes may twitch, this is also known as rapid eye movement (REM) sleep, in which it is thought that dreaming occurs for both babies and adults; and deep sleep when a baby is very still.

State regulation A baby's ability to remain calm when faced with high levels of stimulation.

Stimuli External events that influence a baby's behaviour.

Sudden infant death syndrome (SIDS) Sudden unexplained death of an apparently healthy baby. Previously referred to as "cot death".

Supplementary feeding Giving a baby a bottle of formula or breast milk as a top-up feed after she has finished a breastfeed.

Swaddling To wrap a newborn baby firmly in a blanket so that her head and arms are held close to her body, mimicking the sensation of being in the womb.

Synapse The junction between two neurons (nerve or brain cells) across which nerve signals can travel.

Transitional object An object other than the parent, for example a blanket or soft toy, to which a child becomes attached for comfort. This is an important step towards a child becoming independent.

Trimester A period of three months; pregnancy is divided into three trimesters.

Ultradian rhythms Patterns of physiological activity, that occur more than once in 24 hours, for example a baby's sleeping and eating pattern.

Vernix The waxy substance that protects a baby's skin *in utero*.

Vestibular system The sensory system within the inner ear that sends information to the brain about changes in movement or body position.

Vital signs External indications, such as chest movement caused by breathing and the presence of a pulse that confirm that a person is alive.

Wakeful states The four states through which a baby progresses while she is awake: drowsy; calm-alert; active-alert; and crying. The duration varies with age.

White noise A noise, such as the sound of a washing machine or a vacuum cleaner, made up of all of the different frequencies of sound. As a result it blocks out any distracting noises that might frighten, distract, or over-stimulate a baby.

resources

support and child health

Allergy UK
www.allergyuk.org
Provides advice on odourless washing powders and other allergy tested products

Association of Breastfeeding Mothers
www.abm.me.uk
0844 412 2949

Association for Postnatal Illness
www.apni.org
020 7386 0868

Baby Sense
www.mybabysense.co.uk
0845 833 2282
Provides advice on sensory parenting in order to keep your baby calm and content; also sells baby accessories

Best Bear
www.bestbear.co.uk
0870 720 1277
Help with childcare issues; vets nannies and childminders

British Association for Behavioural and Cognitive Psychotherapies
www.babcp.co.uk

British Association for Counselling and Psychotherapy
www.bacp.co.uk

British Association of Occupational Therapists and College of Occupational Therapists
www.cot.co.uk

British Red Cross
www.redcross.org.uk
0844 871 1111
Provides first aid training courses

Child Accident Prevention Trust
www.capt.org.uk
020 7608 3828

Cry-sis
www.cry-sis.org.uk
0845 122 8669
24-hour helpline for parents with crying babies or sleep problems

Fatherhood Institute
www.fatherhoodinstitute.org
0845 634 1328

The Foundation for the Study of Infant Deaths
www.fsid.org.uk
0808 802 6868

Health visitors
www.healthvisitors.com
Advice on parenting from health visitors

Home Start
www.home-start.org.uk
0800 068 6368
Supports families across the UK

Kangaroo Mother Care
www.kangaroomothercare.com
Information on kangaroo care for parents and health professionals

Kids Health
www.kidshealth.org
Provides advice on parenting and child health

Meet A Mum Association
www.mama.co.uk
0845 120 3746
Support for mothers who are feeling isolated or lonely

The Multiple Births Foundation
www.multiplebirths.org.uk
020 3313 3519
Advice from healthcare professionals for parents of twins or more babies

National Childbirth Trust
www.nct.org.uk
0300 330 0770
0300 330 0771 – Breastfeeding helpline
Organizes antenatal classes, parent-and-baby groups, and breastfeeding counselling

NHS Choices
www.nhs.uk
Provides online medical advice and health information
England, Wales, and Northern Ireland 0845 4647
NHS 24 Scotland 08454 242424

Parentline Plus
www.parentlineplus.org.uk
0808 800 2222
24-hour helpline on all aspects of parenting

Postnatal Illness
www.pni.org.uk
Web community support for postnatal illness from fellow sufferers and survivors of PND

the **babysense** secret

Postnatal Illness Care Practice
www.postnatalillnesscounselling.co.uk
01727 853 400
Counselling and therapy for postnatal illness

St Andrew's Ambulance Association
www.firstaid.org.uk
0141 332 4031
Provides first aid training courses in Scotland

St John Ambulance Association
www.sja.org.uk
0870 010 4950
Provides first aid training courses

Twins and Multiple Birth Association
www.tamba.org.uk
0800 138 0509

Working Families
www.workingfamilies.org.uk
0800 013 0313

shopping for your baby

Baby Concierge
www.babyconcierge.co.uk
020 8964 5500
Suppliers of co-sleeper cots

Baby Mattresses Online
www.babymattressesonline.co.uk
01254 777 603
Supplies cot mattresses and reflux wedges

Baby Sense
www.mybabysense.co.uk
0845 833 2282
Sells baby accessories such as swaddling blankets, sleep bags and white noise CDs and provides parenting advice

Baby Sleep Shop
www.babysleepshop.com
01425 656 060
Sells everything from wedge pillows to black-out blinds

The Essential Oil Company
www.eoco.org.uk
01256 332 737
Supplies essential oils suitable for babies

John Lewis
www.johnlewis.com
0845 604 9049
Supplies ready-made black-out linings for curtains

Mothercare
www.mothercare.com
0845 330 4070
Sells wide range of babycare equipment, from buggies and cots to plastic bags for storing expressed breast milk

Nappy Makers
www.nappymakers.com
Suppliers of fabric nappies

National Association of Nappy Services
www.changeanappy.co.uk
0121 693 4949
Provides information about nappy laundry services in the UK

National Childbirth Trust
www.nctshop.co.uk
0845 8100 100
Sells a huge variety of equipment and clothes including co-sleepers, portable black-out blinds, organic cotton baby clothes, reusable nappies, baby massage oils, bucket baths

Weleda
www.weleda.co.uk
Sells blackthorn berry juice

premature babies

Bliss
www.bliss.org.uk
0500 618 140
Provides support to parents of premature and sick babies

Little Steps
www.littlesteps.co.za
Help and advice for parents of premature babies; sells book *Prematurity – Adjusting your Dream* by Welma Lubbe

Prem2Pram
www.prem2pram.co.uk
Supplies premature baby dummies, clothes, and accessories

Twins UK
www.twinsuk.co.uk
01670 856 996
Supplies baby nests for premature babies

suggested reading for breastfeeding

S. Cox, *Breastfeeding with Confidence*, Finch Publishing, 2004
K. Megaw, S. Strachan & M. Faure, *Feeding Sense*, Metz Press, 2010
S. Trotter, *Breastfeeding: the Essential Guide*, Trotters Independent Publishing Services Ltd., 2004

references

Als, H. *Toward a synactive theory of development: Promise for the assessment and support of infant individuality.* Infant Mental Health Journal Volume 3 Issue 4, Pages 229–243

Anders, T. *Biological Rhythms in Development* Psychosomatic Medicine, Vol. 44, No. 1 (March 1982)

Baldwin Dancy, R. *You Are Your Child's First Teacher.* Celestial Arts, 1989

Bly, L. *Motor Skills Acquisition Checklist*, Therapy Skill Builders 2000

Brazelton, T.B. & Greenspan, S. *The Irreducible Needs of Children.* Perseus Publishing, 2000

Brazelton, T.B. & Nugent, J.K. *The Neonatal Behavioral Assessment Scale.* Mac Keith Press, Cambridge, 1995

Brown, J., Fratar, L., Matsui, I., & Waddington, C. *Breastfeeding your Premature Baby*, 1998

Davis, L. & Keyser, J. *Baby talk: 8 easy and fun ways to improve your baby's language skills* http://parenting.ivillage.com/

DeGangi, G. *Pediatric Disorders of Regulation in Affect and Behaviour.* Academic Press, 2000

DeGangi G., Wiener, A., Long, T., Battaile, B. *Sensory Processing of Infants Born Prematurely or with Regulatory Disorders.* Physical & Occupational Therapy in Pediatrics Vol. 16(4) 1996

Drehobl, K. & Fuhr, M. *Pediatric Massage for the Child with Special Needs.* Therapy Skill Builders, 1991

Dunn, W. (2004). A sensory processing approach to supporting infant-caregiver relationships. In Sameroff, A., McDonough, S. & Rosenblum, K. [eds.] *Treating Parent Infant Relationship Problems: strategies for intervention.* Guilford Press, New York. pp. 152–187

Dunn, W. *Infant Toddler Sensory Profile.* The Psychological Corporation, 2002

Einon, D. *Learning Early.* Marshall, 1998

Eliot, L. *What's Going On In There.* Bantam Books, 1999

Elliott, L., Henderson, J., Northstone, K., et al. *Prospective study of breast feeding in relation to wheeze, atopy and bronchial hyperresponsiveness in the ALSPAC.* Journal Allergy Clinical Immunology: 2008

Faure, M. & Richardson, A. *Baby Sense: Understanding your baby's sensory world.* Metz Press, 2002

Faure, M. & Richardson, A. *Sleep Sense.* Metz Press, 2007

Greenspan, S. *Greenspan Social–Emotional Growth Chart: A Screening Questionnaire for Infants and Young Children.* Psychcorp, 2004

Host, A., Halken, S., Muraro, A., et al. *Dietary prevention of allergic diseases in infants and small children.* Paediatric Allergy Immunology, 2008

Kennel, J. & Klaus, M. *Parent-infant bonding.* 2nd ed. St Louis, MO: C.V. Mosby. 1982

Kitzinger, S. *The Crying Baby.* Viking, 1989

Klein, A. & Ganon, J. *Caring for your premature baby.* HarperCollins Publishers 1998

Krantz, M. *Child Development.* Wadsworth, 1994

Leach, M. *Nutritional needs of the newborn.* Neocare, 2001

Lombard, A. *Sensory Intelligence.* Metz Press, 2007

Lubbe, W. *Prematurity: Adjusting your dream.* Little Steps, 2008

Madden, S. *The Preemie Parents' Companion: The Essential Guide to Caring for your Premature Baby in the Hospital, at Home, and Through the First Years.* Harvard Common Press, US, 2000

McClure, V. *The International Association of Infant Massage Manual for Infant Massage Instructors.* IAIM, 2005

McClure, V. *Manual for Infant Massage Instructors.* International Association of Infant Massage, 2005

Morris, D. *The Naked Ape.* Jonathan Cape and McGraw Hill, 1967

Murphy, A.P. *The Seven Stages of Motherhood: Making the most of your life as a Mum.* Pan Books, 2004

Murkoff, H. *The Real Parenting Expert is ... You.* Newsweek Special 2000 Edition

Murray, L. & Andrews, L. *The Social Baby: Understanding babies' communication from birth.* CP Publishing, 2000

Murray-Slutsky, C. & Paris, B. *Exploring the Spectrum of Autism and Pervasive Developmental Disorders.* Therapy Skill Builders, 2000

Paller, A., Hornung R., et al. *Infant Skin and its special needs.* Johnson & Johnson Compendium of Infant Skin Care 2001

Porter R., Raimbault C., Henrot A. & Saliba E. *Responses of Pre-term Infants to the Odour of Mother's Milk.* Chemical Signals in Vertebrates 11. Springer New York, 2008

Ratey J. *A user's guide to the brain.* Little Brown and Company, 2001

Raymond, J. *Kids, Start your Engines.* Newsweek Special 2000 Edition

Richardson, A. *Toddler Sense.* Metz Press, 2005

Sammons, W. *The Self-Calmed Baby.* St. Martins, 1989

Schaffer, R. *Mothering.* London, Fontana, 1977

Schneider, E. F. *The power of Touch: Massage for infants.* Infants & Young Children. Jan 1996 8 (3) 40–55

Sharpe, W. *Baby talk: enhance your baby's language development.* http://www.partnershipforlearning.org

Sheridan, M.D. *From Birth to Five Years.* Routledge, 1991

Sicherer, S.H. & Burks, A.W. *Maternal and infant diets for prevention of allergic diseases: understanding menu changes in 2008.* Journal Allergy Clinical Immunology 2008.

Smith Roley S., Blanche, E. & Schaaf, R. *Understanding the Nature of Sensory Integration with Diverse Populations.* Therapy Skill Builders, 2001

St. John, J. *High Tech Touch: Acupressure in the Schools.* CA: Academic Therapy Publications, 1987

Stoppard, M. *Know Your Child.* Dorling Kindersley, 1991

Sunderland, M. *The Science of Parenting.* Dorling Kindersley, 2006

Thygarajan, A., Burks, A. *AAP recommendations on the effects of early nutritional interventions on the development of atopic disease.* Current Opinion in Pediatrics: 2008

Tracey, N. *Parents of Premature Infants: Their emotional world.* Whurr Publishers, 2000

Tsiaras, A. & Werth, B. *From Conception to Birth: A life Unfolds.* Random House, 2002

Turner, R. & Nanayakkara, S. *The Soothing art of Baby Massage.* Landsdowne Publishing, 1996

Weiss-Salinas, D. & Williams, N. *Sensory Defensiveness: A Theory of Its Effect on Breastfeeding.* Journal of Human Lactation, Vol. 17, No. 2, 145–151 (2001)

Willemse, S. *Developmental Care for babies.* Course attended 2003

appendix a
criteria for infants with a regulatory disorder

Some children are more sensitive to sensory input and do not integrate it adequately. This can lead to extreme fussing, poor sleep habits, feeding issues, and emotional irritability. The checklist below is included to assist you if you are concerned that your baby is significantly more irritable than average and may have a problem with sensory input. If your baby is over six months of age and displays at least two of the following traits, you may wish to have him assessed by an occupational therapist who treats babies and is specialized in sensory integration to determine whether he has a regulatory disorder. See Resources, p.214, to find an occupational therapist.

Sleep disturbances A sleep disturbance is defined as a persistent problem in the regulation of sleep/wake cycles, and involves difficulties in falling asleep and staying asleep, which are not associated with parental mismanagement. The criteria for sleep disturbance are:
- The baby takes over 30 minutes to fall asleep, even after calming techniques and bedtime routines have been carried out.
- Frequent wakings (more than two) in the night, that are unrelated to nutritionally necessary or habitual night feeds.

Difficulty self-consoling The baby is unable to soothe himself by bringing hands to mouth, looking at certain sights, or listening to voices or sounds. Once upset, the infant requires extreme efforts to calm down. This condition differs from normal unsettledness in that the caregiver spends from two to four hours a day over a period of three weeks or longer, attempting to calm the baby.

Feeding difficulties In order to qualify as suffering from a feeding disorder, the baby must display at least two of the following behaviours:
- Does not have an established, regular feeding schedule.
- Demonstrates distress around the process of feeding, with regurgitation and spitting out of food, particularly when eating textured or lumpy foods.
- Eats only soft foods.

- Had difficulty latching on to the breast for longer than five days as a newborn.
- Will not tolerate the change from the breast to a rubber or silicone teat.

Distress with changes in routine The baby becomes very distressed by changes or transitions from one activity to the next, and this is shown in prolonged periods of crying or fussing (over five minutes) that occur at least three times per day.

Distress with routine caregiving and play experiences which offer a sensory challenge The baby responds by crying, withdrawal, or other negative behaviours when confronted with normal everyday sensory stimulation involving touch (e.g. being held by parent), movement (e.g. boisterous play with parent), sight and sound (e.g. in a busy environment, such as a supermarket). These behaviours include at least three of the following:
- Resists cuddling; pulls away or arches.
- Resists being swaddled.
- Is distressed at having his face or hair washed.
- Hates being placed in the car seat.
- Resists being placed in certain positions (e.g. on back or stomach).
- Avoids touching certain textures or getting hands messy.
- Doesn't want to wear clothing or wants to wear too many layers or very warm clothes.
- Fears of being swung in air, involved in boisterous play, or roughhoused.
- Is excessively startled or distressed by loud sounds (e.g. vacuum cleaner, door bell or barking dog).

Emotional stability The baby displays fussiness, irritability, negative moods, and a tendency to rapidly escalate from a contented mood to distress without any apparent cause. In many cases, this is very disruptive to the family. The child is never very happy and (over nine months) does not initiate interaction with the caregiver.

Adapted from: *Criteria for inclusion in research* by DeGangi, et al (1996); *Diagnostic Classification: 0–3 Manual*

index

the **babysense** secret

index

219

acknowledgments

author's acknowledgments

There are many ways in which writing a book can be likened to the labour of love that raising a child entails – the many sleepless nights, moments of frustration and peaks of elation. Like nurturing a baby, it takes teamwork, and I would like to thank the team that worked with me.

The professionals who I am privileged enough to call colleagues: Kerry Wallace, Ann Richardson, Lizanne DuPlessis, Dr Simon Strachan, Kath Megaw, Dr Mark Tomlinson, Sheila Faure and Welma Lubbe – thank you all for shaping the way I think and for the perspectives and advice you have each contributed over the years.

The special people I work with daily, who provide me with support and encouragement and assist in the many different aspects of my work – Antoinette Scandling, Haydn Heydenrych, Nina Otero, Nancy Mtambeki and Liz Kossuth, my deepest gratitude.

The mums – both the parents of my little patients and of course all the Baby Sense mums who daily share with me over email, Facebook and in consultation the journey of parenting new babies and even offer to read my chapters as I go along.

Peggy Vance, who listened to my concept, believed it was something mums must hear and would not let *The Babysense Secret* go. Thank you, you have been an amazing advocate for this work.

Emma Maule, Penny Warren, Nicky Rodway and Glenda Fisher from DK and our photographer Vanessa Davies, with Emma Forge's wonderful art direction – to work with you all has been incredible – your creative energy and ability to listen to my feedback and improve on all of it has made the compiling of *The Babysense Secret* a pleasure.

Finally to my own children, James, Alex and Em, who made the sensory personalities come alive in their very different characters, thank you my precious children for sharing mummy and being patient when the computer was stealing my attention.

Thank you to you all.

publisher's acknowledgments

The publisher would like to thank Susannah Marriott for editorial consultancy; Jemima Dunne for proofreading and endmatter compilation; Hilary Bird for the index; Joanna Dingley, David Isaacs, and Kathryn Meeker for editorial assistance; Romaine Werblow, picture librarian; Jenny Baskaya for picture research; Steve Crozier and Gary Kemp for help with retouching images. At the photoshoot, DK thanks: Alli Williams, make-up artist; Charlotte Johnson, art director's assistant; Alyson Walsh, stylist and prop buyer; Katie Newham, stylist and assistant to stylist; Issy Wield, photographer's assistant.

Thanks to the models: Rae Baker and Harriet Wisbey; Susanna and Ben Bauer; Sofia and Maya Berggren; Michelle Bridge and Maya Lee; Heidi Carr and Noah Messias; Rachel Chan and Niamh Chung; Lucy and Ruby Chapman; Karen and Henrietta Davey; Solania L. De Freitas and Milin Kushwah; Jacqueline and Francis Denny; Katherine Ellis, Scott Millar and Samantha Millar; Sara Faulkner and Thomas Murray; Giovanna Franchina and Leonardo Diallo; Joanne and Esme Green; Leigh and Isla Summer Haynes; Emily and Lucian Hotchkiss; Lynette Jenkins-Raji and Miracle Raji; Pippa and Leo Heald; Nathalie and Charlie Heath; Emma and Harry Hutchinson; Johanna and Lucas Kemp; Helena and Barnaby Lemanski; Carrie Love and Siamak and Dylan Tannazi; Hat Margolies and Aurora Grace Barber; Ajay and Venaya Patel; Natasha Estelle and Melody and Zeb Pepper; Michelle and Edward Phillips; Sarah Reeves and Imogen Andrews; Viv and Aaran Ridgeway; Annabel and Hattie Robinson; Ijeoma and Timeyin Ryan Samuel-Metseagharun; Caroline and Mae Vernon; Charlotte and Charlie Whetham; Katie and Summer Wilson; Charlie and Somerset Young; Justyna, Majid and Nicole-Anne Zohreh.

picture credits

The publisher would like to thank the following for their kind permission to reproduce their photographs:
(Key: a-above; b-below/bottom; c-centre; l-left; r-right; t-top)
12 Baby Sense: Pippa Hetherington (bl). **18** Getty Images: Frank Herholdt (tl). **20** Photolibrary: Neil Bromhall (bl). **21** Getty Images: Stephen Chiang (t). Science Photo Library: Ian Hooton (b). **22** Baby Sense: (tl). **23** Alamy Images: Paula Showen. **54** Getty Images: Mauro Speziale (b). **59** Getty Images: Yellow Dog Productions. **62** Science Photo Library: Mauro Fermariello (cl). **72** Alamy Images: Trevor Smith (c). Corbis: (tl). Getty Images: Photodisc (br). Photolibrary: Bruno Boissonnet (cl). Science Photo Library: AJ Photo (crb). **73** Science Photo Library: Mark Thomas. **74** Alamy Images: allOver photography (tl). Science Photo Library: Mark Thomas (t). **76** Science Photo Library: Mark Thomas. **77** Photolibrary: Jim Olive (t). Science Photo Library: AJ Photo (bl). **78** Alamy Images: allOver photography (b). Science Photo Library: Mark Thomas (tl) (t). **79** Alamy Images: John Krstenansky. **80** Getty Images: ERproductions Ltd (tl). Science Photo Library: Mark Thomas (t). **81** Photolibrary: Deloche (b). **82** Science Photo Library: AJ Photo (tl); Mark Thomas (t). **83** Getty Images: James Porter. **84** Science Photo Library: Mark Thomas. **85** Science Photo Library: Antonia Reeve. **86** Science Photo Library: Mark Thomas. **87** Science Photo Library: John Cole. **88** Science Photo Library: Mark Thomas (t). **89** Getty Images: Washington Post. **90** Getty Images: Photodisc (tr). **103** Alamy Images: Mira (t). **109** Getty Images: LWA. **110** Getty Images: LWA (t). **112** Getty Images: LWA. **113** Getty Images: Emma Innocenti. **114** Getty Images: LWA (t). **116** Baby Sense: Pippa Hetherington (br). **118** Getty Images: LWA. **120** Getty Images: LWA (t). **122** Baby Sense: Tess Fraser Grant (tl). Getty Images: LWA (t). **124** Getty Images: LWA (t). **125** Getty Images: Digital Vision (t). **126** Getty Images: LWA (t). **132** Alamy Images: Picture Partners (bc). **151** Getty Images: Derek Lebowski (tr). **157** Baby Sense: Tess Fraser Grant. **175** Photolibrary: Picture Partners (cr). **176** Baby Sense: Tess Fraser Grant (bl). **205** Getty Images: Jupiterimages. **208** PunchStock: Brand X Pictures (br)

All other images © Dorling Kindersley
For further information see: www.dkimages.com

acknowledgments